SOCIAL SELVES

SOCIAL SELVES

Theories of the Social Formation of Personality

IAN BURKITT

SAGE Publications

London • Newbury Park • New Delhi

SAGE Publications Ltd
6 Bonhill Street
London EC2A 4PU

SAGE Publications Inc
2455 Teller Road
Newbury Park, California 91320

SAGE Publications India Pvt Ltd
32, M-Block Market
Greater Kailash – I
New Delhi 110 048

British Library Cataloguing in Publication data

Burkitt, Ian
  Social selves: Theories of the social formation
  of personality.
  I. Title
  155.2

  ISBN 0–8039–8384–0
  ISBN 0–8039–8385–9 pbk

Library of Congress catalog card number 91-50852

Typeset by Ann Buchan Typesetters, Shepperton, Middlesex
Printed in Great Britain by J. W. Arrowsmith Ltd, Bristol

Contents

Acknowledgements

I am indebted to many friends and colleagues who have provided help, guidance and useful suggestions during the preparation of this study. I would particularly like to thank David Ingleby, Richard Kilminster and Ian Parker for their insightful and constructive comments on the project at different stages of its development. Robert Ashcroft originally inspired my interest in this topic and also made perceptive comments on an earlier draft. My thanks also go to Brian Burkitt, Eileen Moxon, Hilary Rose and Keith Tester for their help and encouragement. Karen Phillips as commissioning editor at Sage has provided a very positive atmosphere and useful advice that have helped in the completion of this project. I am also grateful to Kathleen Temple and Caroline Pratt for their careful and efficient help in preparing the manuscript.

Many of those I have thanked here would not necessarily agree with my analysis, providing different perspectives which would have taken the work in very different directions. The responsibility for the study and any faults within it is therefore entirely mine.

To the memory of
my father and mother,
William and Irene Mary Burkitt

CHAPTER ONE
Society and the Individual

The view of human beings as self-contained unitary individuals who carry their uniqueness deep inside themselves, like pearls hidden in their shells, is one that is ingrained in the Western tradition of thought. It is a vision captured in the idea of the person as a monad — that is, a solitary individual divided from other human beings by deep walls and barriers: a self-contained being whose social bonds are not primary in its existence, but only of secondary importance. This understanding of people as monads creates one of the central problems of the social sciences, a problem that has become known as the division between society and the individual. What, it is often asked, is the relationship between society and the individual? The question assumes from the very outset that these concepts represent two opposing entities which are fundamentally divided. The problem then becomes one of creating theories which can conceptualize the 'links' between the social and individual worlds, an enterprise doomed to failure because of the dichotomous way that the problem is conceptualized in the first place.

Alongside this dichotomy, and related to it, there exists another problem in understanding the social nature of individuality. This is, not only do people in the Western world feel separated from the others with whom they live and who make up their society, they also feel divided within themselves, riven between the selves they present in relations with others and the individuals they feel themselves to be deep down inside. The armour that protects and separates us from others appears also to drive a deep wedge between our feelings and our ability to express them in public. People often believe they present a 'face' to others, and hide their true feelings inside. The connection between our actions and thoughts, on the one hand, and our emotions on the other, is severed and appears to dissipate. It feels as though, not only are we divorced from others, but from our own selves as well. In philosophical terms, this reflects in the understanding of humans as divided between body and mind, a situation in which the emotions are seen to pull us in one direction while our rational consciousness attempts to temper the affects and pull us in another.

However, suppose we tried to understand human beings from a different perspective, as social selves rather than self-contained individuals. From such an angle we would try to see humans inside their essential connections to other people — those with whom we live and from whom we learn. In this view society and the individual are not two separate entities, for humans are always in social relations from the moment they are born and they remain part of a network of other people throughout their lives. The fact that we feel isolated from others and, thus, from our own selves, says something about the type of social relations in which we live in the modern world, rather than anything about our essential nature as human individuals.

This work will be devoted to building a coherent theoretical understanding of humans as social selves. In doing so, I hope to move beyond dichotomous and dualistic visions of society and individuals, to see humans in terms of their essential social relations with others. This does not lessen the notion that humans are individuals, but grapples with the possibility of understanding individuality as socially based: a view which seems contradictory at first glance but which will become clearer. Such a view, however, would also undermine the understanding of humans as living an essentially dualistic life within themselves, divided between conscious rationality and emotion. Again, I hope to show how this experience is rooted in the type of social relations in which we live and is not an unchangeable component of the human condition.

The result of this work, then, will be to offer a unified theory of social selves which overcomes the dichotomies I have described here. This theory must show how individuality is socially based and how, on this basis, every aspect of the personality is interconnected — consciousness and emotions, needs and unconscious strivings. Like the relations we have to others which make up our society, the interconnections between different aspects of the self do not always appear as evident: yet if we take a holistic view — seeing the personality as a whole — then something of these essential interconnections will emerge. Like the differences between persons, the many facets each one of us has in our personality are differentiated and divided in the way we relate to other people; they are not pregiven aspects of the self with which we are born. The model of personality I offer here must also reflect this.

Because of the denial of dichotomies and dualisms in this work, I will draw upon insights into the social formation of the self from across the disciplines: from sociology, social psychology, psychology, linguistics and philosophy. In attempting this task, I will act as synthesizer and theoretical bridge-builder between different disciplines in order to develop a theory of the social formation of personality that serves as an adequate model for further theoretical and empirical work.

However, before I move on in the main body of this work to look at theories which show how the self is socially developed, I first of all wish to outline theories which suggest a basic division between society and the individual. The remainder of this chapter will therefore be devoted to some of the dominant strands of philosophy, sociology and psychology which have taken as their focus the isolated individual or 'monad'. In philosophy and psychology, in particular, I am interested in those theories which have stressed the essentialist nature of personality, underlining the view that the individual is prior to society and constitutes the basic 'building block' in social relations. Sociologists have attempted to show how this understanding of humans as self-sufficient individuals is actually a product of the society and culture in which we live. Yet despite this viewpoint, many sociologists also fall into the dichotomy of seeing the individual as separate from society. I will develop a critique of these ideas as a preliminary to what follows, where more integrated theories of the social nature of individuality are presented.

For now, I wish to study the consolidation of the view of human selves as monads within the work of rationalist philosophers in the period of the Renaissance. It is in the thinking of these philosophers that the idea of individuals as separate, distinct and unique monads is clarified into a systematic body of knowledge. Although many of these philosophers did not realize it at the time, their vision was based on changes occurring in the polity during their own period of history, and it is within this framework that the notion of humans as monads must be placed.

The Emergence of the Monad

For Norbert Elias — a sociologist of knowledge — the self-perception that individuals developed during the late Middle Ages and the early period of the Renaissance (from roughly the fourteenth to the fifteenth century in Europe), was one in which people began to view themselves as increasingly isolated from the others who formed their society. This self-perception, or phenomenology, was linked to changes going on in the social relations between people in this period of European history. For Elias (1978b, 1982), it was the increasing centralization of the state formation under the direct rule of the aristocracy and, with it, the predominance of more abstract and regular rules that governed the behaviour of those living in the court society, that created the change. Increasingly throughout the period of the Renaissance (which lasted until about the end of the seventeenth century) there was a very gradual switch from a reliance on external rules and punishments to control people's behaviour towards a situation in which the more abstract rules that governed conduct became internalized within individuals as self-controls. People no longer steered their behaviour by controls emanating from outside, but by social controls which had been built-in to the self. These controls, then, moved more to the centre of individual psychology, strengthening the ability to control one's own actions. As Elias says:

> This is the core of the structural change and the structural peculiarities of the individual which are reflected in self-perception, from about the Renaissance onward, in the notion of the individual 'ego' in its locked case, the 'self' divided by an invisible wall from what happens 'outside'. It is these civilizational self-controls, functioning in part automatically, that are now experienced in individual self-perception as a wall, either between 'subject' and 'object' or between one's own 'self' and other people ('society') (1978b: 257).

It is therefore no accident that this very idea of the self as locked inside its own thought processes and perceptions, divorced from other people and from its own emotions, should be found in three key rationalist philosophers from the Renaissance period. For example, René Descartes (1596–1650) believed that the self-experience of the individual as a distinct and unique personality is given in the human ability of thinking. The central sense of self that we refer to when we say 'I', only appears because we can refer to ourselves in such a way, and this very ability rests in our capacity to think. As Descartes says in his *Second Discourse* of 1637:

> I think therefore I am, was so certain and so evident that all the most extravagant suppositions of the sceptics were not capable of shaking it . . . I thereby concluded that I was a substance, of which the whole essence or nature consists in thinking . . . so that this 'I', that is to say, the mind, by which I am what I am, is entirely distinct from the body, and moreover, that even if the body were not, it would not cease to be all that is (cited in Khan, 1983: 18).

In the above we see clearly Descartes's view that because the whole essence and nature of the individual consists in thinking, then the body must be of an entirely different order. This style of thinking creates the problem which has become known as Cartesian Dualism, where the rational thought process is totally divorced from bodily and worldly experience. When Descartes was reflecting on his own existence in this manner, he expressed the feeling that his thinking was special and unique, defining his own individual nature, yet somehow distinct from his body to which he felt it had no relation. In fact, Descartes considered the body to function like a machine — an automaton which was the very opposite of rational thought and the free choice this bestowed. Descartes's own experience, which is universalized into a theory of human experience in general, paints a picture of human being as divided between two modes of experience: the automatic sensations and impulses that arise from the body, and the rational conceptions of the world which are given by the mind. The problem of Cartesian Dualism is that Descartes could not account for the ability of humans to bring these two modes of existence together to create a unity both in their being and in their experience of the world (see Kenny, 1968).

The Renaissance view of the individual is perhaps most clearly expressed in the philosophy of Leibniz (1646–1716), particularly in his doctrine of monadology. This doctrine states that because the individual is the one indivisible entity which is capable of perceiving objects in the universe, then the existence of all other things must depend on the human individuals who perceive them. This includes the relations that exist between monads, so that the individual is seen as the primary reality while all relationships are only secondary phenomena. At any moment in time, each human monad — as a primary reality — has its own unique quality which is dependent on its individual point of view (see Broad, 1975: 98–9). Each separate individual is a particular window on to the world with its own outlook. While Leibniz does not separate the perceiving mind from the rest of the body (for he sees the unique, perceptive monad as resting in the total functioning of the biological organism, including the natural drives) he does, nevertheless, see each monad as essentially separate from all others. This is because, as each monad sees the world from a different vantage point, every monad will become a world in itself with its own outlook.

Leibniz thus reflects the spirit of his age, hardly surprising given what Elias has said above, because he was a philosopher employed by various aristocratic courts. The problem his philosophy presents, however, is that if individuals are as distinct as Leibniz believes, how is interaction between people possible? To overcome this difficulty, Leibniz developed the 'doctrine of pre-established harmony' which claims that because God is the creator of each individual, their internal states will be inclined toward one another by virtue of their common origin, despite their different outlooks (see Broad, 1975; MacDonald Ross, 1984). However, as each person retains their own particular point of view, such interaction is limited, so that individual monads remain essentially divided.

The notion that individuals are essentially divided from others, as well as from the objects of their world, is also central in the work of Immanuel Kant (1724–1804), who was a member of the middle class German intelligentsia. Kant believed there existed a screen that separated humans from the world as it existed 'in itself'. This screen exists because he thought humans could never make sense of their experiences if impressions gained from the world were communicated directly to the mind by the senses. If this were the case, people would be bombarded by such a welter of sense impressions and information that it would be impossible to sort them into an ordered form. He therefore inferred that there must be certain categories that are ever present where humans exist, which enable them to order and classify the world. In this sense, the categories are 'a priori', meaning they are present prior to experience: they cannot be learned from experience but must be present in a priori form, so as to enable us to categorize the world, impose a rationality upon it, and therefore also to learn about it.

The rationality of human beings is thus part of what Kant refers to as transcendental subjectivity, meaning it cannot emerge from experience nor from bodily sensations, but only from the categories that precede experience and sensation, translating these into an ordered form. The transcendental subject therefore consists of the categories and rules which are given to all humans prior to experience and which make that experience possible (Körner, 1955: 35).

However, this creates a split between subject and object, for a gap is opened which cannot be bridged between the world as the subject perceives it through the categories (called the phenomenal world by Kant) and the world of real objects as they exist independent of human consciousness (called the noumenal world). Human individuals, as Kant perceives them, are so isolated inside their own shell they feel themselves to be separated from everything that is perceived as 'outside'. Besides this, Kant's subjects also feel themselves to be divided within, between a rational and moral imperative, on the one hand, and emotional drives on the other. Just as he believed there must be a priori categories that order our sense impressions, so Kant inferred there must be a priori categories that create an imperative for individuals to act in a moral way, ordering and taming the will and desires. In the same way that our sense impressions would have no coherence without the ordering categories, so too would our emotional lives be disordered were it not for the categorical imperatives giving them a moral structure.

Once again, then, we find the notion of humans as divorced from the world around them and from their own emotional lives, living only within consciousness itself, as though in a case. This is something we have encountered in all the philosophers considered here, a vision linked by Elias to the changing social structure of the times, which in turn produced changes in the structure and formation of the personality. The centralized and relatively stable state structure led to more abstract and regular rules that governed conduct, which became instilled more deeply in each self. This created the feeling that individuals were divorced from each other, from their own emotions and from the natural world which surrounded them. Indeed, a study of Kant's philosophy and personality structure suggests that his division of experience between an a priori rationality and a disorganized physical and sensual world, may be a reflection of Kant's own fastidiousness and distaste for anything with sexual connotations (Feuer, 1970). However, as Elias states below, this vision and these feelings about our lives are not just confined to the Enlightenment philosophers, but extend into the modern day.

> The idea of the 'self in a case', as already mentioned, is one of the recurrent *leitmotifs* of modern philosophy, from the thinking subject of Descartes, Leibniz's windowless monads, and the Kantian subject of knowledge (who from his aprioristic shell can never quite break through to the 'thing-in-itself') to the more recent extension of the same basic idea of the entirely self-sufficient individual (1978b: 252–3).

I will return to Elias's vision of the socio-genesis of individual personality in Chapter Seven. For now, I want to look at the more recent idea of the self-sufficient individual and the way that the formation of the modern self is considered by sociologists.

The Modern Self

For sociologists such as Marx, Simmel, Weber and Durkheim, who were working in the nineteenth and early twentieth centuries, the problems posed by the apparently self-sufficient individual were tackled sociologically rather than philosophically. This meant that the modern self, who appears alienated from society, was seen to be a product of the changing nature of the relations between humans in the age of industrial capitalism. Such an isolated self was not taken to be an evident fact of human nature, as it had in previous epochs.

For Karl Marx (1818–83), the apparent division between individuals and their society was something that reached its zenith with the full development of capitalist social relations. Here, property ownership is concentrated in the hands of the bourgeois class, who own the means of production. Unlike the feudal period, where labourers owned small plots of land or their own tools, in capitalism the working class is separated from the means to earn a meagre subsistence and must sell its labour power in order to survive. Property is no longer tied to the community of individuals but becomes the possession of predominantly one social class. The same process also occurs with the state — which Marx saw in its legal, administrative and governmental function as regulating and managing the social relations that support the system of private property ownership — for this in its 'political' role becomes separated from the everyday relations of people in 'civil society', standing above individuals as a regulative body. Under such conditions, the state represents an 'ideal community' which supposedly binds people together in 'society', which stands over and against the isolated individuals of civil society.

In more traditional power relations, particularly in feudalism, political power and ownership were identified with individuals rather than with a system of government through the state. Power and property were embodied in the person of particular individuals — feudal lord and knight, or king and prince — and all individuals in this society were tied together in relations of *personal* dependence. All took their identities from their place in the social hierarchy and also from the social functions they performed. As Marx claims, 'the more deeply we go back into history, the more does the individual, and hence also the producing individual, appear as dependent, as belonging to a greater whole'. He then states that, 'only in the eighteenth century, in "civil society," do the various forms of social connectedness confront the individual as a mere means toward his private purposes, as external necessity' (Marx, 1973: 84).

This is not exactly true, for Elias has already shown that this process started much earlier in court society, probably around the fourteenth century. But what Marx is pointing to is an extension of this process of the appearance of a separation between society and the individual that now, in capitalism, extends to the whole of the population. In capitalism, power passes into the hands of an impersonal state apparatus maintaining the conditions for the economic domination of the capitalist class. Social relations within civil society no longer appear as personal relations between individuals, forming themselves instead as 'objective dependency relations' (Marx, 1973: 163–5). In these relations people feel they are no longer interdependent with other human beings, but that they are confronted by an external 'environment' which takes the shape of an objective system. This is the feeling that Marx (1875) described as 'alienation', a condition that springs from the fact that people are estranged from the means of production, from the social relations which connect them to others, and also from their own nature as social beings who must produce their means of subsistence in order to survive.

Because people are divorced from the social relations they share with others, in which they take on an identity, they are now forced back into the realm of 'private', as opposed to 'public' life, where they exist as isolated individuals. Ironically, the society in which people feel themselves to be alienated and isolated as never before, is also the society of the most advanced division of labour and, therefore, of social relations in general. Here, where people specialize in particular tasks within the workplace and within society, they are more interdependent with others than at any other time in history. Yet because, in the division of labour, people play such a small part in one overall task, and because of the nature of impersonal capitalist power relations, they feel themselves to be alienated and totally *independent* of all others. It is within these relations we find the illusion of the totally self-sufficient individual.

In the division of labour, then, social relations begin to take on an independent existence, creating a division in the life of each individual, as Marx and Engels put it, 'insofar as it is personal and insofar as it is determined by some branch of labour and the conditions pertaining to it' (1970: 83–4). The total result of these factors, for Marx, is that, '*objective* dependency relations also appear, in antithesis to those of *personal* dependence . . . in such a way that individuals are now ruled by *abstractions*, whereas before they depended on one another' (Marx, 1973: 164).

This is a viewpoint also shared by sociologist Georg Simmel (1858–1918), who found the basis of individual differences in contemporary society in the division of labour and attendant forms of social specialization (Frisby, 1984: 76–83). Like Marx, he sees the idea of the isolated individual as a product of the breakdown of traditional, communal relationships in modern mass societies. For Simmel (1978), the individuals in mass society are bound together and ruled by abstractions, such as the value of money, rather than by close personal and emotional ties that united traditional groups. In the advanced division of labour, people are also linked through interdependencies across much wider areas, creating associations between individuals who have no personal contact. The result of this, for individuals, is spelled out in Simmel's essay on city life (1971: 324–39), which he believes is founded on the money economy. Here, individuals, linked by abstract values, are part of some of the largest social groups in the world, each individual interdependent with all the others; and yet people who live in the metropolis feel isolated and alienated, part of the 'lonely crowd'. This is because people are, as Marx would put it, only bound together by objective rather than personal dependencies, and also by abstract values such as money. For Simmel, this is precisely the setting in which individuals become isolated and there appears to be a division between them and their society — amidst some of the largest and most complex social groups in existence.

Emile Durkheim (1858–1917) is also in agreement with Simmel and Marx on the importance of the modern division of labour as the basis for the formation of greater differences between individuals. Durkheim (1984) says that in simpler forms of society, individuals are bound to others through a 'mechanical solidarity', where a person will totally embody the beliefs and values of the group, taking their identity directly from the immediate culture. In contrast, modern societies are marked by an 'organic solidarity', in which people are bonded because they are dependent on one another due to the different functions they fulfil within the division of labour. However, given that each individual occupies a very different place and role within society, people begin to see the world from very different points of view. What Durkheim calls the 'collective consciousness' — the values and beliefs of any society which unites the population — begins to break down under such conditions, for 'each mind finds itself directed towards a different point on the horizon, reflects a different aspect of the world and, as a result, the content of men's minds differ from one subject to another' (Durkheim, 1969: 26). Social individuals thus come to experience themselves like Leibniz's monads.

People who are alienated from each other's thinking in this way can find themselves in the condition Durkheim called *anomie*, which is a lack of moral regulation to structure individual actions. This occurs when so many moral positions emerge within a society it becomes impossible for individuals realistically to choose any system of values to guide their actions. In modern society, individuals are not only isolated, they are also without collective values and in a condition of moral uncertainty. One of the main expressions of this is the doctrine of individualism, which places the highest value on the rights of the individual for freedom of thought and action. Durkheim (1969) argued against this doctrine in its utilitarian form, which states that each person pursuing their own self-interest inevitably results in the best ultimate outcome for society. In Durkheim's view, nothing could be more destructive of social solidarity. However, Durkheim thought the trend toward individualism was positive providing that people realize it is a particular type of social organization which guarantees individual rights. If this is the case, people will not consistently place their individual interests before society, but will realize they derive their freedoms from their association with others — from their shared humanity. It is, therefore, humanistic beliefs and the ideology of individualism which act as a collective consciousness and hold society together in the modern age.

While Durkheim was able to draw some positive aspect from the appearance of a division between society and the individual, this was not echoed in the work of Max Weber (1864–1920). He saw the modern world and the isolated form of individuality it produced in a similar way to Marx, as resulting from a transformation of relations of personal dependence into relations of impersonality and rational calculation (see Sayer, 1991). However, for Weber, the main element in this process was not the formation of the capitalist economy, but the development of forms of rational ethical action that had strengthened in the Judeo-Christian strand of the Protestant religion. It is in this Protestant ethic that we find the basis of capitalism (Weber, 1985), for protestantism demands that individuals should not only do single good works for the glory of God, but that they live a life of good works bound into one overall rational plan. This ever encroaching system of rationalization soon began to permeate every aspect of life: it begins first in the rational ordering of monastic and military life, where the hours of the day are rigidly divided up for specific duties: it then spills over into economic life, where rational methods of book-keeping and labour discipline come to be employed. But perhaps most importantly, for Weber, rationalization pervades the methods of government, giving rise to bureaucratic styles of administration.

The abstractions that rule the lives of individuals are not, for Weber, purely economic and centred around the private ownership of property. This is only one upshot of rationalization. Bureaucratic methods of management also play a part in the development of abstract systems that dominate people's lives, resulting in their ultimate isolation as individuals. In such systems we find the separation of the institutions of ruling — whether they be in the state or in types of workplace management — from the person of any particular ruler, as well as from the persons who are ruled. Political power is then embodied in the apparatus of government and in abstract systems of rules. Because individuals must order their entire lives according to such rational systems, they come to embody the rules as part of their own personality rather than as aspects of specific actions or behaviours. This is something which Elias traced in the period of the Renaissance, the increasing trend toward the *internalization* of ethical rules that govern not only a person's actions, but structure their entire personality. Individuals use these ethics to order their own life and self into a coherent whole, yet these rules detach people from the concrete social contexts in which their actions are shaped, and place barriers against the free expression of sentiments between individuals. The identity of persons is then structured as much by discipline and strict self-control, as by their place in the community of other individuals. The result of this, for Weber, is the existential loneliness of the individual, divorced from the roots of social life and social being.

However, despite the sociological and historical perspective on the separation of individual and society, in their theoretical work many of the sociologists we have studied here fell into the trap of seeing this division as essential to human life. Durkheim (1938), for example, saw a sharp divide between sociological and psychological study. He believed sociologists should be concerned with 'social facts', such as the phenomena arising from group life and collective consciousness, while psychologists are primarily occupied with facts about individuals and individual consciousness. This seems to suggest that Durkheim fell prey to the idea that there inevitably exists a 'social' and an 'individual' realm to each person's life, and that the two are so sharply cut off from one another they can be studied by separate disciplines. Thus Durkheim implies there are aspects of individuality which are not social and need not be studied in that context. This is reflected in his image of human nature, in which Durkheim portrayed egoistic individual wishes and desires which are in constant conflict with the collective consciousness and internalized moral values. Individuals are therefore divided each within themselves between individual and social consciousness and their corresponding emotional claims.

It is because of this that Anthony Giddens (1971: 228) has said that Durkheim's theory produces an image of human personality as homo duplex, 'in the sense that there is an opposition in every individual between egoistic impulses and those which have a "moral" connotation'. Moreover, 'those needs connected with physical survival in the material world are not assimilated to those impulses which are rooted in social commitments'. Thus, individual and collective consciousness appear to have a very different basis and work according to different rules, making the relationship between individual and society problematic. Instead of seeing the social relations between individuals as shaping collective consciousness and the moral order, Durkheim sees morality as devised 'outside' the realm of individual action. Morality must then be imposed upon the consciousness and desires of individuals. Society thus appears as something forced upon individuals from above rather than as something in which people are actively involved.

For Georg Simmel, it was the problem of subjectivism that dogged his essays on sociological method. Here he expresses the view that because of the fragmentation of modern urban society, it is impossible to discern any totality or unity in the social group and, thus, to develop a theory of its overall structure. Therefore, a macro study of society, which treats social activity or collective representations as objective things, is impossible because society can only be understood in a micro analysis, through the subjective viewpoints of the individuals in which the social group is constituted. For Simmel (1971: ch. 1) the only unity in society is that which the individual perceives in their own consciousness and acts upon in their social exchanges. Consciousness does not rest on the social order, as it did for Durkheim, but the social order rests on the unity of consciousness.

The difficulty Simmel faces here is that the individual and their consciousness appear prior to society. This can be seen in his notion of 'sociation', the process he thought sociology should concentrate its studies upon, where individuals combine their actions into unified group activity through face-to-face interaction. This interaction comes into play because of prior psychological impulses and categories which could be said to be purely of an individual nature. However, despite his sociological work on the alienation of people in city life, this means that Simmel has an ontological view of individuals as essentially asocial. He claims humankind need not have created social associations as its general form of life, for 'this was not, so to speak, the only logical possibility. The human species could just as well have been unsocial' (1971: 36). So, after showing how the isolated individual is a product of changes within the social group, it appears that in his methodological statements, Simmel reverts to a form of

Leibnizian monadology which sees isolated individual consciousness as separate from, and prior to, social relations. The result of
Simmel's theorizing is that he creates a separation between society
and the individual, which, in his sociological studies of city life, he
showed to be the product of a particular form of society rather
than a universal fact.

A similar problem of individualism and subjectivism arises in
the work of Max Weber (1968), when he tries to distinguish
between the categories of 'social action' and 'non-social action'.
For Weber, only those actions directed by rational orientation to a
system of values are to be considered as social action, whereas
actions governed by emotional impulses are designated as 'behaviour' and regarded as non-social, by which we must take Weber to
mean their source is purely 'individual'. Here we find Weber
perpetuating not only the division between individual and society,
but also the dichotomy between the body and the mind in his
dualism of rationality and emotion in the steering of activity.
Likewise, personal identity is not regarded by Weber as something
developed by individuals in their interconnections with others.
Instead, personality is held to be an ethical ideal, attained only
when the *individual* becomes fully responsible for their own
actions according to their freely chosen values. Personality then
becomes an ideal to which individuals aspire but which few
achieve.

The problem with this moral philosophy of Weber's is that in
portraying the existential dilemmas of individuals, searching for
meaningful expression in often restrictive and individually prohib-
itive societies, society and culture appear as external forces
operating against isolated individuals. Human beings are held
apart from their culture, the two only becoming joined when the
person makes a commitment to a particular mode of life which will
become their vehicle for self-expression. Weber's main concern
then becomes the subjective meaning complex through which
individuals rationally choose their own actions and make commitments. Because of this, his work has often been characterized as
'methodological individualism', which is 'a doctrine about explanation which asserts that all attempts to explain social (or individual) phenomena are to be rejected . . . unless they are couched
wholly in terms of facts about individuals' (Lukes, 1973: 110).

This way of seeing individuals as separate entities who confront
their cultures is reflected in the work of the American sociologist

Talcott Parsons (whose first work was published in the 1930s and who continued to work until his death in 1979). Parsons saw social life as composed out of different, conflicting life orders which 'interpenetrate' one another (an idea taken not only from Weber but from Kant's philosophy, see Munch, 1981, 1987). The social order is composed in the interpenetration of four 'subsystems' — the behavioural organism, the personality, the social system and the cultural system (Parsons, 1964) — in which the social and cultural systems must be present prior to social action in order to create the conditions which make it possible (Bauman, 1978: 132). If this were not the case, then individuals would clash with one another and society would resemble Hobbes's vision of a war of all against all. The social and cultural systems are therefore 'normative orders' which lay down values and rules through which individuals structure their actions and achieve social order.

For Parsons, the personality system is the result of the internalization by the behavioural organism of cultural values and norms, which provide a subjective framework of meanings through which individuals can voluntarily structure their actions. However, critics such as Dennis Wrong (1961) believe this model of personality creates an over-socialized view of individuals. Wrong labels this as 'homo sociologicus', an image in which people are seen as happy to conform to social rules out of a need to win the respect of fellow social beings. The conflict between individuals and their social rules is ignored, turning people into nothing more than the products of their cultures. In reply to Wrong, Parsons (1962) claims that the values which constitute personality may conflict, because they are drawn from different aspects of the cultural system. This means that individuals will never be blindly conformist.

Perhaps a more fruitful line of criticism is that Parsons characterizes the social order and its subsystems as independent of human action to such a degree that it is difficult to explain how these life orders were created in the first place. Parsons attempts to solve this problem by theorizing two primary actors — ego and alter — who, in their original interactions, begin to form the normative framework of the cultural and social systems. However, this creates a theoretical dualism between pre-social and social beings. It also raises a problem that I will call the 'double reduction', in which some form of social action is seen as necessary prior to the normative order and which creates it, while this order is in turn regarded as the necessary *precondition* for social action. On the one hand, social order is reduced to the acts of originally isolated individuals, while on the other, individual acts are reduced to the norms of the social order. This presents us with a circularity which is impossible to unravel and perpetuates the theoretical separation of society and individual.

In fact, the only sociologist (if that is a wholly correct description of him) to emerge with any workable theory of the continual and necessary reproduction and reconstruction of society by the individuals who compose it, is Karl Marx. However, I wish to leave his description of the dialectics of social relations and social activity until Chapter Five, where I shall begin to consider a Marxist foundation for psychology. I now to turn my attention to the way that the problem of the division between society and the individual, and the resulting view of the individual as monad, plagues not only sociology but psychology as well.

The Psychological Monad

The psychology of personality is a discipline which so often begins from the assumption that the individual as a separate entity from others is a fact given in nature. The isolated individual therefore becomes not a historical and social product but a biologically given entity whose individuality is contained inside itself from birth. This is a particularly persuasive branch of psychology, because such an image of humans corresponds closely to the everyday understanding we have of ourselves in the West, which forms part of our 'common sense'. Such an image of individuals is found most clearly in trait theory, which claims that those traits which make up the personality or character are part of a genetic inheritance uniquely combined inside each individual. As the American trait theorist Gordon Allport put it, the centre of nature's most 'lavish concern' is 'the integral organization of life processes into the amazingly stable and self-contained system of the individual living creature' (1937a: 3).

This view of Allport's is very similar to Leibnizian monadology, with its idea that the biological organism is a stable and self-contained system which is the centre of all nature. Also, the idea of the individual as a self-contained system separated spatially from all other people, is monadology to a T. However, when Allport claims that individuals are self-contained, it is necessary to show what constitutes the container in which they are encased and kept separate from others. For him, the dynamic organization of each individual is separated from others because, 'when we say the dynamic organization lies within the individual, we mean merely that it lies within the organism i.e., "within the skin" ' (Allport, 1937b: 30). The skin is thus seen as the boundary which naturally separates all individuals. Furthermore, the dynamic organization that lies within the skin and characterizes each person, is made up of the innate psycho-physical components — or traits — that are combined to create the unified system of personality. These psycho-physical systems are the raw material of the personality, comprising of such elements as inherited levels of intelligence and physical build, which combine to determine a person's character. Allport's definition of personality is what he calls 'essentialist', in that, 'personality is the dynamic organization within the individual of those psychophysical systems that determine his characteristic behaviour and thought' (1937b: 28).

In his later work, Allport (1955) began to concentrate on the changes that occur in the psycho-physical system of the individual as it adapts to the 'environment'. This is a position which can also be found in the work undertaken in Britain by Hans Eysenck (1953), which stresses the primary role of the psycho-physical systems of personality that determines each individual's unique adaptation to their surroundings. Eysenck, however, does place greater emphasis on personality types, which are made up of an amalgamation of traits that operate in unison. Such personality types have been characterized by Eysenck as being found within three basic dimensions, which he called 'introversion–extroversion', 'neuroticism' (stable–unstable) and 'psychoticism'. All personalities can be classified and measured as belonging to a certain type somewhere within these dimensions. Eysenck believed that genetic factors play a major role in determining our personality type and, thus, the way we act in order to adapt to the environment. Later in his career, he estimated that genetic factors are at least two-thirds responsible for the differences between the personality dimensions (Eysenck, 1982). What characterizes and composes an individual personality is therefore largely to be found inside the organism of the person.

The approach of Allport and Eysenck was extended by Raymond Cattell who returned to focus on the trait, rather than type, as the essential structural element of personality. Traits are understood as predispositions that govern the way we act and determine the personality we will become. However, Cattell included in his inventory many more traits than either Allport or Eysenck, also allowing for the fact that some traits may be learned rather than simply inherited. In his view, traits describe general patterns of action rather than fixed tendencies and may vary according to the situation in which the person acts, along with the emotional state of the person while in that situation (Cattell, 1979). However, while Cattell's trait theory is more sophisticated, taking into account learning and the effects on behaviour of different situations and emotions, it is still based in monadology and individualism. We are told nothing about the social contexts in which people learn and in which they act, nor about the effect that social structure may have on the shaping of predispositions of the personality. In general, trait theory assumes a basic separation between the 'outside' society and the 'inside' of the personality, which, at least in its basic adaptational predispositions, is shaped by internal organic forces.

A similar viewpoint to this, reminiscent of Leibnizian monadology, can be found in the psychoanalytic theory of the personality devised by Sigmund Freud (1856–1939). He had a vision of the human body as a mechanism that accumulated and discharged energy through a process that is usually labelled as his 'hydraulic theory of biological functioning', whereby, just as in an hydraulic system incorporating water, pressure from the underlying source tends to accumulate as it is dammed up and needs to be discharged if the system is to go on functioning properly. Similarly, in the human body, the organism must achieve homoeostasis, in which the internal energy level is kept manageable so as to protect against overstimulation and the possibility of the body's ceasing to function properly. The welling up and discharge of energy means that, for Freud, the human personality operates on a basic principle which he calls the 'pleasure principle', whereby the organism finds an outlet for energy and can release it satisfactorily, causing the sensation of pleasure.

Infants operate mainly along the lines of this basic principle, which explains the dependence upon their mothers in the early stages of life. The dependency is based on the need for protection, because energy and impulses cannot always be discharged safely, as the environment is not geared solely to the purposes of human pleasure: indeed there are many dangers in the world that threaten the existence of human beings if we do not attend to them and take due care. In order to survive in the world and adapt, humans must develop another principle which counters the impulse for immediate satisfaction. Freud called this the 'reality principle', which must partially work against the desire for pleasure, until such a time when the impulses can be gratified safely, or when it is likely the most pleasure will be obtained. Thus the internalization of the reality principle means that individuals are forced to become more consciously aware of the reality of their surroundings and the stimuli that exist around them, as much as they are conscious of internal stimuli and pressures. The reality principle therefore forces individuals to develop a heightened consciousness which Freud calls the 'ego' or the 'I' (see Bettelheim, 1985, for a discussion of the translation of Freud's terminology). This is related to, and partly opposed to, the 'id' or the 'it', which is composed of the life energies that work according to the pleasure principle.

In every personality, then, there is tension and conflict between these two agencies in the psyche, the 'I' representing the rational and conscious command of action, the 'it' representing those forces which propel and drive the actions of the individual. The 'I' is suspended between threatening forces: on the one hand, the 'it' whose impulses compel the person to act, on the other hand, the stimuli from the environment which arouse the senses, but also warn of danger. These two forces are often perceived as hostile and threatening, which is why Freud labelled the inner drives as 'it'. Many of these drives may well be too threatening for the person to comprehend, in which case they become denied and repressed, existing as unconscious impulses within the personality. Besides the two agencies of 'I' and 'it', Freud also acknowledged another aspect of the personality which he called the 'super-ego' or 'over-I', which is composed of cultural values and rules that people must abide by when expressing their wishes or desires. The 'over-I' is therefore the internalized moral commands, which act as another force in the psyche which seeks the repression of certain drives or impulses.

In his later work, Freud (1930) thought the level of repression that culture and civilization demanded of its members was intolerable, and he began to contemplate the possibility that human civilization may not survive. The reason for this is that he began to posit the existence of a death instinct that competes for dominance with the life energies. The death instinct is the power behind the destructive tendencies of humankind and, because of this, is the greatest threat to civilized coexistence. However, one of the problems with Freud's theory at this point, is that he begins to understand culture simply as a repressive superstructure which must stifle some of humanity's most basic tendencies — such as aggression and destruction — in order to survive. It is true that some of these more disruptive energies can find a legitimate outlet in a culture by sublimation — that is, by being redirected to accepted goals rather than their original, prohibited aims. Yet Freud feels doubtful whether this can be entirely successful, fearing that anti-social tendencies may overturn civilization.

However, in seeing culture as a superstructure erected over the base of human energies, Freud is led into a problem similar to that faced by Durkheim with the model of homo duplex. That is, the basic needs and energies of the individual — the life energies searching for pleasurable satisfaction, or the destructive tendencies threatening to wreak havoc — are not assimilated to the moral and rational impulses rooted in the social bonds between people. There appears a sharp divide between conscious rationality, or 'I', and the 'it'-like drives, as well as a radical breach between the deep-seated energies of the individual and the moral demands of society. Individual consciousness then appears as a Leibnizian monad, hemmed in by the terrors it perceives in the 'it', on one side, and in the environment, on the other. In fact, this is not the only likeness between Freud and Leibniz, for the latter philosopher also saw energy as the key to the functioning of the total monad. Leibniz's notion that each part of the monad is an organ, a small body and perceptual system within the larger monad, is very similar to Freud's notion of unconscious perception: particularly the idea in his work on dreams (Freud, 1900) that in sleep the mind may perceive aspects of the body that it is unaware of in waking life, especially in the case of malfunctioning organs which signal their disease in the images of the dream. However, the main point for us here is that in employing a form of monadology in his work, Freud recreates in psychoanalysis all the basic dichotomies associated with this approach: most notably, the dualism between the conscious mind and the emotions, as well as the division between individual and society.

Like Leibniz, both psychoanalysts and trait theorists also get caught in the dualism between mechanism and vitalism, the mechanists seeing the laws of action as lying in the interrelationship between parts within a whole, while the vitalists place emphasis on the spontaneity of the parts in generating action. For Leibniz, an individual monad was subject to change because of spontaneous developments within its own nature and, also, because of the adaptation of the monad to the system of which it is part. However, the monad is the most important element because it is prior to the totality of which it is one element. Something of this can be seen in both trait theory and psychoanalysis, which place emphasis on the internal functioning of individuals and how this is changed through the person's active adaptation to the environment. The monad, however, remains the primary element. As can be seen from this brief description, two dimensions of monads are clearly recorded in these theories, consisting of the active and passive: the monad is active when its spontaneous development determines the way it adapts to surroundings, and passive when determined by the surrounding system.

These two positions have come down to us in philosophy and psychology as a division between active and passive views of human nature. They are reflected in a division between idealist and materialist philosophy, the former reflecting the active view of human individuals while the latter expresses the influences of the environment in determining or limiting the ways in which people behave. This dichotomy is mirrored in two very different psychologies of human personality — personal construct theory and behaviourism. Personal construct theory is elaborated in the work of George Kelly (1955), who thought that human beings acted like scientists, constructing theories of the world in which they lived. Humans do not simply respond in a mechanical way to their environment, for we have the capacity to represent it in a theory and draw from this theory some meaning to events. This will help to predict the outcome of things that happen to us and give people some active control over the environment.

In Kelly's view, people are constantly interpreting and reinterpreting their environment, building mental pictures or maps (known as cognitive structures or templates) which are used to get a grip on the world, to construct and change it through knowledge. Humans are therefore constantly making and remaking the reality in which they live, as well as their own selves, for individuals work with the meaning of events rather than just by responding to them. People are never the victims of circumstances, in this view, unless they passively allow themselves to be shaped by them. Personal construct theorists take this viewpoint because they do not believe there is a reality independent of our representations of it: equally, there is no independent truth of the reality of things, just different interpretations which construct the world in different ways. Furthermore, the cognitive structures or templates we use to construct and understand the world, are not things that could be found in people's heads. They are the result of efforts to understand and interpret the world, and as those efforts are continued, the templates will change. The personality of individuals at any one moment then becomes seen as the sum total of their construct systems — the way they view the world and themselves.

One problem with personal construct theory is that, in its idealistic understanding of how people construct the world, it fails to recognize any material limits on the way in which people can interpret and reinterpret their environment. It also sees activity as a purely mental phenomenon and not a practical endeavour that engages all human faculties — the senses, the emotions and the mind. Indeed, the theory of Kelly tends to ignore the emotions and motivational processes altogether, instead seeing humans as simply interpretive creatures (something which is mirrored in information-processing models of humans, picturing us like computers). As in all the approaches we have considered so far, this tends to separate mind from the body, the relation between the two becoming problematic. Also, the relationship between reality and representation becomes tenuous, the 'two' being held quite rigidly apart, as though our personal constructs were something that not only filtered reality but acted as a barrier to separate us from it. Here, the mind is seen as purely a subjective phenomenon, separated from the world it represents and constructs.

An opposite approach to personal construct theory, one which reflects materialist philosophy, can be found in behaviourism. This was pioneered in the early part of this century by the psychologists I.P. Pavlov and John B. Watson, who claimed that animal and human behaviour should be understood as a series of responses that have been conditioned by stimuli in the environment. A more up to date version of this theory can be found in the work of B.F. Skinner (1953, 1971), who argues that behaviour is conditioned in a number of ways, primarily through reinforcers. These are consequences that follow a particular response and, if the results it produces are positive, will reward the behaviour with a pleasurable stimulus. It is then highly likely that the particular action will be repeated. However, there is also negative reinforcement where the outcome of a response will be unpleasant. This negative reinforcement can either be removed to increase the frequency of the behaviour it makes painful, or it can be deliberately applied as punishment to make that behaviour less frequent. In general, then, the behaviourists believe that human activity is largely structured by the stimuli in the environment.

The problem here is that people are seen as passive receptors and reactors to the environment around them. This approach has been somewhat altered in the strand of behavioural psychology which has become known as 'social learning theory'. In this method, advanced by theorists like Rotter (1982), Bandura (1977) and Mischel (1971), as much emphasis is placed upon the internal influences on activity as the external ones. Bandura and Mischel, in particular, lay emphasis on the cognitive locus of control in human behaviour alongside the conditioning of action by the situation the person is in. Mischel has put this down to the influence on his theories of both Julian Rotter and George Kelly. In social learning theory, then, allowance is made for the fact that humans learn through symbolic and cognitive processes that create within them the power of self-regulation bestowed by the consciously functioning mind. The mind is thus able to transcend the immediate situation, the stimuli of which are no longer an unmediated influence playing upon human responses. What is now of central importance is the interaction between the person and the environment, and the way in which the two reciprocally determine one another. However, in social learning theory, cognition is not simply a construct of the individual theorist, but is determined by past experiences in particular situations. Cognition, therefore, allows us to learn and adapt but it cannot be separated from our responses to the environment and to other people.

While social learning theory is undoubtedly a promising approach in the study of personality, going some way to resolving the idealist and materialist positions, there still exists a number of problems. Most notably, these are that the theory tends to pay very little attention to motivation and the emotions. Although these factors are recognized, little is said about them, and their relationship to the cognitive functions is therefore left unclear. Similarly, while the approach is labelled *social* learning theory, there is virtually no analysis of the social relations in which people learn and which determine the structure of personality. Society and the individual, and the mind and the emotions, are not connected in any satisfactory way, leaving a trace of monadology in the isolation of the conscious self from other aspects of personality and from other people.

Out of the Monad: the Dialectics of Social Individuality

As I have previously said, I am attempting here to overcome many of these dichotomies and dualisms in the social scientific understanding of individuality, particularly in its attempt to go beyond a monadological view of the personality. The effort to understand humans as social selves is being made in order to overcome the dualisms between society and the individual, along with those that are seen to exist inside the self, particularly between the mind and the body (or emotions). In this study I hope to develop a holistic view of human individuals, as well as a full picture of their sociality. In short, what I am trying to do is to show how individuals derive their identity from their place within social relations and interdependencies, despite appearances to the contrary that exist in the modern world. The structure of the chapters will follow closely the arguments of those social scientists who have taken the view of sociologists seriously, and seen the separation of society and individual as an illusion peculiar to our society. To understand fully the nature of personality, they have attempted to put the individual back into her or his social context. They have tried to avoid the pitfall which ensnared many of the founders of sociology, seeking not to become a prisoner of modern appearances, but to see deeper into the reality of social being and social selfhood, by not separating society from individual, and by integrating the body and the emotions back into a theory of social relations and social action. Not all the theorists I will consider have been successful in these endeavours, yet all have made attempts to overcome age old dichotomies and dualisms.

This study is structured into two halves. In Part One, I will look at the work of those who see the social formation of identity as closely bound up with discourse and language, which binds together the social group. Chapter Two will concentrate on the work of George Herbert Mead, whose social psychology is, I feel, greatly undervalued and widely misunderstood. He saw the collectivity of communicating individuals as preceding the self-conscious identity of any singular person, because identity is based in the structure of communication within society. Furthermore, the discourse between social individuals is seen to be based in the network of social relations and interactions, a basis many contemporary discourse theorists ignore. Mead is therefore by no means an idealist, who does not connect discourse to practical activity in a material reality. In Chapter Three, I will look at the attempts to extend this type of social psychology in the work of the ethogenic school, which utilizes the sociological research of Garfinkel and Goffman — who also emphasize communication — and tries to integrate this with the personal construct psychology of Kelly. Chapter Four will look at the way in which other social psychologists have tried to connect ethogenic theory to current French philosophy, which sees discourse as irrevocably bound up with power. In this way, it is hoped that links can be forged between the construction of identity and the wider frameworks of the social power structure.

However, I criticize the methodological bases of the ethogenic school and the French philosophers, for reverting to idealism and some of the older philosophical dichotomies. Many of these dichotomies I believe have been resolved in the Marxist dialectical method, which looks at the way in which people create their world through activity within particular social and historical locations, utilizing the forces these place at their command. It is my view that this method is fully compatible with many of the insights from the pragmatist approach of Mead, particularly in the sense that practical social action is seen as the foundation of communication, meaning and identity.

In Part Two, therefore, I concentrate upon approaches which see the basis of identity located in the social relations and interdependencies between individuals which structure their action and communication. Chapter Five will look at the Marxist psychology of Lucien Sève, while Chapter Six will be devoted to the psychology of the cultural-historical school — particularly the work of Vygotsky. It is here that we will see many of the links between Marxism and pragmatism coming to full fruition in a theory of how the self and mind is socially and culturally structured. In Chapter Seven, I will return to look at the work of Elias, to consider his theory of socio- and psycho-genesis of personality, bringing the social and historical structure of personality into clear view. This approach brings to full realization an understanding of individuality as socially based.

Finally, Chapter Eight is reserved for conclusions, to draw all these strands together and see whether, upon the methodological synthesis I have created, a new theory of social selves can be developed that may be useful for future theoretical and empirical work in the social sciences. My ultimate goal is to create a clear view, which has been progressively elaborated through the whole work, of how social relations and the self are irrevocably intertwined. The route I have taken to reach this goal, through American, European and Soviet theories of the person, is clear in my mind, but unfortunately filled with opportunity costs. There are many lively and revealing debates currently going on in the social sciences about the construction of identity in studies of gender and race. I have chosen not to concentrate on these approaches because I want to highlight a different set of theories that address the same problem — the social formation of identity — from a different angle. However, nothing I have to say here is in opposition to that literature; rather, I feel that many of the points I want to make here are entirely complementary and may be of some use to people researching issues of gender and race.

Indeed, the discussions presented here will be useful to people interested in the formation of human identity from whatever approach they may be working. It is my hope that I may be able to clear some methodological pathways towards a better theoretical understanding of the necessarily social nature of human personality, of the way in which we are all social selves.

PART ONE
Personality as Social Discourse

CHAPTER TWO
Language and the Social Self

The first theorist whose work I will review in this study of the social formation of personality is the American philosopher and social psychologist, George Herbert Mead (1863–1931). I shall begin with Mead because he is one of the few Western thinkers who, in the early part of this century, tried to build a theory of the social origin of human selves, overcoming many of the dichotomies and dualisms we noted in the previous chapter. In particular, Mead's work goes a long way toward resolving the debate between mechanists and vitalists, which is mirrored in contemporary psychology in the opposition between behaviourism and personal construct theory. In contrast to these two present day branches of psychology, Mead understood that a theory of human behaviour could not be separated from a theory of the mind, developing a standpoint which has become known as 'social behaviourism'. This position involves a radical redefinition of the mind which sees human thought as part of the wider system of social activity.

In developing this standpoint, Mead was influenced by the pragmatist philosopher William James, who believed that human consciousness could not be studied through introspection if it were to be the subject of an objective science. James (1912) redefined consciousness as an *objective function* in the adaptation of humans to their conditions of existence, instead of an originally subjective phenomenon which could only be revealed introspectively. Consciousness thus becomes an element and a function of objective behaviour rather than a given entity within the subject. Mead took this pragmatist philosophy of mind a stage further by showing how consciousness arises as a function of *social* behaviour, as well as being a function in evolutionary adaptation. Mead therefore had a biosocial theory of the mind and self, one which went beyond the theories of James.

Social behaviourism also promises to resolve the dichotomy between society and the individual, because if the approach is correct, then there is no separation between 'collective consciousness' and 'individual consciousness', for consciousness is always socially based. Although the former terms belong to Durkheim, Mead was aware of a similar dichotomy in the work of one of his teachers during a period of study in Leipzig, the philosopher Wilhelm Wundt. Wundt noted a difference between what he labelled as *Völkerpsychologie*, which is concerned with collective phenomena arising from the 'folk' or community, and 'individual psychology' which is based in physiological, sensory processes. Collective psychology could not be studied in terms of the individual mind, for it is concerned with such things as language, religion and myth. However, individual psychology could be investigated experimentally under laboratory conditions, being a product of the mental processes. Mead's approach was aimed at breaking down this dualism, by showing how there is no separation between collective and individual levels of analysis: indeed, in social behaviourism, the communication between individuals in the collectivity is a precondition for what takes place in individual consciousness.

The theories of Mead therefore went some way towards tackling the divisions created between behaviour and mind, and also the empirical and introspective approaches in psychology. Because of this, Mead's work is highly relevant to modern psychology. Unhappily though, as Rob Farr (1990) points out, Mead's social behaviourism has had little impact on psychology due to the fact that Mead taught mainly in the department of philosophy at the University of Chicago, and that his work was largely utilized by the 'Chicago school' of sociologists. Since that time, his theories have been seen mainly as sociological. However, with the impact of cognitive theory and social learning theory, a more receptive audience may be forming within psychology for Mead's work, and Farr (1987) has already begun to spell out its relevance for psychology. I hope that what I have to say here will also convince psychologists of Mead's relevance to the discipline.

The basic thesis that Mead propounded was that the 'mind' and 'self' are formed within the social, communicative activity of the group. He was therefore one of the first theorists to explore the notion that personality develops within discourse. I have used the term 'social discourse' in the title to Part One to denote Mead's point that discourse and language is a *social activity*, and can never be the personal property of the individual. We will come to a more detailed discussion of this point later in the chapter, but from now on I refer simply to 'discourse' and 'language', assuming they are essentially social phenomena. Here we find the distinctive roots of Mead's social behaviourism.

Social Action, Gesture and Consciousness

The remarkable feature of Mead's social psychology, then, is that he aims to show how the personality — along with intelligence and self-awareness — arises only in society. However, along with the division between the individual and the social, Mead was also highly critical of the Cartesian dualism between the body and the mind, as well as the more general dichotomy between nature and rationally organized society. Mead's own views were greatly influenced by the theories of Darwin and the notion of the adaptation of species to changing ecological conditions. For Mead, the human mind plays an adaptational role in the sensuous activity of the human species within evolution. The mind is the instrument which enables humans to adapt to the natural conditions in which they live and, through their bodily activity, to modify the environment in order to make survival more likely. Unlike Darwin, Mead therefore recognizes that human life is unusual in that human groups are capable of selecting and recreating aspects of their own environment through intelligent activity. And in contrast to Descartes, Mead does not see the mind as a divine attribute, emerging from the heavens rather than the earth. Instead, the mind is seen as part of the process of the human body adapting itself to a given material world. Consciousness, intelligence and self-determined activity are viewed as capacities which are emergent in the concrete conditions of adaptive activity within the social group.

This is the reason for Mead's position becoming characterized as 'social realism', or more commonly, 'social behaviourism', because he understands the activity of the species and social group as a primary reality which is the foundation for the development of consciousness and the self. It is only in this sense, however, that Mead can be regarded as a behaviourist. His position must be distinguished from behaviourists such as Pavlov and Watson whose theories centre on the responses of the human body to stimuli within the environment. For such behaviourists, consciousness and the mind are regarded simply as secondary processes, emerging as a response to the environment. This behaviourist position continues the dualism between the human individual and their material world, for stimuli are seen to be located within the 'external' environment, while responses are purely physiological and arise 'inside' the individual. For Mead, human responses were to be regarded as socially organized, originally by the adaptation of the individual to the social group, and later by the use of language, through which individuals incorporate into their own self the attitudes of the entire group. In this sense also, Mead's theories are to be distinguished from behaviourism, as they allow for the conscious awareness of the *meaning* of social activity, and therefore for the possibility of the social redirection and moulding of the impulses. Human behaviour is thus not an endless string of nervous responses, but is consciously attuned social conduct.

It is this aspect of Mead's work that commentators usually stress. His work is normally presented as providing for the social sciences a theory of the social formation of human cognition and intelligence, and from this a sociological perspective on personality. However, as Andrew J. Reck points out, Mead saw human instinct, impulse and habit as determining factors in human activity. Reck says that, for Mead,

> The task of intelligence is not to replace the noncognitive factors, but to reorganize them, to mould them together in such a way as to maximise the possibility of their satisfaction. In some instances the noncognitive elements in human nature have to be modified or rechannelled, if other basic human interests are to be gratified (1964: xxxviii).

In Mead's theory, then, humans are to be thought of as possessing a nature, just like the other animals of the world. The difference between Mead's understanding of human nature and the way in which the term is generally used, is that Mead sees the nature of human beings as social. That is, the instincts and impulses of humans are not set in a fixed pattern, but are conditioned by the experience of the social group as a whole. Also, as Reck points out above, the human impulses are not thought of as compartmentalized, each with their own fixed goal: instead, Mead is clear that the impulses are to be thought of as an organization, meaning they are moulded *together*. And the process in which they are moulded is that of social activity. To Mead, it is wrong to proceed by trying to pin down an act to any one instinct or impulse, in which case the

motive is always seen as preceding the act. Instead, the organization of the body's impulses is created within the activity of the
group which exists in a definite material world. For Mead, then,
what he calls the 'social instincts' are

> found to be subject to modification by experience, and the nature of
> the animal is found to be not a bundle of instincts but an organization
> within which these congenital habits function to bring about complex
> acts — acts which are in many cases the result of instincts which have
> modified each other. Thus new activities arise which are not the simple
> expression of bare instincts (1917: 212).

However,

> Back of all this type of organization of instinctive conduct lies the social
> life within which there must be cooperation of the different individuals,
> and therefore a continual adjustment of the responses to the changing
> attitudes of the animals that participate in the corporate acts. It is this
> body of organized instinctive reactions to one another which makes up
> the social nature of these forms (1917: 213).

In Mead's theories, then, the centre of focus shifts away from
adaptive activity in a material environment — although this
remains a background factor of social activity — and moves
towards a theory of the way individuals in a social group must
adapt to one another through their actions. This does not mean
that Mead believes that all human impulses are benevolent and
cooperative ones, and later in his career he talked of two opposing
groups of instincts, the hostile and the friendly (Mead, 1929).
However, for Mead, even the hostile instincts have a social
function. These impulses unite particular social groups against a
common enemy, who is located either within or outside the group,
and to defeat whom the group must pull together. Yet even the
hostile and friendly instincts are open to modification through
social organization. If a truce is called between warring factions
and a new alliance formed, then the hostile feelings will be
transformed into ones of goodwill. These feelings emerge and
change within group activity, and they are moulded by the way in
which social relations are structured between members of a group,
or between different groups.

The key factor in all of this remains the way in which humans
shape their actions so as to adjust to one another. And Mead
understood that central to this process of mutual adjustment is the
system of social communication. Initially, this communication

takes place through gestures, in which individuals in a group signal their responses to others who then use this signal as a stimulus to adjust their own response. In social activity we continually ask ourselves questions, such as: Is the other person reacting to my actions in a hostile or friendly manner and, depending on this, what should my next action be in order to continue the interaction or bring it to a satisfactory conclusion? The gestures, then, are closely linked to the social organization of the instincts, and are dependent on human bodies adjusting themselves to one another within the structured relations of a social group. Certain responses will be called out in individuals by the stimulus provided in the actions of others. Through these responses the conduct of individuals is adjusted to the conduct of the whole group, especially where the responses are appropriate to the corporate act.

However, there is another factor which emerges in the process of mutual adjustment through gestures, one which Mead regarded as of central importance in social interaction. This factor is the emergence of self-consciousness, for the adjustment of one's actions to those of the group involves the individual's being thrown into an attitude of self-reflection, in order to select what they believe is the appropriate response. This is one of the ways in which Mead challenged the accepted wisdom in the psychological theories of his day, in particular the theories of Baldwin, whose work centred mainly upon the concept of imitation. In Baldwin's theory, human learning occurs primarily by the imitation of conduct, which is copied directly by one person from the model provided by others. While Mead agreed that imitation played a part when infants learned responses that had been socially devised within their group, he felt that imitation was not central to social conduct as a whole. This is because, in social life, human conduct differs, and the response required from another human being in social interaction is not a direct copy of the act that went before it, but an act which is *appropriate* to the *social situation* in which the person is involved. What is required is an appropriate *response* to that situation and the action taking place within it, not an imitation of the actions of others. It is important that the act one undertakes is considered in its social context and is designed as a stimulus to others involved in the interaction, to draw from them the desired response. In social interaction, for Mead, the act of an individual is both a response to the situation *and* a stimulus to provoke action in another person. This is to get the other to respond in an appropriate way, so as to carry on the interaction.

To Mead, this is precisely the point at which self-consciousness develops in individuals, at the very same moment in which social consciousness emerges and people begin to sense there is a meaning to activity. In this instance, people are thrown into a subjective attitude, being forced to design their actions so as to respond adequately to the social situation and call out the necessary responses in others. This tends to occur in societies as they become more complex and the function of group members differs: here, the action of one person serves as a stimulus for the response of the other, and so on. Social consciousness and self-consciousness is awakened in people, for individuals must become aware of the totality of activity in the group, and the place of their own self and that of others within it, in order to plan their actions according to their role. It is in this process that Mead finds the roots of human communication, for

> The probable beginning of human communication was in cooperation, not in imitation, where conduct differed and yet where the act of the one answered to and called out the act of the other (1909: 101).

What is important to us at this point in Mead's analysis, is that we can see how he does not place subjective meanings and mental reflections as prior to the social formation — as did many of the theorists whose work we examined in Chapter One. Instead, Mead theorizes the social organization of communicative interaction as the foundation upon which selves and minds arise, thereafter their mutual development going hand-in-hand. In interaction, acts are social and therefore primarily objective; they produce a response from others in the social group and, in so doing, they also produce a result for individuals. That is, they force upon them the subjective attitude in order to design actions that are better attuned to the social group and will also call out desired responses from others. The objective act therefore produces the capacity for subjective reflection. Through the subjective attitude, individuals monitor their own responses in the social situation and attempt to channel them into actions which are calculated to be both appropriate and provocative.

The subjective attitude therefore opens up the possibility that the emerging self-consciousness can direct impulses which occur involuntarily or instinctively into actions which are reflectively considered and calculated. The agency of self-consciousness thus intervenes between the stimulus and the response in order to produce actions which are considered in a social context. It is under these conditions that the *interpretation* of the action or gesture of the other becomes possible, where one can reflect upon their possible meanings and choose the response which will answer the other's intentions. In these circumstances, a person is now responding to their own self as another would: that is, one is responding to one's self as a social object and taking the social attitude — the attitude of others — towards it. This is the point at which self-consciousness emerges, a development that only occurs in social life. As Mead observes:

> In these social situations appear . . . a consciousness of one's own attitude as an interpretation of the meaning of the social stimulus. We are conscious of our attitudes because they are responsible for the changes in the conduct of other individuals. A man's reaction towards weather conditions has no influence upon the weather itself . . . Successful social conduct brings one into a field within which a consciousness of one's own attitudes helps towards the control of the conduct of others (1910a: 131).

In this mutual social stimulation, Mead has noted the importance of communicative interaction, because it is through communication by gesture, and later by language, that one can signal to others one's own subjective attitude without going through the entire act which the gesture signifies. A gesture, then, implies two things. First, it is a collapsed social act, an indication to the other members of the group of the act that is likely to follow, or that would follow if one were to enact one's subjective attitude. Second, the gesture is the expression of the subjective attitude and a vehicle for the expression of emotional responses. However, it is important to stress that the gesture is not the direct expression of the responses. This is because it is only in the social process that gestures can become signs which are significations carrying meanings for all the members of a social group. What Mead calls the 'significant symbol' — the symbol or sign which becomes accepted currency in social communication — does not, therefore, gain its meaning as a direct result of emotional expression. Rather, it gains its meaning from the part it plays in social interaction, and only then can this social meaning serve as the conductor for emotional expression. Like the meaning of all social acts, the meaning of the gesture as a sign is objectively established in society before it becomes part of any subjective attitude.

This is why, for Mead, the role of language is of crucial importance in the process of social communication, and in the emergence of the self and the subjective attitude. It is because language is a truly objective, or as Morss (1985) puts it, 'impersonal' system of communication through which the attitudes of the whole group — rather than just particular individuals — can be communicated. Language is the ultimate form of social intercourse. It is to the role of language in the development of the social self that I now turn.

Language and the Social Self

Language takes prime place in communication above the gestures, for Mead, because it is through the vocal gesture that one can respond immediately to one's own action. That is to say, the vocal expression of one's attitudes brings to immediate attention one's responses, allowing the individual to better reflexively adjust his or her own actions to those of others. In doing so, they respond to their own words and their meanings as others will do. Also, other people use language as the medium through which to communicate their responses, so giving us an objective sense of the way in which we have affected them and, through this, an objective sense of our own self. As Mead says:

> The individual experiences himself as such, not directly, but only indirectly, from the particular standpoints of other individual members of the same social group, or from the general standpoint of the social group as a whole to which he belongs. For he enters his own experience as a self or individual, not directly or immediately, not by becoming a subject to himself, but only in so far as he becomes an object to himself just as other individuals are objects to him or in his experience; and he becomes an object to himself only by taking the attitudes of other individuals towards himself within a social environment or context of experience and behaviour in which both he and they are involved (1934: 138).

Language is the most important element in this process because it is through language that people internalize the attitudes of the social group and, on this basis, form their subjective attitudes. It is only in language that such a general, impersonal standpoint can be communicated, against which individuals can react to their own selves and organize their responses accordingly. This is because language itself is an impersonal, social system. Language provides individuals with a thoroughly objective standpoint through which they may become objects to themselves. Like Wittgenstein (1953) and de Saussure (1974), Mead views language as a system which is independent of the intentions of individuals considered as singular entities. It is the place of a word or gesture in a sentence or a wider system of signification which gives it its meaning, not any attribute peculiar to it as a sign, nor the intention of the speaker who utters it. This is what Wittgenstein meant when he referred to the 'language-game', that it is the place of a word in an overall strategic system which gives it its sense and meaning. The word is defined against other words or signs, and these are used in organized sentences to create and convey ideas or concepts.

However, Wittgenstein saw the language game as connected to the entire non-linguistic field of social behaviour. So it is for Mead, who sees that language is always connected to the non-linguistic field of social interaction, so that a word or a gesture largely derives its meaning from its connection to social meanings. In turn, social meaning refers to the meaning that an act takes on from the place it occupies in the totality of interaction in the group. Yet for Mead, the original and primary function of language remains as a medium for the more successful mutual adjustment of individuals within their social activity.

Because of its objective function within the social group, Mead also agrees with Wittgenstein that there is no such thing as a private language which describes private experience. For Mead, experience is always articulated in terms of a language which refers to socially defined meanings and concepts, even when the dialogue in question is an introspective one. The interpretation of one's own responses, therefore, does not always reveal to us the meaning of an action in any direct terms, for the responses of the self can only enter awareness when the individual gains an objective view of their own self. This can only be attained through language, by taking the attitude of the others towards the self. Even when we are alone, our introspective thinking takes place in the form of an internal conversation with our own self, mediated by social language and meanings. Against methodological individualism, Mead is claiming that personalities do not emerge through their own private experience, but only in social experience, where 'other selves in a social environment logically antedate the consciousness of self which introspection analyses' (Mead, 1910b: 111).

The foundations for what seems like the most private of all human functions, the activity and processes of the mind, are not private at all: the mind and the self only emerge in a social process of interaction, communication and the development of language. Mead was one of the first to devise an argument that I shall refer to many times — that what we call 'the mind' is in fact a conversation held internally with a person's own self, which is based entirely on language and social meanings. Mead gives the following description of the social self:

> The self which consciously stands over against other selves thus becomes an object, an other to himself, through the very fact that he hears himself talk, and replies. The mechanism of introspection is therefore given in the social attitude which man necessarily assumes towards himself, and the mechanism of thought, insofar as thought uses symbols which are used in social intercourse, is but an inner conversation (1913: 146).

For Mead, there are two sides to this social self. There is the objective presence of the self within the group which acts as a stimulus to others; and then there is the subjective attitude of reflection which treats as an object the responses of the body to others in interaction. Mead has labelled these two faces of the self, which are continually in dialogue, the 'me' and the 'I'. Both faces are social and only emerge together in discourse, but the 'me' represents the unique identity a self develops through seeing its form in the attitudes others take towards it, while the 'I' is the subjective attitude of reflection itself, which gazes on both the objective image of the self and its own responses. The 'I' makes possible the inner dialogue between the responses to others, on the one hand, and self-consciousness on the other. The latter, having been established through language, reflects the meanings, morals and values contained in discourse. The 'I' thus facilitates the inner conversation between these mutually interdependent aspects of the self. As Hans Joas (1985: 83) eloquently puts it, 'the "me" is the individual as an object of consciousness, while the "I" is the individual as having consciousness.'

The two faces of the social self are difficult to describe because, as Mead points out, consciousness cannot become an object to itself, and so the 'I' can never appear as an object of contemplation. The 'I' *is* the individual as having consciousness, so that as soon as an impulse or an object enters consciousness and is articulated through the inner conversation as an idea, wish or desire, it becomes an object in contemplation and therefore part of the 'me'. The 'I' is the process of thinking, yet once the thought is born and becomes tangible, it belongs to the 'me'. In the inner conversation, the 'I' articulates thoughts and the 'me' hears them expressed, recognizing the voice as its own. The self which can think of itself as an 'I', is the memory image of the self which, in the last moment, acted towards others and towards itself as an object. Thus:

> the stuff that goes to make up the 'me' whom the 'I' addresses and whom he observes, is the experience which is induced by this action of the 'I'. If the 'I' speaks, the 'me' hears. If the 'I' strikes, the 'me' feels the blow. Here again the 'me' consciousness is of the same character as that which arises from the action of the other upon him. That is, it is only as the individual finds himself acting with reference to himself as he acts towards others, that he becomes a subject to himself rather than an object, and only as he is affected by his own social conduct in the manner in which he is affected by that of others, that he becomes an object to his own social conduct (Mead, 1913: 143).

This is fairly abstract, and a practical example of how the 'I' and 'me' work together may help. Such an example can be found in the case studies of the neurologist Oliver Sacks (1985), who describes the case of a patient called 'Jimmy', a man in his fifties who had a large portion of his brain destroyed through alcohol abuse. In particular, Jimmy has inadvertently destroyed that part of the brain where the memory functions are located. Such is the extent of his brain damage, all Jimmy's memories of events after he was aged seventeen have been wiped out. The significant point about this case for us is that Sacks remarks that it was impossible to make Jimmy aware of his problem — that he was a chronic amnesiac — for his condition was so bad, as soon as he was informed he was an amnesiac he instantly forgot again. While Jimmy was an 'I', still able to think and speak and listen to others, he was unable to develop an adequate 'me', for his memory was so poor it did not allow him to become an object to himself with a clear identity. He could not say to himself, 'Now the doctor has told me the problem "I" know who I am: this is "me", an amnesiac.' Because he was not able to do this, Jimmy had no adequate sense of his own self nor of his predicament.

Returning to Mead's theory, he claims that because the 'I' is the self as having consciousness, it is associated with the fundamental sense of our own self; it is that which we believe we truly are. But as we can see from Jimmy's example, an 'I' cannot function properly without the 'me' and, indeed, the subjective sense of self would never have developed if the self as a social object had not arisen in the first place. Yet because the 'I' seems the closest to our 'inner' sense of self, as opposed to our objective identity, and is the agency which can objectify and communicate the impulses and responses, it is more closely associated with the *active* sense of the self. However, it must not be confused with the innate or the socially conditioned responses, for the 'I' is a psychic agency which only develops in social activity along with the 'me'. The 'I' is contemplated action-in-progress, while the 'me' stands beside objectified past actions and is identified with them. The 'me' on its own would be totally without unity, as it breaks down into many different selves, each one associated with past social acts in different social circumstances. The objective self will have many aspects to it, and possess many capacities stored from past experience which can be used in the future. And it is the active 'I' which draws on these resources as it moves into the future, its reflective function planning activity in accordance with the 'me' — or parts of the 'me' — of past acts, while its active function executes these plans in activity. As John Shotter says of this theory of the self, 'we must imagine ourselves to be not an object-like thing as such, but a mobile *region* of continually self-reproducing activity' (1989: 139). And it is in activity that the 'I' draws together the different aspects of the self to create a unity among them. The self, then, is only created and sustained as a mobile region of self-reproducing social activity.

This is the difference between Mead's theory of the 'I', conscious of its own self-identity, and the theory of Descartes. Whereas Descartes saw the individual, conscious 'I' as a primary reality, Mead argued for the primacy of social relations and activities, which are necessary preconditions for the emergence of the self. It is this which prevents Mead's theory from becoming individualistic like the philosophy of Descartes, Leibniz and Kant.

Mead's description of the social self went even deeper than this, for his notion that the self is created in discourse meant that certain aspects of the personality were bound to mirror the general values and morals of the group contained within discourse. He theorized another aspect of the 'me' as a monitor and censor of actions, thought and speech. This monitor and censor is a running current of awareness which attends over the mind and its imagery; it criticizes, approves, suggests and plans the next stage of conduct in accordance with the 'I'. It is at this point in the psychic process that the morals and values implicit in discourse are strongly felt within the inner conversation of the mind and self. Mead says:

> We assume the general attitude of the group, in the censor that stands at the door of our imagery and inner conversations, and in the affirmation of the laws and axioms of the universe of discourse . . . Our thinking is an inner conversation in which we may be taking roles of specific acquaintances over against ourselves, but usually it is with what I have termed the 'generalized other' that we converse, and so attain to the levels of abstract thinking, and that impersonality, that so-called objectivity we cherish (1924: 288).

Here we see Mead spelling out the different levels of the thought process that we have been outlining so far. Initially, thought and self-awareness arises from interpersonal processes, largely through communication by gesture. Later, as more sophisticated forms of language emerge, the inner conversation which we call 'thinking' takes on an impersonal form, because the conversation in our minds is no longer with actual persons, but with a 'generalized other': that is, the values and morals of the group which are embodied in discourse.

A remarkable parallel emerges at this point between the 'generalized other' as a monitor and censor, and the concept of the 'super-ego' in Freudian theory. For both Mead and Freud, there is an agency in the psyche which represents social attitudes and seeks to channel the impulses towards accepted social goals and objects. The difference between the two theorists is that, in many cases, Freud proved to be an individualist, seeing the impulses and the instincts as primary forces which demand their own satisfaction, no matter what the cost to others. Mead, on the other hand, tries to show how all aspects of the self are social — the impulses, the objective self-image and the subjective attitude. Despite this, both Mead and Freud see the censor within the personality establishing itself in exactly the same way; first, through the attitudes of the parents towards the child, and then later in life, through the generalized attitudes of the group implanted in social consciousness by language. Thus, originally the psychic process has a dramatic content, with real characters playing a part in the inner conversation, while later in life this psychic process becomes purely linguistic and more abstract. As Mead explains:

the child can think about his conduct as good or bad only as he reacts to his own acts in the remembered words of his parents. Until this process has been developed into the abstract process of thought, self-consciousness remains dramatic, and the self which is a fusion of the remembered actor and this accompanying chorus is somewhat loosely organized and is very clearly social. Later the inner stage changes into the forum and workshop of thought. The features and intonations of the dramatis personae fade out and the emphasis falls upon the meaning of the inner speech, the imagery becomes merely the barely necessary cues. But the mechanism remains social, and at any moment the process may become personal (1913: 146–7).

So, initially, the parents and their attitudes reflect the moral character of society, and are the gateway to the wider social group. Slowly, as children begin to learn the language of the group and more about its culture, they find society opening up for them more directly. This is reflected in the way that children of different age groups play together. In very young children, we find that they tend to imitate the roles of adults with whom they are in direct contact, whether it be parents or teachers. Later in childhood, this play will gradually take on more of a story or theme, as children learn to anticipate the actions of others and become capable of responding appropriately in accordance with the role of the character they are playing. Here, a child is showing the capacity to assume the attitudes of others depending on the course of social activity. This ability can be seen in more abstract form as children begin to play organized sports. In these, children must be able to understand the rules of the game and, also, the general movements of all those players who are involved, in order to fit their moves in with the rest. As well, they learn to pit their wits against their opponents. Here we see reflected the growing ability of the child — which develops through the social process — to take the generalized attitude of the group towards themselves and, thus, be capable of treating the self as an object. As individuals they are becoming self-aware, by responding to themselves as another would, through the generalized attitudes of the group.

It is through these different processes that Mead believes individuals gain a sense of their own personalities, over against those with whom they interact, and against the general attitudes within the group communicated in language. I now want to look at the way Mead's theory of the social self overcomes many of the dichotomies and dualisms I outlined in Chapter One.

Overcoming Dichotomy and Dualism

As I noted at the beginning of this chapter, Mead's view of the self overcomes many of the problems generally found in the social sciences because he does not demarcate a social and a personal region. He does not see the individual as the founding reality, with society emerging only as an epiphenomenon — the result of individual actions or intentions. Instead, for Mead (1909: 98), 'it is evident that human conduct was, from the very beginning of its development in a social medium'. This means that Mead does not split the evolution and development of the body, self and mind from the material world in which individuals live; and this includes the social life that people have always lived, from the very beginning, with others. He theorizes no pre- or non-social realm or being which exists prior to society.

The model that Mead develops of the social self should not, therefore, be confused with the model of homo duplex developed by Durkheim, or the ideas propagated by Parsons. In their theories, the social individual became subject to the social and cultural systems, while the 'behavioural organism' and its desires were left partly non-absorbed in the cultural realm of symbols. For Mead, the body has evolved in a changing material and social world, so that instinct, impulse and desire are always directed at others: they can never be thought of as non-social. The fact that the balance of human nature can be modified according to social organization and meaning does not lead Mead to conclude that the body's natural responses are suppressed by society. The activity of the body in the social world and the dynamic of the psyche, are both processes of adjustment, modification and negotiation: neither the body nor the mind are self-enclosed processes, but instead are interdependent and in constant mutual adjustment and modification. Indeed, as Reck mentioned earlier, it is in minded social activity that the non-cognitive needs of the body may be better satisfied.

Also, for Mead, cultural standards and the psychic monitor and censor are not normalized as they were for Parsons. In Mead's theories, meaning and moral standards of behaviour exist only in change, through a constant process of mutual adjustment, and not in a stabilization of values through any mechanism of 'institutionalization'. Meaning can only exist in reference to that about which there is doubt, about objects or actions which are problematic and require constant attention, readjustment and redefinition. In Mead's work, it is through the solution to conflicts and problems that meaning arises, through the effort to readjust activity towards an object by the redefinition of its meaning. Activity and thought is therefore implemental; it is not a means of finding perfect stability but of adapting through change. This need to adapt and change mitigates against the conservative function of certain aspects of social morality, and against the monitor and censor functions of the 'me'. Mead presents this in its dramatic, psychical form.

> Assuming as I do the essentially social character of the ethical end, we find in moral reflection a conflict in which certain values find a spokesman in the old self or a dominant part of the old self, while other values answering to other tendencies and impulses arise in opposition and find other spokesmen to present their cases (1913: 148).

Solution to these psychical dilemmas is not found internally but, 'is reached by the construction of a new world harmonizing the conflicting interests into which enters the new self' (Mead, 1913: 149). The more conservative values are linked to the past and to the past self, or the 'me', while the need for change and adaptation is expressed through the 'I', which is the self of present activity moving toward a planned future. Both the past and the future are reconstructed in the present, according to the problems and conflicts which must be solved, and this draws attention to certain aspects of the past and certain possibilities for the future. In the case of moral conflicts, Mead shows that these can only be solved by seeking an objective social basis on which to attempt to resolve them, and only then can a new self emerge that has settled the conflict between the part of itself tied to the old values, with that part tied to the new.

In the process of what Mead calls 'reconstruction' in society, the culture, symbols and signs employed in interaction are not simply stabilizing elements, as they were in the work of Durkheim and Parsons; they are also the means that the implemental mind uses to adapt to conditions of existence through change. Symbols and signs are emergent and not normalized or transcendental features of social life. The same is true of Mead's concepts of 'role' and 'generalized attitudes' of the group. Here, he is not falling into the trap of what I have called the 'double reduction', where individuals create their own roles, which then become part of the cultural system that 'acts back' to determine their actions. Instead, Mead shows how individuals reconstruct the past, according to problems or conflicts they must solve in the present, to make for a better future. A role is the function an individual performs in this objective activity of adaptation and, as this is constantly changing, so are the roles of individuals and the social demands which are placed upon them. In taking part in the reconstruction of social life, we ourselves play a part in constructing new roles and new selves, so that we are never wholly determined by them.

Mead, then, was not a functionalist in the same way that Durkheim and Parsons were, seeing it as the function of individuals to support the social system through their roles. In contrast, Mead stressed that the social self has concrete functions of its own: it is functional only in that its psychical activity facilitates change and adaptation, and not to the extent it is rigged to unchanging norms. In a changing social world, such rigidity of personality could have apocalyptic consequences for humanity. Nor must we think of the 'real' individual as hidden behind social roles, their being masked and coerced by them. For Mead, the self only develops as part of objective social activity and can therefore be studied as a social object — that is, an object to others which is invested with meaning and, thus, takes on a new dimension in the course of its existence. In human terms, this new dimension is the personality. Society and personality do not represent separate systems which 'interpenetrate' each other, as Parsons thought, but instead, for Mead, they evolve from the very beginning in tandem with each other.

This also leads to a different theory of society in Mead's work, because, from the adaptational point of view, society is an ever changing and emergent organization of activities which is always in the process of meaningful reconstruction. Forms of interaction that become institutionalized and stable are only the base on which further change can take place in areas of conflict. Yet the altered perspectives and objects involved in this change only serve to throw other, previously stable meanings and interactions, into doubt and thereby into conflict and flux. The social process is a *process*: it solidifies into stable interactions and meanings here, only to liquefy into conflict and uncertainty there. Its stability in one quarter allows imaginative reconstruction in another. The creative and also changeable force in this process is the minded self — the personality — whose life is contained within the social interweavings in which it develops self-awareness, capabilities and characteristics. It then objectifies these again in social interaction only to be altered itself by the changes it produces.

Yet of all the dualisms that Mead's work seeks to overcome, the Kantian dualism between subject and object, between consciousness and world, is perhaps foremost. Mead's own theory of consciousness revolves around two levels, as Natsoulas (1985) has recently pointed out. These are, consciousness qua experience and consciousness qua awareness. The former equates with the physiological fact of an animal having consciousness of experience in a definite environment and the latter, with the animal which can bring that experience of conduct up to the level of awareness. To do this, the active body must have developed a self; that is, a sense of 'I' and 'me' against which to refer their experience. However, it must be stressed that for Mead neither level of consciousness is to be regarded as a priori to experience. Both these levels depend on the pattern of activity of the body, and it is this activity that will shape the experience of the environment. In consciousness qua experience, experience is organized by the adaptive activity of the species within its environment. In consciousness qua awareness, consciousness becomes organized by the communicative activity of the social group, which — as we have already seen — leads to the development of individual self-consciousness. Activity can now be self-consciously planned by the self which can reflexively refer its own responses to the consciousness of social meanings and, in this way, determine its interventions in the world. For Mead, then, the way things are experienced does not rest on the qualities of the mind, but on the way those qualities have been shaped through activity. Natsoulas quotes Mead on this subject:

> When one goes back to such a conception of consciousness as early psychologists used, and everything experienced is lodged in consciousness, then one has to create another world outside and say that there is something out there answering to these experiences (1985: 65).

However, as Natsoulas remarks (1985: 65), in Mead's view there was only one world, the world that 'is variously experienced depending on the organism's behaviour in the total sense'. In this light, Mead's theories belong amongst twentieth-century theories of relativity, where a real objective world is not denied, but individuals 'slice' that reality according to their activity within it. It is only in the activity of different species and, later, different persons, that this same world is experienced from a slightly different angle, yet always with a common thread of experience running through it. And it is only when humans attain consciousness qua awareness that they can begin to distinguish what they self-consciously 'know' from the objective world of experience. That is, they can distinguish their own subjectivity from objective existence. But the two are not compartmentalized from the very beginning: it is only in the process of acquiring self-conscious knowledge that the facts we develop about the world can be distinguished from the world itself. This also means that the knowledge we develop about the world can, in some instances, closely approximate the reality of our experience, for there is not another world which is always outside our consciousness. So,

> for Mead, there is no world beyond the world that is experienced, no world beyond to which experience 'answers' echoically. There is only the one world in which all animals exist though they may experience this world differently, from different 'perspectives' (Natsoulas, 1985: 66).

This runs against the Kantian and rationalist view of the self and its experiences that I outlined in Chapter One. In this view, the nature of the objective world was subjectively given and, therefore, the experience of the subject, or self, was always tenuous in its link to reality: ultimately it relied on the grace of God, who designed the objective world and its principles in line with the subjective categories in which it was seen. There were two worlds in Kant; the subjective and the objective world. For Mead, nothing could be further from the truth, for human beings are always part of their material world: their thinking does not structure it, rather, they structure their own thinking to solve objective, material problems. It is only at this point that the material world becomes subject to human ideas, imagination and judgement, when problems or conflicts restrict human action and we are forced into the subjective attitude to solve the problem and reconstruct activity. There is a dialectical relation between the material and the mental in Mead's work, in opposition to the Kantian one-way street. To Mead, it is our sensual, bodily contact with the world and with each other — finding its medium in the gesture — on which activity and meaningful practice are based, out of which emerge knowledge and ideas. Also, what Kant saw as the active 'I' of the personality, which he took to be given in individuals as a ray of pure apperception, Mead shows to be a product of meaningful social activity. Thus, categories of self-consciousness and moral thought and action are constantly being redrawn in society, but always within the boundaries set by experience.

Far from seeing the personality as an organization contained 'within the skin', as Allport put it, Mead has shown to what extent the inner organization of the self rests on the dialectical interchange with everything that is outside it: that is to say, its material environment as it is mediated through social activity and communication. It is always possible to make a distinction between internal and external experience *in an analytical sense*, but we can no longer believe there is a natural and invisible wall that divides the two in reality. To think of the personality as a monad, a pre-sealed primary reality out of which emerges social relations, is to cling to a supernatural notion of the self. Mead says that:

> Our whole religious thought has gone upon the assumption that the personality was a fixed substance . . . a something given at birth and to be carried eternally. Through its faculties large stores of knowledge may be acquired and it may be developed in character but its essence is a fixed entity (cited in Mills, 1986: 194).

Mead contrasts this view with his pragmatist social psychology, where

> from this standpoint, perfect individuality or a fully developed personality, instead of being something given and simply to be recognized, is the result of deep and profound consciousness of the actual social relations. Furthermore, as a prerequisite of this consciousness, we imply the formation of the most extensive and essential social relationships whose control must lie within themselves and in their interaction upon each other rather than in any internal judgement. From this standpoint personality is an *achievement* rather than a given fact (cited in Mills, 1986: 197).

When Mead refers above to the formation of extensive social relations as a prerequisite for social consciousness, he is talking of the social relations that play a part in the constitution of our experience before we become profoundly aware of them and, hence, he is talking of consciousness qua experience. Thus, there is not only the self-conscious side of the personality but, also, the entire consciousness of experience — or, as Helminiak (1984) calls it, in relation to Freud, the 'preconscious' — in which self-consciousness is set. In Mead's work this does not emerge as in Freud's, out of the unconscious instinctual drives, but instead is cast by the whole realm of experience that we take for granted, which has been established by the social relations which predate us as individuals. Even where activity has become problematical and social objects and social relations have to be self-consciously reconstructed, the new arrangements can always slip out of consciousness and turn into habits. These unthinking patterns of conduct were seen by Mead as necessary to the entire economy of our conduct. We can then turn our attention to other instances where there are problems and conflicts in interaction. Here, the reverse can have happened, where what was previously preconscious and taken-for-granted in social life, becomes self-conscious and open to reconstruction. If the problem affects enough people, there can be a huge shift in organized social conduct.

This is similar to Heidegger's (1967) notion of 'being-in-the-world', where the function of objects is constituted by habitual everyday activity in the material world, and the meaning that objects have for us is the part they play in that habitual activity. Our own 'being' stems from this 'being-in' the practical activity of life. But the more obvious parallel to Mead's work is that of his fellow pragmatist John Dewey (1922), who also enquired into the role of habit in human behaviour. Mixon (1980) comments on this work, saying that, for Dewey, habit is not the repetition of acts, but acquired predispositions to ways or modes of response. A person inclined to anger easily may commit a murder, yet the act to which his or her habit predisposes them may happen only once. Our habits are governed and limited by our capacities, even in the most simple things we do, such as our movements and bodily carriage. These habits are largely unconscious within the economy of our activity, and so to control or alter a habit means bringing the unconscious attitude into self-conscious awareness. Thus, like Mead, Dewey sees habit as largely preconscious, as the way in which our responses are modulated in social activity in order to give rise to further social acts. As Mixon (1980: 178) says, 'physical, emotional, and cognitive ways of behaving can be conceived of as organized, skill-like capacities or habits'. Dewey saw these as a necessary element in social adaptation, believing that the idea most people have of habit being fixed and unchanging is due to the type of social conditions in which we live:

the reputation habits seem to have as resisting re-adaptation to changed conditions is because social conditions demand from a large part of the population a kind of unthinking activity that results in an abnormal type of habits (cited in Mixon, 1980: 182).

So habits are set within the overall network of activity within the group, and it is here that the preconscious, or consciousness qua experience, is formed. Self-consciousness, or consciousness qua awareness, is developed within communicative interaction, in the same social network of activity which forms the seat of experience. Thus we have seen how the pragmatist school of social psychology, particularly in the work of G.H. Mead, theorizes the development of human personality under social conditions. This occurs in the social organization that arises from the mutual adaptation of conduct, an adaptation that takes place in activity through the medium of communication. It is in this communication, particularly through language, that individuals become self-conscious and gain control over their own responses within social activity. The attitude of the generalized group also enters consciousness through language and plays a part in the control of behaviour.

Mead's theories of the social development of personality are therefore a far more satisfactory way of understanding the self than the ideas we looked at in Chapter One, and avoid the dualism that is so often set up between the self and society. However, Mead is sometimes criticized for the lack of a theory of society in his work. It is on exploring this criticism that some flaws begin to open up in his theories.

Mead and the Theory of Society

One of Mead's students, Herbert Blumer (who actually coined the term 'symbolic interactionism' to designate Mead's approach), has summarized the contribution made to social psychology and psychology by his former teacher. While Blumer's account of symbolic interactionism differs substantially from Mead's (see Joas, 1985: 6), he nevertheless realizes Mead's contribution to the social sciences, saying that:

He reversed the traditional assumptions underlying philosophical, psychological, and sociological thought to the effect that human beings possess minds and consciousness as original "givens", that they live in worlds of pre-existing and self-constituted objects, that their behaviour consists of responses to such objects, and that group life consists of the association of such reacting human organisms (Blumer, 1969: 61).

However, 'in making his brilliant contributions along this line he did not map out a theoretical scheme of human society' (1969: 61). This is despite the fact Mead has already made clear that he sees other selves in a social environment logically antedating the individual self. Furthermore, these selves are locked into patterns of communicative social activity which becomes the basis for individual selves and minds. Even the intentions and motives of individuals are to be found in these group processes, for, 'the objective of the act is then found in the life-process of the group, not in those of the separate individuals alone' (Mead, 1924: 280). It follows logically from this position that the key to unlocking some of the secrets of the self is the study of the social group in which the individual is active.

Despite this, Mead did not develop any consistent theory of the wider social formation, which means that one of the dichotomies he is less successful in solving is that between the macro and the micro processes in society. Even though he identified language as an impersonal system and, therefore, a macro structure, he did not provide an adequate theory of the formation of processes at a macro level. Nor did he develop an adequate theory of the link between such macro structures and the micro processes of every-day interaction. Because of this, it often appears that Mead left intact the dualism that existed in the work of sociologists like Simmel, between macro and micro processes in society.

For example, while Mead has hinted that the division of labour is an important feature of the macro level of society — because it is the objective basis for the differentiation of roles and therefore individual identities — he has no overall theory of the social processes that led to the greater complexity of this division. Mead says that, in the division of labour, the individual

always and necessarily assumes a definite relation to, and reflects in the structure of his self or personality, the general organized pattern of experience and activity exhibited in or characterizing the social life-process in which he is involved, and of which his self or personality is essentially a creative expression or embodiment (Mead, 1934: 221–2).

Yet there is no investigation into the general organized pattern of experience and activity of which the individual personality is a creative expression. Mead was also concerned by the divisions which separate and segregate human beings, through national-mindedness (Mead, 1929), and also by attitudes of hostility to certain groups within our own society (Mead, 1917).

However, Mead thought that the conflicts created between groups, by nationalism or by prejudice, could be overcome by greater communication both within and between societies. He thought that the problem was

> that of overcoming the distances in space and time, and the barriers of language and convention and social status, [so] that we can converse with ourselves in the roles of those who are involved with us in the common undertaking of life (Mead, 1924: 292).

Only when these divisions are broken down through more adequate forms of communication, can a universal morality be created through which conflict can be settled more peaceably. In understanding that conflicts can only be settled objectively, before the subjective attitude becomes less conflict-ridden, Mead has shown that he sees the truly humanized personality as only arising under more humanized and democratic social conditions.

Yet while Mead envisaged a new social organization with greater possibilities for communication as a solution to many of our problems, he did not analyse Western social organization in the twentieth century, which creates groups with both common and divergent interests. With his emphasis placed solely on communication, Mead has failed to analyse other areas of power and inequality in society. He does not talk about economic inequality, nor does he consider the question of ideology. That is, certain groups in society have the power to impose beliefs and values on the rest of the population which are accepted as the basic facts of life. This is largely because these ruling groups also control other aspects of social organization which structure the everyday lives of individuals and groups, making these values appear to be simple common sense.

Because of this failure to identify power relations in society, Mead cannot begin to consider how social divisions and inequalities are reflected in the self through social organization. As Roberts (1977) points out, Mead plays down the internalization of social conflict within the personality through the idea of the 'generalized other'. If society is in conflict, then the generalized values that we appropriate psychically to steer our conduct will also be, in part, contradictory. The absence of any notion of the repressed unconscious, to supplement Mead's idea of the habitual preconscious, could also be seen as the result of a lack of internal conflict in the pragmatist theory of the self. Mead does not consider that contrasting social meanings or moral values might create motives for action in the personality that oppose one another, with the result that the weaker motive may be repressed by the more powerful one.

In the next chapter I will turn to contemporary interactionist theories to see if they have managed to compensate for these errors of omission and analytical blind spots. For now we must remember Mead's achievement: he has largely overcome the theoretical dichotomies that often emerge in thinking of the relation of individual to society, and he has put forward one of the most comprehensive theories of the social self.

Conclusion

In this chapter I have tried to show how Mead's theory of the social self is a great advance upon other models of personality to be found in the social sciences. His theories resolve many of the dichotomies and dualisms that emerged from Chapter One. This is largely because he refuses to see any aspect of the self as asocial, yet at the same time he does not reduce the individual to the level of a cultural cypher. Mead demonstrates how individuals develop their subjectivity in the network of social interactions and meanings, and that this subjective attitude has both a moral and a cultural aspect, as well as a personal and innovative sense. Social meanings are given a personal sense and application through the 'I' that develops in the social self. But this 'I' can only arise in social communication, where first we get an objective sense of our own self, which is the 'me'.

However, while realizing that the social structure of the group is always creatively embodied in the self, Mead did not deal thoroughly with the formation of any particular society, nor did he dwell on the ramifications of social conflicts for the individual psyche. This left the exact nature of the contemporary social self — or the social self of any specific period in history — unexplored. He did not consider the power relations that exist in society on a macro, or a historical scale, and the extent to which these limit the scope for consciously chosen actions within the social group. This led him to overlook the possibility of constructing a theory of the repressed unconscious like that in psychoanalysis, where more powerful or more socially acceptable motives can gain dominance within the personality over other impulses which are socially prohibited and repressed. I want now to ask whether more contemporary theories inspired by interactionism can solve some of these problems. However, I do not wish to lose sight of Mead's contribution: he has developed a consistent theory of the social self and, in so doing, has provided insights into personality formation that are indispensable for the social sciences.

CHAPTER THREE
The Self in Everyday Communication

A contemporary theorist who has tried to advance the type of social psychology begun by George Herbert Mead, is Rom Harré. He has embarked on a philosophical project which attempts to synthesize elements drawn from micro sociology, social psychology and psychology, around the conceptual framework provided by the 'ethogenic' social sciences. This is a term for those social sciences which try to discover the belief systems or methods people employ in their everyday lives to give meaning to their actions and by which they construct their own identities. The framework ethogenics provides is an interpretive one that seeks to discover the collective meanings and rules people develop to negotiate and manage the daily process of interaction. A number of social psychologists and philosophers have now formed a loose grouping around this methodology, and Harré has recently proclaimed ethogenics as the 'new psychology'. In this chapter I will consider the extent to which Harré and the ethogenic school have been successful in advancing the methodological breakthroughs made by Mead. I shall also ascertain how the 'new psychology' deals with the problems inherent in Mead's work, which centred on the lack of a macro theory of society and an inability to theorize about psychological contradictions and repressions. But first, I want to examine the roots of the ethogenic approach, which are to be found in contemporary micro sociology, in particular the ethnomethodological school of Harold Garfinkel and the dramaturgical interactionism of Erving Goffman.

Micro Sociology

Although it seems paradoxical, in many ways the micro sociological approach is a logical development from the grand systems theory of Talcott Parsons. I say that this appears paradoxical, because an approach which concentrates on the achievements of people in constructing and maintaining their everyday world, seems far removed from the large scale ambitions of Parsons.

However, both systems theory and micro sociology have one central theme in common: the question of how social order is possible, and what are the preconditions which must be present for the members of a social group continually to make the possibility of social order an everyday reality.

It is this achievement of moral order, normally regarded as commonplace by most sociological theories, which is the central focus of the work of Harold Garfinkel and the ethnomethodological school. This approach views the real world in which people live as the organized activity of everyday life, which is achieved in an artful, yet taken-for-granted, way by members of the social group. In this accomplishment, the 'members' employ known and well used procedures — their 'ethno-methods' — which social scientists must try to understand if they are to make sense of everyday actions. The ethno-methods are composed of the rules and resources which can be used by members to construct, account for, and give meaning to the everyday activity of the social world.

> Ethnomethodological studies analyze everyday activities as members' methods for making these same activities visibly-rational-and-reportable-for-all-practical-purposes, i.e., 'accountable,' as organizations of commonplace everyday activities (Garfinkel, 1967: xii).

We can see from the above one of the central principles of ethnomethodology: that is, the activities through which members produce and manage their organized everyday affairs, stem from the same procedures through which members account for their actions. This is because the competence of members in constructing the social world is contained in their implicit and explicit understanding of it, and this, in turn, is displayed in the way they account for that world and their own actions within it. Ethnomethodology is not itself a theory of social action within the everyday world, but instead employs a sensitivity to everyday accounting practices in order to discover the formal properties of commonplace, practical common sense actions, from within actual social settings. It is interested purely in the question of how a social order is constructed and maintained, and in the formal properties of settings in which this is achieved.

Through this perspective, Garfinkel restates Kant's concern with the possibility of a moral order, seeing it not as an awesome, 'cosmic' question, but as a technical problem. For Garfinkel, the moral order consists of the rule-governed activities of everyday life, which is a common sense world that is simply assumed by members as a set of 'background expectancies'. These are the unnoticed features of discourse whereby people's statements are recognized as common, reasonable, understandable, plain talk. Such properties of discourse are conditions under which individuals are entitled to claim to know what they are talking about, and through which they can recognize the legitimacy of what others say. Because of the background expectancies we can anticipate that what we say and do will be recognized and understood by others. But more than this, we can presume that it *ought* to be understood by any rational and reasonable person and, therefore, these expectancies are regarded as morally binding.

Common sense understanding therefore relies on the enforceable character of action in compliance with the taken-for-granted expectancies of everyday morality. It also portrays for members the real conditions of their society, yet this reality can only be produced and reproduced by members if they are motivated to comply with the background expectancies of the moral order. This motivation consists not only of the persons' 'grasp of and subscription to the "natural facts of life in society" ' (Garfinkel, 1967: 53), but also their commitment to honour such facts must be bound by the desire to achieve the self-esteem of being seen as a rational, reasonable and competent member of society. A person does this by utilizing what everyone knows is a pre-established corpus of socially warranted knowledge, and speaks and acts according to its precepts.

To Garfinkel, this is also cause for introducing a new concept of the person into sociology which, in his view, had previously regarded individuals as 'judgmental and cultural dopes'. That is to say, social scientists had tended to see the actions of individuals in employing their cultural symbols and signs as purely epiphenomena — processes which were only secondary to, and wholly determined by, the cultural system itself. Garfinkel hopes to reinstate the study of the actions and judgements of individuals through ethnomethodology, by putting back into the practical realities of everyday life the common sense rationalities of members. Through this perspective, ethnomethodology looks at the nature, production and recognition of reasonable, realistic and analysable actions in daily life.

There are many apparent similarities between this approach and the micro sociology of Erving Goffman. He continues the study of the technical achievement of the production and reproduction of everyday life, but in a subtly different manner. Goffman moves from the analysis of the practical necessities and the preconditions for the achievement of a moral order, to the study of the expressive techniques used by individuals to achieve and maintain that order. In particular, he concentrates on the expressive ability through which individuals develop their capacity for managing the impressions others receive of them. Through their ability to manage impressions, individuals also create a definition of the reality of a social situation which others must initially accept.

Like Garfinkel, then, Goffman is concerned with how order is created in society and how agreement between interacting individuals is produced and sustained. This is achieved by individuals suppressing their immediate, heartfelt feelings, and in their place conveying a view of the situation it is felt others will find at least temporarily acceptable. Goffman (1969) regards this as simply a surface agreement, a veneer of consensus, which is engineered by the social 'actors' concealing their own desires in order to pay lip service to values they feel obliged to respect. A situation such as this is understood by Goffman to be a working consensus, in which the participants contribute to a definition of that situation. Together they reach not so much a real agreement as to what actually exists but an agreement over whose claims concerning what issues will be temporarily honoured.

In forming the working consensus, the information that the individual possesses or acquires about others is all important, for it is on this basis that the individual builds up a definition of the situation and plans lines of responsive action. Individuals' initial projection of their own self commits them to the image they have fostered, and limits them in the future in any attempt to appear as someone different. Thus, as interaction progresses, there may well be additions and modifications to the initial information that actors possess, but it must grow out of and be capable of being related to the initial definitions worked out by participants. Individuals can make greater claims about their own self, and about the situation, at the beginning of an interaction than they can once the interaction is under way: at this point, they find themselves and others bound by the moral claims and demands they have made through their initial definitions. If the individual can live up to or surpass their definitions of the situation and their own self-projections, then that person has a right to the respect of other participants in the encounter. Should the person fail in this task, then they will lose the respect of others and experience feelings of shame.

Again, like Garfinkel, Goffman is not concerned with the content of activity, nor is he interested in 'the role it plays in the interdependent activities of an ongoing social system' (1969: 13). Rather, he is concerned with the techniques of impression management and the common contingencies of situations associated with the employment of such techniques. He sees the problems of individuals presenting themselves and their actions before others as 'dramaturgical' ones. That is, they are problems akin to those of actors on a stage who must make their performances believable and convincing to the audience. Goffman therefore employs an analogy in understanding how individuals produce and manage their social encounters, seeing these as problems to be dealt with by stage craft and stage management. Individuals present an impression of themselves through their expressive abilities, which is essentially a performance that creates a 'front': that is, an image of the person's own self that is projected to others. Through the moral order, however, individuals are held to the fronts they have created, and these carve out the individual's 'moral career'. This is bound to the image individuals have created of themselves and, through this, the expectancies that others develop of them and the moral demands they feel justified in making of them. In his work on asylums, Goffman (1961) shows how the role of 'mental patient' sticks to those who have been designated as mentally ill through the expectancies of others, thus becoming a moral career that the individual finds hard to shake.

Goffman, then, makes a distinction between the self as a character and as a performer. The self as it appears to others in interaction is a performed character, a dramatic effect that arises from the scene as the actor presents it, including the presentation of personal characteristics. Whether or not this character is a true reflection of an individual's personality is of no concern to Goffman, for he does not distinguish between true and false selves. Instead, what is of importance to him, is whether the presentation of the social setting and the self which the individual makes will be credited with respect by others or discredited. Upon this depend the characteristics that will be attributed to the individual by others.

In contrast to this, the person as a performer is one who trains as a social actor and learns their part. Being a performer means developing all the capabilities and capacities of the actor. It also means having all the fantasies and anxieties of the actor, courting in one's performances the possibility of triumphant successes and dismal failures, the joys of winning the adulation of the crowd and the shame of being booed off stage. Interestingly, Goffman does not attribute all the capacities of the performer to social learning, for

> These attributes of the individual *qua* performer are not merely a depicted effect of particular performances; they are psycho-biological in nature, and yet they seem to arise out of intimate interaction with the contingencies of staging performances (1969: 224).

As we will see later on, this tends to open up the dichotomy between the biological and the social being in Goffman's work, which undermines some of the theoretical advances made by Mead. But also Goffman's theories do nothing to overcome the dualism between macro and micro social processes, for Goffman does not even have the intent of constructing a macro theory of society in which to fit his discoveries about the construction and reconstruction of everyday life. He tends to assume, in Parsonian manner, that social establishments are 'closed systems' (1969: 211), and that the study of the relation between such establishments is of a different order of facts from the study of daily life. Even in one of his last published essays, Goffman (1983) was still wrestling with the problem of the relation between the interaction order at the micro level of society, and the social institutions and social structure at the macro level. All Goffman could do was to advocate that there was a 'loose coupling' between the two orders, but he could not specify how they were linked, nor what effects the two orders had on one another. His main case was still to argue 'for treating the interaction order as a substantive domain in its own right' (1983: 2).

I will return to a critique of micro sociology later in this chapter. For now, I wish to look at the way this approach has been generalized as an ethogenic social science and utilized by the 'new psychology'. In this, I will mainly concern myself with the work of Rom Harré, as this is the most systematic statement of ethogenic psychology. However, I want also briefly to consider how, on closer inspection, the new psychology breaks down into different elements, each resting on a separate branch of interpretive sociology.

The Construction of Social and Personal Being

In Harré's social psychology the central elements from both ethnomethodology and dramaturgy are incorporated into his theory of social and personal being. From Goffman's work Harré takes over the analogy of social life as a stage performance, and allocates a central role to expressive activity within society, for this is the medium through which impressions of the self are conveyed. From Garfinkel's analysis Harré retains the attitude that the accounts people give of their actions are also identical to their resources for producing social action.

For Harré, of central importance in such a theory of human activity is the conversation that takes place between people in social life. Conversation is the mode through which information is exchanged between individuals, and through which people make presentations of themselves and their settings. In this way, individuals not only construct and maintain their social interactions, they also construct their own personalities through the presentation of the self and the way they account for their actions. Persons in conversation therefore becomes the primary mode of life. As Harré says,

> I take the array of persons as a primary human reality. I take the conversations in which those persons are engaged as completing the primary structure, bringing into being social and psychological reality. Conversation is to be thought of as creating a social world just as causality generates a physical one (1983: 64–5).

This theory of the primary structure, where conversation is seen as creating a social world and conversational accounting practices are identical with the resources for producing acts, reminds one of Benedetto Croce's (1913) remark that 'In the beginning was neither the Word nor the Act; but the Word of the Act and the Act of the Word.' That is to say, social reality and social activity are created at the point where conversation begins between individuals, for it is through language that society and the self are created. Harré also uses this theory to make a distinction between two very different orders of reality — the expressive order which constitutes society, and the practical order which is physically structured by causality. In physical reality objects are located in space, locked in causal relations with one another — relations of push and pull, the mechanics of the universe of matter and motion. In the primary structure of social reality, what exists instead of locations in space are persons, and what takes the place of causal relations is conversational interchange. It is in this structure that the social and psychological world is created.

It is at this juncture that Goffman's expressive order emerges which constitutes human society. And for Harré, it is here that social being develops where individuals find the means of truly expressing themselves, displaying their worth as human beings and impressing on others what sort of person they wish to be seen as. Therefore, the expressive order of society and the psychological realities constructed within it, form as secondary structures out of the primary structure. It is out of the primary mode of people in conversation that there develop accounting practices, rules and conventions, along with the styles of self-presentation, which are of central importance to Harré's social psychology. As Harré, Clarke and De Carlo say of this approach,

> the focus of interest becomes the actions for which human beings can be called to account. The method involves the analysis of those accounts in search of the meanings the actors give to their actions and the rules and conventions which they follow (1985: 24).

Like Garfinkel, Harré does not want to see individuals as judgemental dopes, whose actions are 'caused' in a mechanical way by any external force — environmental, cultural or historical — working on them. Instead, human agents are to be viewed as responsible and autonomous individuals who use accounting practices, rules and conventions to construct their everyday activities and give meaning to them. They are also held to account by others for the actions they undertake, and are thereby turned into morally responsible agents. Individuals are therefore knowledgeable and self-aware about the things that they do, relying on the information they have about people and settings in which they are involved. Through this information, they can structure their actions in a moral way, having to live up to the impressions they give others of their own self, and placing demands on others according to the information they possess about them. In this way, individuals present an image of themselves in a dramaturgical fashion, just as Goffman described, in order to win the respect and admiration of their fellow actors. Harré believes that this is a basic need which has motivated people to act socially in all places and times.

Separate from this expressive order, Harré subsumes the world of work and production under the heading of the 'practical order'. This would include all the features of society described in the political economy of Karl Marx. Also included in this order would be any non-conscious, unpremeditated reflex responses of human individuals, for Harré would classify these as taking place through biological systems of causality, rather than as freely chosen conscious acts. Any responses which are caused by an external or internal force are labelled as 'behaviour' by Harré, as opposed to the 'acts' which are consciously planned and accounted for, in which the new psychology is primarily interested.

Harré believes that at most places and times the expressive order is dominant over the practical order (except, perhaps, in nineteenth century Western Europe where Marx carried out his analyses), a fact which can be evidenced in a remarkable feature of human society which is termed 'elaboration'. This is where the rituals and conventions in society far outstrip the activity necessary merely to survive physically, which means that these social practices are used largely for expressive rather than practical purposes. Elaboration is a universal feature of all human societies because it allows expression and, therefore, the satisfaction of the basic need of people to win the respect of others.

It is within this expressive order that the individual's social being is constructed. Social being is largely dependent on the presentation of oneself in public, the parts or roles that an individual plays in social life, and the way the person accounts for her- or himself. In turn, social being is wholly dependent on the social script of rules, resources and conventions, and the activity and conversation that takes place in the social scenario of everyday situations. Each person may develop their own style of playing a role, which gives their part a personal twist, yet the style of self-presentation that is called for will largely be determined by the situation that calls it out.

Social being is therefore synonymous with the parts that people play in social life and the way they perform them. Harré makes a distinction between this 'social being' and 'personal being' because he wants to distinguish between the roles that individuals play and their inner sense of being. This is often felt by individuals to be different from the social image that they project. Here we find a distinction similar to the one made by Mead between the 'me' and the 'I', or the objective and subjective sense of self. Also like Mead, Harré notes that persons will have different aspects to their social identities depending on the different situations in which they are involved, referring to these as 'personas'. Harré, Clarke and De Carlo describe 'persona' as

> the public way people present themselves to one another, masks adopted in everyday life. Common sense suggests we should contrast persona with personality, but when one actually studies persons passing through the social world, through a great many situations and scenes, through many settings, playing many distinctive parts, 'personae' and 'personalities' cannot be distinguished. As people pass through distinctive situations, not only do they do different things but they display distinctive personalities by displaying distinctive personae (1985: 142).

However, distinct from the personas that individuals develop in everyday situations, there is also forged what Goffman referred to as 'character', based on the moral judgements that others make of a person's actions related to the values of the local moral order. Harré agrees with Goffman, that a person's character is closely bound up with their moral career, and this is related to the winning and losing of honour and respect within the expressive order. Harré says:

> an essential element in the understanding of the social activities of human beings derives from their attributions to each other of permanent moral qualities. I have called this attribution 'character'. It is made up of the attributes that a particular group of people ascribe to an individual on the basis of the impressions they have formed of him on the basis of his expressive activities. These attributes, or rather the beliefs that people have as to these attributes determine the expectations that a group form of a person. They are the foundations, as individual beliefs of the willingness of others to defer to and praise an individual or to denigrate him, or simply to ignore him. They are the ultimate basis of his moral career (1979: 313).

In Harré's view, social activity and the personality and character an individual displays within it, are based on their performance in expressive interaction. But behind the performance lie the rules and resources of the moral order that an 'actor' draws upon to structure their performance. The degree to which the individual has command over the rules and resources of everyday life will determine their 'competence' in self-presentation. The distinction between competence and performance follows the example laid down by the linguist Noam Chomsky, who used the term 'competence' to describe the grammatical rules of the language in a culture, and the term 'performance' to describe the everyday application of these rules in the speech acts of members of the culture. Harré draws on this theory of language to make a distinction between the competence of social actors, in terms of their linguistically formed knowledge of the rules and conventions of society, and their ability to translate this into an appropriate performance depending on the situation they are in and the type of person they are judged to be. Ultimately their personality depends on performance and therefore on the rules and resources in the person's command. For De Waele and Harré, this is how personality is to be defined in their theoretical schema.

> [Personality] is to be identified with the resources upon which a person draws in giving form and meaning to his actions as social performances. These resources are the basis for what one could call his social competence. So in a general way this theory falls into the competence–performance category of theories of human behaviour (1976: 193).

Here we can see De Waele and Harré drawing on linguistics as well as social psychology to achieve a more integrated ethogenic approach to personality formation. Harré also tries to bring into the ethogenic synthesis the personal construct theory of George Kelly that I described in Chapter One. However, Harré wants to show that personal constructs — or what he calls 'templates' — are not at all personal in origin, for they are collectively developed in social communication. For him, the templates are collectively based, yet individually modified constructs which form the plans and blueprints for a person's social activity. The basis of the templates is in cultural resources, such as shared systems of knowledge and belief, and only when these are developed at the social level do they shape individual constructs. Again, we see why the accounts people provide of their own activity and personality are so important for the new psychology, because they lay bare the beliefs, rules and reasoning-procedures that are at the heart of the construct system that composes the self. The basis of ethogenic social psychology is, therefore, the development of hypotheses about the system of beliefs that actors possess and which they use to produce meaningful actions in the social world. The hypothesis of the rules which structure these actions will also serve as a model for the templates and constructs which are instrumental in their production and fundamental to the self.

Analysing communal and personal beliefs is thus important in the new psychology because these are seen to be at the core of personal being, our own inner sense of self. As I have already pointed out, this idea of personal being is similar to Mead's theory of the 'I' within the self, only he saw this as the subjective side of objective social actions, whereas for Harré, subjectivity is based in the beliefs a person holds about their own self existing as a certain type of social and moral actor. Theories and beliefs about what it is to be a person in society, and about the type of person one actually is, are at the centre of the experience of one's own self. For Harré,

> a person is not a natural object, but a cultural artefact. A person is a being who has learned a theory, in terms of which his or her experience is ordered. I believe that persons are characterized neither by their having a characteristic kind of experience nor by some specific genetic endowment. They can be identified neither phenomenologically nor biologically, but only by the character of their beliefs (1983: 20).

And

> By believing the theories in which concepts like the self have a place, we so structure our experience as to create them: different theories, different mental organization. Everything that appears to each of us as the intimate structure of our personal being, I believe to have its source in a socially sustained and collectively imposed cluster of theories (1983: 21).

Through the possession of a theory of the self, then, a person 'orders, partitions and reflects on its own experience and becomes capable of self-intervention and control' (Harré, 1983: 93). It is therefore through the possession of theories and beliefs that people are empowered as social agents, with a self against which to plan and construct their activities. But self-consciousness and self-intervention are not enough on their own to describe personal being, for they are entirely dependent on social rules and cultural resources for their existence; they cannot help us to understand how each person is in many ways unique. Like Mead, Harré sees the self as constructed in social communication, and psychological processes are similarly understood as based on socially learned linguistic devices. Yet, for Harré, there must be something within these devices that allow each person to become unique within the mechanisms of their own cognition. This he believes is found in the linguistic practice of metaphor, through which individuals transform social structures and linguistic rules into unique thoughts, plans and styles of role performance which are entirely their own. Thus,

> Personal being arises only by a transformation of the social inheritance of individuals. It is essentially a semantic transformation and arises through the use of cognitive processes typified by metaphor to transform social inheritance (Harré, 1983: 23).

Metaphor allows us a leeway to develop our own personal style, by applying cultural and cognitive rules to particular situations imaginatively rather than literally. Thus, in the ethogenic method, there is no psychological property that corresponds to the sense of 'I', only a set of theories and beliefs about there being such an 'I'. These are appropriated through everyday language use and metaphorically transformed, functioning to enable us to believe that our self and our consciousness is ordered into one single, unified and unique autonomous being. In a quotation which summarizes the spirit and method of the new psychology, Harré states that:

> The fundamental human reality is a conversation, effectively without beginning or end, to which, from time to time, individuals may make contributions. All that is personal in our mental and emotional lives is individually appropriated from the conversation going on around us and perhaps idiosyncratically transformed. The structure of our thinking and feeling will reflect, in various ways, the form and content of that conversation. The main thesis of this work is that mind is no sort of entity, but a system of beliefs structured by a cluster of grammatical models. The science of psychology must be reshaped accordingly (1983: 20).

To summarize Harré's claims about the personality, he is saying that we must regard it as a duality between the social being — as seen in the personas and character created in public-collective life — and the personal being, which is the self that is created by the learning and stylizing of a self-concept. This creates a private-individual experience which is not necessarily shared. Thus in any expressive order, there is always a degree of separation between the public world in which we find our social being, and the private world in which we create a personal sense of self and idiosyncratically transform our social inheritance. However, Harré's theory and the micro sociology on which it is based, tend to continue many of the dualisms in the social sciences that we are trying to overcome. For the reasons I will set out below, this leaves his theory of social and personal being somewhat wanting and settles none of the problems left to us by Mead.

The Reopening of Theoretical Dualisms

One of the problems in micro sociological analyses like those of Garfinkel and Goffman is that they see themselves purely in analytical terms, searching out the technical issues of the production and reproduction of everyday life. The maintenance of a moral order is solely a question of how the members of a group achieve order in their daily lives, rather than an enquiry into the substance of that morality. Ethnomethodology and dramaturgy do not ask the questions, why this morality in this era? or, why do certain beliefs and values have a meaning for people in a certain place and time? Thus ontological and historical questions are replaced with (cross-) cultural analyses into the different methods people use to achieve moral order.

This has led Bauman (1978) to characterize ethnomethodology as a 'transcendental analytic', which is to say that it is not interested in the actual social objects or meanings that are produced by members, but in the necessary preconditions for the very production of meaning itself. In this way, ethnomethodology bears many similarities to Kantian analyses, in that it is not so much concerned with objects or meanings, as with the manner of the social production of the meaning of objects and the preconditions that must be present for meaning to emerge. The information that members possess about the setting of action and about each other — the background expectancies that they share — are all preconditions for the production of meaningful, moral action. Yet ethnomethodology cannot tell us how information is acquired in the first place. It must be present as a precondition for social action to take place, but how is it accumulated prior to active involvement in the world, and how is such information agreed upon by members so that it may form the background expectancies of moral activity?

Ethnomethodology cannot, therefore, tell us why people ascribe to different background expectancies in different cultures and historical periods, nor why these change over time in all societies. While it wishes to describe and analyse the practical achievement of moralities, it cannot explain how such background expectancies are anchored in the *practical reality of people's socially structured experience*. This must centre upon a person's place and activity in a wider network of social relations and interdependencies which are structured in a particular way — having developed and continuing to develop through a particular historical process — and which place expectations upon individuals. The rationality and morality of everyday action could then be seen, not just in a technical light, but ontologically. Why this morality in this age? Only now the ontological question is transmuted into a sociological one: what role does a certain morality play when its everyday production and maintenance is seen in terms of the logic of social relations as a whole in which individual lives are set? The question still remains one in which the activity of individuals plays a central role: except now this activity is not analysed in a sociological vacuum. It must be viewed in terms of wider social structures and interdependencies.

Unfortunately, Goffman falls into exactly the same trap of setting aside the 'macro' question of the content of activity and its role in society, maintaining the macro/micro divide that was evident in the sociology of Simmel. The questions Goffman attempts to answer are ones dealing with sociation, or the way in which individuals form social groups and maintain them through the use of expressive techniques. This leaves the back door wide open to smuggle in the asocial view of individuals as existing prior to the social group. This is because the social group is not seen as primary; rather the individual is the fundamental unit and it is only from a collection or an array of individuals that society forms as an epiphenomenon. Unlike Garfinkel's 'transcendental analytic', Goffman's interactionism tends towards subjectivism, for it stresses the meanings that individual actors give to situations and the impressions they foster of themselves. On numerous occasions in Goffman's work we are told that it is 'the individual' who defines the situation and their own characteristics.

Micro sociology reopens all the old dualisms, not just that between macro and micro processes. The reality of objective experience is also thrown into doubt, for reality is only what actors define it as. Although Garfinkel tries hard to rid the social sciences of subjectivism, he and Goffman — who is not so successful on this count — raise the spectre of a new form of solipsism. This was the old philosophical view that reality was simply what we imagined it to be. Taken to its logical conclusions, is not micro sociology advocating a similar thing: that reality is only what it is socially and meaningfully constructed to be? We could ask of this approach whether there are no external limits to how we socially define the world?

Stemming from this, Goffman's work opens up another dichotomy between the 'front' that a person adopts as a moral character and the self of the performer who manipulates the mask. While Goffman refuses to broach the question of which is the most 'real', the presentational front or the self of the actor who is behind it, he still makes it appear as though there are two selves: the self who is a mask and the residual self that it hides. Goffman appears not to understand what Mead so clearly illustrated, that the subjective self and its capacities are a consequence of the individual's objective sociality. So difficult was it for Goffman to explain the self of the performer, he briefly even contemplated a biological foundation for their acting abilities, missing Mead's point that the body and its capacities are shaped in social interaction as much as the personality. In fact, for Mead, the mutual adjustment of bodies in the social world was the basis for the development of more elaborate forms of symbolic and linguistic communication out of which the self was constructed. This led to no bifurcation of practical and expressive activity in Mead's theory, nor to any dualism between the body and the self.

This is not the case in Goffman's analysis. As in Durkheim's model of homo duplex, Goffman says that our 'human' self and bodily impulses are restrained by the creation of the social self. Quoting Santayana, Goffman (1969: 50) wants to show how, through morality and self-knowledge, 'our animal habits are transmuted by conscience into loyalties and duties, and we become "persons" or masks'. Or following Durkheim, he wants to illustrate how

> The expressive coherence that is required in performances points out a crucial discrepancy between our all-too-human selves and our socialized selves. As human beings we are presumably creatures of variable impulse with moods and energies that change from one moment to the next. As characters put on for an audience, however, we must not be subject to ups and downs. As Durkheim suggested, we do not allow our higher social activity 'to follow in the trail of our bodily states, as our sensations and our general bodily consciousness do' (Goffman, 1969: 49).

Once again this creates the vision of humanity as homo duplex, whose physical impulses and personal desires are not assimilated to the moral order of loyalties and duties. The human self is riven in two between the biological being and the social actor. Furthermore, the socialized self is described wholly in terms of the model provided by homo sociologicus. That is, as Dennis Wrong claimed, an oversocialized individual who can do nothing but act in the way she or he believe others expect them to, in order to win the respect and favour of fellow actors. As this is the sole motivation of the socialized person, there is little hope of individuals ever challenging socially accepted norms or deviating in their activity, except perhaps because of some underlying pathology. This also stems from the rather overintegrated view of society that Goffman has inherited from Parsons, where social norms are taken to be a homogenous system with little variation. An individual therefore has scant choice except to model their actions according to generally accepted principles.

But perhaps the main failing of Goffman's dramaturgical approach is that even he has finally to admit 'that this attempt to press a mere analogy so far was in part a rhetoric and a manoeuvre' (1969: 224). The idea that all the world is a stage has its limitation, and that is, as Goffman notes, nothing real or actual can happen to performed characters in a play, for the action staged there is a contrived illusion. This is patently untrue of everyday action which has real and lasting consequences for those engaged in it. And while professional actors can leave their mask in the theatre at night before they go home — along with their make-up and costume — the selves that we create in everyday life are bound into a long term identity which becomes what we truly are. This was Mead's radical insight: that the objective self of social interaction is the foundation of the subjective, 'inner' self.

The limits of the theatrical metaphor are succinctly drawn by Bruce Wilshire (1982a, 1982b), who makes many of the points that I have made above. In particular, Wilshire believes Goffman's metaphor is limited because he does not draw a distinction between the 'ideal time' in which a play or a performance takes place, during which reality is suspended, and 'world time' which binds all people in its grip. This world time is not limited and fictional but is the real world where our actions have a real consequence, and where the impressions others gain of us are woven into a lasting identity. In this way, persons bring their real experience and a sense of their own self to everything they do, investing their actions and presentations with a meaning that possesses a reality for them. This is true both of individuals in everyday interactions and those who are professional actors who perform fictions on stage. Wilshire sums up many of his points against Goffman in the following way.

> I will maintain that Goffman construes appearances as if they were phantasmic *things* which exist here and now and contained in themselves. Hence he cannot properly distinguish the appearance of an actor's performance in the isolated and ideal time of the play's 'world' from the appearance of our lives offstage which refer beyond the here and now into the future of world-time — the time which holds us as persons and artists in its grip. Hence he cannot properly distinguish between the fictional life of characters in plays from the actual life of persons in society. Persons, for Goffman, mask a basic (perhaps unknowable) asociality behind a phantasmic sociality (1982a: 290).

Yet Goffman never stops to ask what the consequences are for the understanding of social life if the analogy through which one has chosen to study it is ill-fitting. Perhaps this is because, in micro sociology, the model one adopts to analyse social life is thought of as producing the reality one sees. In truly Kantian fashion, the structures of the model or the theory produce the reality they are designed to view. It is these scientific theories, or in everyday life the values and beliefs of agents, which are the underlying mechanisms that produce and structure the way 'reality' appears. As Richard Rorty (1982: 140) says, idealists point out how Kant showed scientific concepts to be, 'merely instruments which the mind uses to synthesize sense-impressions; science, therefore, can know only a phenomenal world'. Like Garfinkel's transcendental analytic, we can never have an understanding of the objects of the world; only the mechanisms through which they are meaningfully produced can be uncovered through analysis. The outcome of this Kantian influence results in the position Rorty describes by rephrasing a suggestion of Berkeley's, so that it reads, 'no idea can be true of anything except a world made of ideas' (1982: 146).

The neo-Kantian position is also at the root of Harré's theories. For him, this philosophical approach means treating

> the social and even the physical environment as a complex product of interaction between persons as active agents and the environment as a plastic construction that can be endowed with causal powers through the meaning-giving acts of agents. Environments do not exist in their fullness independent of the agents who enter them. They are part

created by the way the individuals who enter them assign meanings to the people, activities, settings and social situations they find within them and actively create. Then they are themselves affected by that which they have created (1979: 143).

Prior to the above quotation, Harré was addressing himself to the dilemma I pointed out in Chapter One between a mechanistic approach to human activity, as found in behaviourism, and a vitalistic approach as found in cognitivism. In adopting a Kantian position, Harré is clearly siding with the vitalists, who see the environment as the realization of human attempts to give it structure and meaning. Human actions are not primarily determined by the environment, but are intentional and freely chosen. While Harré does not want wholeheartedly to endorse an idealist position, stressing the importance of structured processes over which individuals have no control, his Kantian leanings take him more in an idealist direction. This can be seen in his view that the environment is only a 'plastic construction', which presumably means that it has no definite form which would register on the senses were it not for the 'meaning-giving acts of agents'.

Harré's conception here would be a positive move toward an agential view of humans, except that, in his embrace of Kantianism, an individualistic and phenomenological outlook begins to reassert itself. As with Kant's philosophy, if reality and sensuous experience are not structured in any discernible way, then how is it that humans are able to create pattern and form in their existence? Kant, it will be remembered, put this down to categories which were transcendentally inherent in human subjectivity prior to experience. Harré tries to translate this position into more modern terminology, utilizing contemporary cognitive theories within psychology, which see the human capacity for categorizing the world as rooted in the cognitive and cybernetic properties of the brain. That is, in innate mental structures and processes which filter and classify information from the world. For Harré, then, the meaning-giving and agential power of humans can be regarded as 'a disposition grounded in a physiologically realized cybernetic property of the brain and nervous system' (1979: 290). However, this resorts to individualism, seeing the constructive and interpretive powers of humanity as based ultimately in *subjectivity*.

This return to individualism is not helped by Harré's adoption of a Renaissance view of the self which he labels as 'architectonic man', 'according to which the unrestricted and undeformed activity of men is to conceive and try to realize a variety of structured forms, a variety controlled only by the demands of mathematical harmony and order' (1979: 5). The fact that the Renaissance view of the self is adopted uncritically leads back to many of the dichotomies and dualisms I described in Chapter One, which Harré attempted to overcome in his theories of social being. The problem is that Harré does not historicize the Renaissance image of the person, showing how it is a product of the social relations people lived in at the time. Instead, he universalizes this image as his 'model of man' which he applies to all human societies, making it appear that this is the way human beings are under all conditions which do not restrict or deform their inherent nature. The notion of 'man' as 'architectonic' therefore appears to describe a presocial human being. This, however, recreates two of the dichotomies a theory of social selves ought to overcome.

First, the dichotomy of society and individual is recreated, for it now appears uncertain as to whether human selves and activities are socially created, or whether the meaning-giving acts of agents are a result of the unrestricted and undeformed activity of 'architectonic man'. This must be the type of person already present in the primary structure — the 'array of persons' — who create harmony and order in the conversation between them. This has to be the case, for while Harré suggests that public conversation is the basis of the self, it could hardly exist prior to active and meaning-giving agents — unless conversation is to be thought of in a transcendental fashion like Kant's a priori categories. Yet this conjures up presocial and asocial images of humans, a view not helped by Harré's assertion that it is naive to think of us as a social species because so many aspects of our lives are solitary. Instead, we have 'invented rather than inherited society' (Harré, 1979: 18), a view which reaffirms Harré's implication that those who were there before society to invent it must have been the presocial, architectonic individuals.

Furthermore, Harré completes his Renaissance view of individuals by taking on board Leibniz's monadology, claiming that it is only because individuals represent the world from their own unique position that we need to join together to dovetail our perspectives within society. Thus humans only become interdependent because we are different to begin with. Yet this is to place individual representations of the world prior to collective representations and undermine the work done by Mead. It also appears to contradict the intent of much of Harré's own work, which aims to show humans as social beings. However, one is now led to wonder whether the notion Harré takes from Goffman, of individuals as 'actors' playing parts and roles, does not also lead him into the dramaturgical dualism of seeing the masks we adopt as phantasmic things which hide a basic asociality. Certainly, there is now a striking similarity between Harré and Georg Simmel, for both have a vision of humans as basically asocial; both also concentrate on the process of sociation, where the individual is given a primary role in constructing society for purposes that are primarily subjective. The impression is given of individuals as the founding reality, while social relations are only the epiphenomena of individual actions and intentions.

Something of the Parsonian dilemma then emerges in Harré's work, where individual actions and intentions are theorized as the basis of society, while these created social orders 'act back' to determine the future actions of individuals. Thus, 'the public and collective orders are created by intentional action, while the orders so created act back upon private and personal skills and beliefs' (Harré, 1979: 4). Yet this is to create the dilemma I called the 'double reduction', where the meaningful and intentional action of individuals creates the social order, yet at the same time the social order is theorized as the *precondition* for meaningful and intentional action. Harré's work clearly demonstrates this dilemma, for the public and collective order is seen as the basis for social and personal being, providing the blueprints or templates for the intentional action of agents: however, at other times, the social order is said to be created by the intentional actions of individuals, which must exist prior to the society individuals invent.

Along with this problem, Harré's Leibnizian vision of individuals as the primary reality means he has been no more successful than Simmel in solving the dichotomy between the macro and micro processes in society. Just as Simmel's emphasis was on the face-to-face interaction in which society was created, so Harré tends to focus on the expressive activities taking place in the 'local moral order'. Nowhere in Harré's work do we find an attempt to connect these local moral orders — with their values and rules that guide social action — to the wider networks of social relations or social power. The view is given of relatively isolated communities that are not connected in any way across space or time, leaving untouched the macro/micro division Mead could not overcome.

The second dichotomy reopened by the neo-Kantian approach is that between subject and object — between the phenomenological view of the world created by the categories of knowledge and theory, and the way that the world exists in 'reality'. Consciousness is no longer given the status of an *objective* function in *practical activity*, as it was in the pragmatism of James and Mead, but is now seen as primarily subjective. Harré's Kantian framework has led him to do away with the dialectical relationship that Mead perceived between the knowledge possessed by humans and their material, practical activity. For Mead, there *is a reality in which experience is set*, and consciousness and knowledge are part of the practical activity which occurs within the objective world to adapt humans to their material conditions. Consciousness, knowledge and belief here depend upon the activity of groups of people and the place they occupy in the world.

Such a position shows Harré's distinction between the practical and the expressive to be extremely unhelpful. In his approach, activity is seen mainly as meaning-giving, and not as practical, physical activity in a material environment. Like Garfinkel and Goffman, Harré does not properly connect the practical activity of human bodies to the communicative, expressive moral order of daily life. Because of this, he fails to show what was so crucial in Mead's work — the *development* of communication, language and subjectivity, and the practical basis of adaptive social activity and the conversation of gestures upon which they develop. Instead, Harré's approach takes on a transcendental rather than a developmental perspective, positing the primary structure of persons in conversation as a prerequisite for the development of the practical and expressive orders. Ultimately Harré's approach is idealist, because people are seen to produce the world in conversation, through their accounts of reality. In pragmatism the opposite would be true, in that it would be activity within the world which is formative of people's accounts.

Thus, in the new psychology we lose many aspects of the methodological and theoretical advances made by Mead, finding ourselves back in an asocial and monadological view of humanity. It goes without saying that from this position Harré cannot repair the divisions between macro and micro processes, between society and the individual, or the practical and the expressive opened up again by the dramaturgical approach. Also Harré cannot tackle any of the problems in Mead's work, for he has no theory of the structure of power relations in society and their role in forming the self, nor any theory of psychological conflicts and repressions. It remains to be seen whether other approaches in the school of new psychology have been more successful.

Practical Hermeneutics and Theoretical Constructivism

John Shotter (1976, 1984) has challenged Harré's idea that people act on the basis of individual plans and rules which ultimately have an innate cognitive basis, or must be assimilated on to one. For Shotter, the 'social powers' that people acquire from their social inheritance enable them to create and sustain moral action in the everyday world. Rather than try to understand this as rule-, plan- or script- following activity, we must grasp the intentional structure of the moral world in which individuals give their actions meaning. It is the moral order that requires interpretation if we are to understand the ways in which individuals are enabled as agents in the social world, not individual plans or cognitive structures.

Shotter's focus therefore shifts from individual performances and sense-making to the interpretation of the moral order created in 'joint activity' between people. Borrowing from Anthony Giddens's (1979) notion of 'duality of structure', Shotter (1983) says that joint social activity does not need to be structured by prior mental representations or ideas, nor by rules or reasoning procedures. Instead, joint activity is a network of ongoing, patterned changes which exist in time and space. Duality of structure suggests that, 'the moment of my control of my action can be informed — not by me consulting an "inner-representation" or "plan", . . . but by what I have just specified in my action remaining "on hand" so to speak, as a structured context into which I can act further' (Shotter, 1983: 33). Structure is not to be found, therefore, in the minds of individuals, but in the activity of a group of individuals. As Giddens says, it is both the medium and outcome of social action. Thus Shotter is concerned more with the structured context of action than was Harré.

However, Shotter does follow Harré's example in placing emphasis on accounting practices in everyday life, but wants to see these in terms of the 'social ecology' — the complex interdependencies that exist between people which shape their joint activity. These ecological strata of interdependencies are unaccounted for by individuals — like Garfinkel's background expectancies —

because they are the implicitly understood and taken-for-granted basis on which joint understanding and joint activity is achieved. It is within this structured arena that common sense understanding and meaning is generated, making the content of activity within social interdependencies of prime importance to Shotter. This is because it is only in the social ecology of joint activity that people are called to account; a practice in which the self is formed.

The background ecology which forms the basis of common sense understanding has a coercive quality for Shotter, for only if we make sense of things in certain institutionalized ways will we be accounted for by others as competent and responsible members of society. Thus we owe our constitution as autonomous beings to our embedding in joint activities and accounting practices that demand of us that we act as free and responsible agents.

But despite his emphasis on the social ecology of joint activities and interdependencies, Shotter still claims that in the social accountability thesis, attention should be directed not to the structure of activity but to the structure and function of accounts of activity in everyday life. An account is an explicit description of the actual content and function of activity, and it is also formative of the actions of individuals. Accounts provide an intelligible framework through which the world is made sense of and in which the powers of the active social agents are forged.

From this position, Shotter (1989) views social life as a text in which joint activity produces a social world of meanings and accounting practices which determines consciousness, the structure of the personality and the future actions of social beings. Like Harré, he is against any theory of human action which produces causal accounts of behaviour, but in place of the dramaturgical approach, Shotter suggests there should be a practical descriptive account of activity. In order to understand the moral world of joint activity, constituted by the texts of accounting practices, we need a 'practical hermeneutics' which aims to interpret the meaning of social activities 'in their doing'. Hermeneutics was originally the study of biblical texts which aimed to extract from them their 'true meaning'. Later, the art of hermeneutics was extended through the interpretive social sciences to the understanding of the meaning with which humans invested their activities.

However, a problem emerges for Shotter in the method he has chosen to study joint activities. If these acts are structured by the social ecology of interdependencies between individuals, then surely it is these which should be the focus of attention in understanding the basis of human action. Using the hermeneutic method we are still confined to studying the individual's intended meanings in producing their activity, even if these are to be located in the text of accounting practices and joint activities, rather than in people's heads. The problem is that Shotter is still relying on the text of accounts to reveal social activities and interdependencies. Yet he has told us himself that these are more often than not unaccounted for in social life and, therefore, beyond recovery by his chosen hermeneutical method. If they are not present in the account they cannot be revealed by hermeneutics. Instead of this method, we need an approach like that of Mead's, which understood meaning in terms of its function within structured, practical interactions. But this is not the approach Shotter adopts.

There is also a chance in Shotter's ecological approach to begin developing a theory of the social unconscious, for if many of our interdependencies remain outside of our powers to account for them, and therefore outside of our awareness, then these form an unconscious layer in the ecology of the self. However, this opportunity is also missed in the practical hermeneutic method, and it remains for Marxist psychologies (explored in Chapter Six) to develop the theory of the social unconscious.

Another variant of the ethogenic approach is to be found in Kenneth J. Gergen's work. He agrees with the general thrust of the ethogenic method, supporting and charting the social constructivist movement which claims that reality is created along with the personality in everyday symbolic activity (Gergen, 1985). Like Shotter, he believes that it is the meaning created in this realm that requires interpretation by the socio-behavioural sciences. Where Gergen differs from the other ethogenic theorists is in concentrating on the role of scientific theory in constructing reality, values and meanings, which can form the basis of daily moral activity. This occurs in two ways.

First, Gergen (1982) believes that scientific theories are not established through the provision of irrefutable proof about their representation of the world, but by establishing a warrant among the population of scientists and everyday actors which institute their credibility as theories. These theories construct the reality we see by investing it with meaning, and the world outlook they foster is sustained thereafter by appealing to what everybody already knows. Proof is then accumulated for the theory by various methods, yet theories are never disproved with evidence which undermines them. Many theories have survived such an onslaught against all the odds. Theories only lose validity when they lose their warrant, and this is when the counter-evidence against them becomes telling.

Second, not only do theories construct the world but, in the case of the social sciences, they interpret the actions of individuals and thereby impute motives for action to them. The reality of social action and the motives which move individuals to act are therefore constructed through the framework of a theory which constitutes that reality as it interprets it. If this theory of society and the self achieve warrant it may change the way that people act and the way they think about themselves. Theory is not simply a description of behaviour, therefore, but is a linguistic system whose function is to change or sustain behaviour. It thus plays a role in power relations within society as a whole, and scientists who propagate a theory that achieves warrant gain a lot of power.

Gergen does try to focus on relations of power in this way. In particular he sees social power as established by different groups achieving warrant for their conceptions of the self (Gergen, 1989). But like the micro sociologists, Gergen cannot tell us why different theories — including theories about the self — should appeal to people in different eras. What is it about these theories that chimes with the experience of people in different times and places? Like Garfinkel and Goffman, he cannot say anything about this process because he offers no historical analysis of phenomena.

This problem occurs for Gergen because, like the rest of the ethogenic school, he assumes a division between the world as it is practically experienced and the world which is constructed by linguistic, theoretical schema. He claims that 'language has created independent and enduring entities in an experienced world of prevailing fluctuation' (Gergen, 1982: 59). Once again, the problem is that of transcendentalism. If the experienced world is one of flux, then language and theory cannot emerge from sensuous experience or activity. Language and theory are transcendental preconditions of knowledge which cannot be derived from practice. The Kantian problem reasserts itself once more, for where does the structure of language, theory and knowledge emerge from if not from humans and their sensuous experience?

Gergen (1982: 207) realizes the problem himself, for he admits that constructivist theories court being charged with an otiose solipsism with the claim that reality is simply a construct of theory. However, Gergen himself cannot offer any solutions to this problem, because he does not recognize any objective, structured experience from which language emerges and against which competing theories could be measured. Such an understanding of practical experience, like that of Mead's, would not mean abandoning social theories of the formation of meaning and the self. However, as I have already claimed, it would mean developing a theory of social action and communication which took account of sensuous, bodily activity in a material social world that is not simply the construct of a theory or a belief. We would then need to see societies as structured social relations and activities which are mediated by language, and the selves that develop within them as practical and linguistic achievements. Both culture and the self must be put back into a socio-historic context.

But this means transcending the ethogenic method, and looking for a basis for an adequate theory of social selves in another direction. This would have to offer a more satisfactory macro theory of society which could then unite social processes on a wider scale with the formation of individual selves.

Conclusion

Looked at in the terms through which I aimed to assess ethogenic theory, there does not seem to have been any significant advance made within this school on the theories of Mead. In equating society wholly with conversation and linguistically created theories, the ethogenic school have placed the emphasis of their analyses solely on interpretation of the meaning of individual's accounts of activity. They have not developed any macro theory of society into which to fit these accounting practices and have thereby continued the dualism between macro and micro social processes. More importantly, the ethogenic approach has led to the reopening of many dichotomies and dualisms which Mead had begun to resolve, most notably that between society and individual, as well as between the practical and expressive realms of activity — the world of material and bodily reality, and the world of human communication and ideas.

Even in other versions of ethogenic social psychology these dichotomies remain, particularly that between the constructions of the world that appear in accounts or theories, and the material reality and limits within which they are produced. While a theorist like Shotter does attempt to overcome the limitations of micro theory and interpretive methodology by stressing the importance of 'joint activity', this is not linked up to any macro theory of social activity or interdependencies. One way out of this dilemma for the ethogenic school is to turn to theories in structuralism and post-structuralism, which attempt to link structures of signification to wider social and political structures. While few have tried to make connections to this body of mainly French social theory, other psychologists have, and the results promise to remove, once and for all, many of the pitfalls that befell ethogenics.

CHAPTER FOUR
Power, Knowledge and the Self

There is one common thread which unifies theories in the ethogenic social psychologies with structuralist theories of the subject;
this is the view that language and knowledge are the organizing
and structuring principles within social life. In the work of both
schools, discourse is seen as synonymous with the social domain.
However, in structuralism and post-structuralism, the roots of
discourse are not traced back to the local moral order. Rather,
discourse itself is understood as the principle element in the
construction of social life. Nor is this discourse seen to be utilized
by an already active individual whose aims and capacities exist
prior to discourse — such as Harré's 'architectonic man'. Such a
theory is a reversion back to the humanist vision of the conscious,
freely choosing, autonomous agent as the primary and constitutive
element of social life. Structuralism and post-structuralism, in
particular, attempt the 'deconstruction' of this humanist notion of
the individual, showing how this vision of humans, and the actual
capacities of agents produced by it, are simply the constructions of
the humanist discourse itself. Once this vision is deconstructed
there is revealed a different type of subjectivity altogether, one
which is diversified and fragmented. This allows for a vision of
both conscious and unconscious processes, for the self is now
understood as a unified entity but, simultaneously, one which
contains many contradictions, some of which become repressed in
the social process of unification. Because of this, the structuralists
and post-structuralists announce the death — in theoretical terms
— of the rational centred Western image of 'man'.

Determination by Discourse: The Death of 'Man'

Structuralism and the De-centred Subject
The anthropologist Lévi-Strauss (1975) studied and compared the
myths of various civilizations in order to draw out from below the
surface differences their common, underlying structural principles.
Just as a linguist translates one language into another by identify-

ing the system of coding common to both, Lévi-Strauss attempts to uncover the hidden rules which structure the system of coding in different languages and myths. In this approach, the structuralists have been greatly influenced by linguists, such as de Saussure, who see humans' perception of the world as constructed by forms of grammar that organize the language through which people can begin to speak and think about their world. From this perspective, Lévi-Strauss took the view that the myths contained in various cultures create an image of the world which reflect the systemic rules and structural principles that are the precondition for their production. Myths do not reflect the reality of the world or of people's existence in any direct or immediate way, instead reflecting the structural principles through which they are produced.

These cultural visions of the world made possible by structural rules, then determine the conscious perceptions that individuals have of their environment and of themselves and their existence. Like Harré, Lévi-Strauss thus believes that the structure of the system of signification and language, which manifests itself in a set of cultural beliefs or myths, creates a cognitive grid through which each member of society can order reality and the activities of the group. The problem that this theory creates for Lévi-Strauss is not unlike the problem faced by Harré in ethogenics: that is, exactly what is the source of origin of the structures of signification which order culture and meaning, and where is the source to be found? The two theorists answer this problem in a very similar way: in the final analysis, the system of language and meaning is rooted in the structure of the human mind:

> myths signify the mind that evolves them by making use of the world of which it is itself a part. Thus there is simultaneous production of myths themselves, by the mind that generates them and, by the myths, of an image of the world which is already inherent in the structure of the mind (Lévi-Strauss, 1975: 340–1).

Here we see how Lévi-Strauss believes that the image of the world created by the categories of the myths and the contents of consciousness, is already contained in a pregiven structure fundamental to the human mind. The elements and the awareness of this structure are always bound to remain unconscious, for we can only uproot it by a structural analysis which looks for its systemic principles in the different layers of culture and consciousness. It is in this sense that Lévi-Strauss overturns the Cartesian view of the rational individual centred around the conscious 'I'. What is now important are the inherent structures of the mind contained in the unconscious.

However, the difficulty with this approach is that the role of humans within culture and society is considered as peripheral, if it is considered at all. Social activity is regarded as unimportant by Lévi-Strauss, for people and their actions enter social analysis only in terms of the roles they are allocated within social ritual and custom, which are governed by myths. He therefore shows how, even when people think they are acting freely, their choices and actions are limited by the structures inherent in their own cultures and minds, of which they are simply the bearers.

Besides this, the work of Lévi-Strauss does not address one of the key problems also left unresolved in Harré's ethogenic theory, in that particular cultures are not linked to social relations or to power structures in any way so as to provide a macro theory of society. Instead, we find ourselves with the problem that social relations and activities are still seen as based in cognitive structures innate in the human mind, so that society is simply the epiphenomenon of the nature of each individual mind.

The structuralist who has tried the hardest to link the formation of personality with the macro structures and power relations of society is the French Marxist Louis Althusser. Like Lévi-Strauss, Althusser wishes to construct a social science in which the Cartesian subject is not assumed to be the primary and guiding element of all social life. For him, the beginning of a new type of social analysis can be found in Marx's mature works, where the main subject of study is not the activity of individuals, but the formation of social relations. According to Althusser, we find here the possibility of a subjectless social science, where the nature and role of individuals need never enter the analysis. Instead, concentration is centred on the structure of social relations and the conditions that must be present for their maintenance and support.

Of vital importance for the existence of any social structure is that the individuals must be created who act as the supports (*Träger*) of social relations (Althusser and Balibar, 1970). The creation of these individuals occurs in the realm of culture, as it did for Lévi-Strauss, except that for Althusser, the emphasis is displaced from myth to the realm of ideology. In Marx's work, this term refers to the dominant ideas in any epoch which legitimate the social structure and make the power relations between individuals appear as natural and timeless bonds which cannot be broken. However, for Althusser, ideology has a constant and an eternal function, in that it arises as a series of 'representations' of the reality in which people live. These representations refer to material reality and to the social relations between individuals, constructing for people the way in which the reality of these things appears. What is therefore reflected in ideological representations is not the reality of the world nor of social relations, but their ideological appearance: it reflects our 'imaginary' relation to the world and to our social relationships.

It is within this imaginary, ideological relation to the social structure that individuals take on a role or a position in social practices which necessitates a certain form of individuation and the construction of a particular identity. Ideology constructs subjects by calling them out, or as Althusser (1971) puts it, by 'hailing' or 'interpellating' them. In fact, many people who believe in religious ideology describe their experience as receiving the calling, after which they play a role in religious practice and ideology. While people may argue that these are their own freely chosen beliefs, Althusser would reply much the same as Lévi-Strauss, that people only believe that their ideas are freely chosen when in fact they are not. The course of our lives is already set for us by our place in ideology where we are made subject to certain ideas. As Hirst and Woolley say:

> This is what the 'imaginary' relation is — it is a form of presentation of the agent's existence in such a manner that a definite pattern of conduct is implicated. For Althusser the imaginary relationship to the totality of the subject's social relations is both constitutive of the subject and the basis for its actions 'as if' it were a free, self-determining consciousness (1982: 134).

However, like the theories of Lévi-Strauss, a problem with Althusser's approach as described above is that it constitutes what he calls a 'theoretical anti-humanism', in that it appears to write the human subject out of history and social activity altogether. Society, social practices and the realm of ideology appear to be constituted outside of human activity and human influence, which only plays a role in supporting these objective structures. Thus human subjects are seen as only the supports of the social system. It is the realm of ideology that constitutes and organizes the idea of autonomous subjectivity, which is merely a cultural illusion. But in seeing ideology as the organizer of the illusion of individuality, Althusser is according ideology a dominant role independent of human activity: it somehow creates representations of the real which *then* construct the subjects needed to support the structure of social relations. This ignores the fact that, in Marx and Engels (1970), ideology was seen as the *expression* of groups of individuals from within their location in concrete social relations and practices, no matter how distorted these ideological expressions were. It was the nature of social relations and practices which caused an ideological view of the world to form, as if in camera obscura, within the consciousness of social beings. Social relations between active individuals give rise to ideology and its contradictions, which is then worked through in human practice. Instead of this, Althusser sees the battle against ideology taking place through a 'subjectless science'. However, as Jorge Larrain says, 'the picture one gets is similar to a battle in heaven between two non-historical and transcendental actors, ideology and science, which are engaged in permanent struggle' (1979: 162). What is missing from this battle is that which Marx placed at the centre of his theories — the social conflict between human groups and classes and its *active* resolution.

Furthermore, the question arises of the nature of humanity which is organized by ideology and constituted as a subject. Just what is the raw material that lies behind the illusion organized by ideology? In trying to resolve this problem, Althusser turned to the work of the French psychoanalyst Jacques Lacan, who offered a structural linguistic reading of Freud's theories of human development. Lacan's argument was that psychoanalysis is a true science because it had identified a new object in the human sciences which decentred the previous philosophical concern with the 'I' of human subjectivity. The new object was the unconscious. Lacan argues that the unconscious is structured like a language and can be understood in this way, not because the unconscious is a language or is produced by it, but because it can be treated as the possible object of structural analysis. Like Lévi-Strauss, Lacan does not see the structure of the unconscious lying on the surface of what we perceive as reality; instead he sees it as the structure which lies underneath our perceptions, and which occasionally interrupts them.

In contrast to this, the conscious subjectivity of persons — the 'I' — is constructed within the 'Symbolic' realm of signs and language, the structured system of meanings and significations. Not only does the conscious subject come into being in the Symbolic, but their sexual identity is also constructed in this realm along with their desires. Lacan is emphasizing at this point the distinction Freud made between the instincts and the drives — lost in the English translation — where the instincts refer to the biological needs of the organism and its inborn responses, while the drives refer to the psychic propulsion and motivation that arises with the emergence of the 'I' (the ego). Because we are constructed as conscious, desiring subjects within the Symbolic, we are bound to live in an 'Imaginary' relation to the 'Real', the latter being that irreducible reality which is always screened out by the Symbolic, continuing to exist as absences which signs and language cannot call up.

One of these absences from the Symbolic and from consciousness is the unconscious. It appears only in the gaps or spaces in the Symbolic, as slips of the tongue, metaphors or in dreams. It thus becomes the object of a structural analysis only because it announces its absence and gives clues to its strivings in the way it uses the semiotic and linguistic systems for its own hidden purposes. Therefore to Lacan (1977a: 29), the unconscious is a creation neither of language nor symbols, but is precategorical and preontological: that is, it is neither being nor non-being, but the unrealized.

The construction of the unified, conscious self out of the undifferentiated, unrealized, non-unitary form of the unconscious occurs for Lacan by a succession of imaginary identifications beginning in the stage Lacan (1977b) calls the 'mirror phase'. Here, the notion of the mirror is used as a metaphor for that stage in the development of the self where the child becomes fascinated by the reflection of its own image. By making itself appear in its own eyes through the aid of the mirror, the child begins to recognize itself as a being separate from others. However, in making itself appear as a conscious, unified being, with a secure and separate self-image, the child at the same moment loses itself as an unconscious, undifferentiated, non-individuated being, who sees and wants everything 'in terms that can admit of no distinction between self and world, inside and outside' (Archard, 1984: 66). Now, in the mirror phase, there are rigid boundaries placed around the child, erected by the restricted barriers of its own ego.

While the mirror phase inaugurates the process of imaginary

identifications and the formation of the ego, this entire process is reinforced in the Oedipus complex. Each infant goes through this complex, in which their conscious subjectivity is called out by the 'discourse of the Other'. That is, its own self is called out by the Symbolic as the child begins its imaginary identifications with the Symbolic functions of the parents. In Freud's original model of the Oedipus complex, a boy child begins to identify with his father because of the sexual desires he feels for his mother. The father is the figure who commands the mother's love in the way the child wishes to, and in order to achieve that wish, the child begins to hope for the death of his father. The successful resolution of the Oedipus complex occurs when the father defeats the wishes of his son by establishing a relationship of authority with him, resulting in the eventual redirection of the boy's sexual desire to women outside the family.

In Lacan's account, the Oedipal triangle is an interplay of symbols rather than the interaction between concrete individuals. The identification that the child makes with the father is imaginary in two senses: first, the identification is constituted on the basis of the Imaginary ego construction in the mirror phase; and, second, the child's identification is with the 'name-of-the-father', which is desire for the power he symbolizes as head of the family with command over the mother's love. The child therefore longs not for the woman who is his mother, but for the 'desire-of-the-mother', meaning that the boy child wishes to be the object of the mother's desire in the same way his father is. Lacan calls this the 'discourse of the Other' because the forces which are drawing the child out as a subject are not within his or her own field as an individual, but are excentric to their being: they are located in the Symbolic realm which is composed of these excentric processes.

Lacan is therefore showing how the self is formed by its imaginary identifications with others in the Symbolic realm, and thus providing the key to personality formation within imaginary relations that Althusser lacked. The theories of Lacan also demonstrate how the basic needs and strivings of the biological organism are transformed by the Symbolic realm into socially constructed personhood and socially recognized desire. He also provides something else for Althusser, for in showing how the child's original identifications and Symbolic constructions of the self are centred around the power and authority of the father, Lacan is demonstrating how power relations within imaginary relations play a central role in personality formation. For Althusser,

> Lacan demonstrates the effectiveness of the Order, the Law, that has been lying in wait for each infant born since before its birth, and seizes him before his first cry, assigning to him his place and role, and hence his fixed designation (1971: 212).

However, a number of problems emerge here for Althusser, stemming from flaws in his own theorizing and that of Lacan. While Lacan has answered some of the problems raised in the Symbolic construction of the self, showing how this originally occurs by the child making emotional investments in the Symbolic realm through its imaginary relations, he can no more explain the presence of the Symbolic than can Althusser. If this must be present before the conscious agent in order to construct them, then what is the source of origin of the Symbolic realm? It must have been created by humans or from where does it emerge? Again the problem is one of theoretical anti-humanism. If the role of human activity in the construction of social and symbolic orders, as well as selves, is to be regarded as only a contingency, how then do we explain the development of these orders? And if, as in Lacan's model, humans are creatures whose primary experience is one of a fragmented world and self, how could they ever have created an ordered vision of the world in their Symbolic realm? Language and culture then appears as something external to the original, biological individual, which constructs the personality from outside.

Ironically for Althusser and Lacan, this vision is actually based on an existential individualism, whereby an essential experience of human subjects is posited against a culture and language which only separates them from that experience. In Lacan's case, the loss or lack that the individual suffers on entry to their culture is the experience of themselves as a fragmented, needful being, whose unconscious processes only disappear on entry into the Symbolic realm. The old problem of homo duplex also emerges at this point, for an 'individual' is theorized whose needs are originally undifferentiated and insatiable, and who must renounce them on entering the Symbolic realm, substituting in their place the socially constructed desires. This reopens the old body versus society dualism. All of these criticisms have been summed up by Carl Shames, who says that:

> [A] popular viewpoint, derived from the structural theories of Lévi-

Strauss, Lacan, and Althusser, holds that individuality is organized as a culturally-based illusion. Cultural structures and conceptions or the nature of language are seen as the organizing factor. This conception, for all its modern sounding terminology, once again posits the biological individual in an eternally external world. If language or cultural institutions are the organizer of the illusions of individuality, what, exactly, is organized? If individuality is an illusion, whose illusion is it? This theory confuses the obvious fact that each individual enters a pre-existing social world with the absurd notion that the social world, in the form of cultural structures, has some existence apart from living individuals. Cultural structures are seen as having a life of their own, somehow implanting illusions in the heads of *homo sapiens* organisms. Far from a revolutionary conception, this theory takes the old dichotomous biology/society model to its most absurd extreme (1984: 54–5).

What Lévi-Strauss, Lacan and Althusser have left unexplained is how 'cultural structures' are integral to the practical and active existence of social individuals, or how the material and cultural worlds are transformed through human practice. Instead, they theorize the Real, the Symbolic and the Imaginary worlds as if they were independent, Parsonian systems in whose interpenetration the 'individual' is constituted. As Shames says so succinctly above, they confuse the fact that each individual enters a pre-existing social world with the notion that the social and cultural world exists somehow independent of the activity of social and historical individuals. Shames rightly points out that this is absurd. The question must now be addressed that the various forms of anti-humanism cannot answer: that is, how does culture relate to the activity and practices of humans in the world? To answer this question would mean allowing some role for human action in the construction of society and selves. It is a question that is left to the post-structuralists, or French Nietzscheans, to address.

French Nietzscheanism: Variations on a Number of Themes

Most of the structuralists considered above can be regarded in general terms as neo-Kantians, in that they give precedence in their theories to an a priori system of categorization which defines the mode of being in which objects appear and can be recognized, and in which the subjectivity of individuals is constructed. For some, the system of categorization exists in the unconscious mind; for others it exists in the symbolic, discursive or ideological orders:

but for all structuralists the emphasis is placed on the symbolic or discursive realm rather than on individual consciousness. These are themes taken up by the post-structuralist school in France, except that they make the transition from the influence of Kant to that of Nietzsche.

The Nietzschean influence shows itself in the joining together of cultural knowledge with the 'will to power' that is thought to produce it. The classificatory system which knowledge provides supports a number of truth claims which are an intrinsic part of the struggle for power in human groups and, in this sense, truth is imposed on the world — on recalcitrant nature — by power. Knowledge is therefore always the intimate of power. This philosophical position of Nietzsche's stems from his disillusionment with the notion of absolute truth, of a universally true knowledge whose axioms hold good for all places and times. For Nietzscheans, there is no absolute truth, only the historical dominance of certain definitions tied to the dominance of particular powerful groups.

The Nietzscheans, therefore, link into the constructivist theses of theorists like Gergen, whose work we discussed briefly in the last chapter. They see the human sciences as playing a central role in the definition of social reality. In turn, this is part of a power regime which also creates a 'regime of truth', forming itself as the fundamental truth which everyone 'knows' and against which all other truth claims are assessed. The social sciences are always in cahoots with regimes of power and are part of the techniques through which the subjection of the population is achieved. Unlike Gergen, then, power does not stem from the acceptance of a scientific discourse as it gains warrant within the population: instead, power relations are channelled through knowledge, which is established or rejected as part of the power plays between individuals or groups.

The most famous of the modern French Nietzscheans in the countries outside France, is Michel Foucault. His work can be read as an attempt to show how knowledge maps out the field of objects and identities around which relations of power can come into operation and discursive practices can be formulated. Foucault (1970) first identified three discourses that emerged at the turn of the nineteenth century and marked out the terrain for new relations of power: these were the discourses on living beings, on language and on wealth. As to the 'humanist' discourses which study living beings, and which give a central role to 'Man' as a conscious agent whose actions are intentional, Foucault believes that this discourse actually produced such human beings as an object for power. Within humanism there was encapsulated the will to truth about human beings themselves, to put human bodies and minds under the microscope of analysis and to uncover humanity's essential elements. However, in attempting to reveal the kernel of humanity, the discourse actually recreates human subjects as they are filtered through the categories of the social sciences. The will to truth and power is enabled by the humanist discourse in which new capacities of human beings are produced. Once we come to recognize this, Foucault believes we must declare the 'death of Man', for this subject lives only in the realms of anthropological discourse.

Initially, Foucault concentrated mainly on a study of the discourses themselves which produced knowledge and identities. Gradually his focus moved to the institutional sites where power operates in the field organized by knowledge, governing the discursive practices of individuals and thus the very nature of their subjectivity. Foucault (1982) was eventually to say that the 'government of individualization' and, through it, the creation of subjectivity, had always been his prime focus of concern.

This can be seen clearly in Foucault's (1977) studies of the prison, where disciplinary practices were used not only to punish but also to reform. The aim of such practices was to create a new, useful individual, one who is subjected to discipline and whose capacities could be utilized as labour power. While the soul is the target of disciplinary techniques, the site on which they operate is the human body; their purpose being to instil self-control within that body and, through it, within the soul as well. The individual is both objectified within these practices — turned into an identifiable object by knowledge upon which power can direct its operations — and is subjectified within them as a personality with the necessary in-built controls over their own body and self. As Dreyfus and Rabinow put it, quoting from Foucault:

> The aim of disciplinary technology is to forge a 'docile [body] that may be subjected, used, transformed and improved' (1982: 153).

> The modern individual — objectified, analysed, fixed — is a historical achievement. There is no universal person on whom power has performed its operations and knowledge, its enquiries. Rather, the

individual is the effect and object of a certain crossing of power and knowledge. He is the product of the complex strategic developments in the field of power and the multiple developments in the human sciences (1982: 159–60).

As we can see from the above, Foucault theorizes power not only as a constraining force but as productive; it invests the body and creates the capacities and dispositions of the individual. There is no individual who exists prior to power relations and who is subdued or coerced by disciplinary technology into subservience. The individual is not the material on which power works, because

it is already one of the prime effects of power that certain bodies, certain gestures, certain discourses, certain desires, come to be identified and constituted as individuals. The individual, that is, is not the *vis-à-vis* of power; it is, I believe, one of its prime effects (Foucault, 1980: 98).

Thus the individual is *produced* by power relations, whose strategies and techniques turn human bodies into a given social subject. For example, in the prison one of the main disciplinary techniques to be employed was 'surveillance', where prisoners were constantly observed from strategic vantage points. These points of surveillance were organized so that the prisoners could never be certain when, or from where, they were being watched. Those who were jailed had then to monitor and regulate their own behaviour according to the disciplines and the rules of the prison, thus practising as 'second nature' the self-controls required of them as good citizens. A different individual is being produced here according to the dictates of power and knowledge.

So far, then, Foucault has identified two modes of objectification through which power and knowledge create the subject. The first mode is constituted by methods of enquiry which designate themselves as social sciences and which create the realities and the subjects of which they speak. In the second mode of objectification, subjects are constituted by 'dividing practices' which are informed by the human sciences. Here, they are categorized, defined and, sometimes, confined according to their perceived differences from others. Through these systems of classification provided by knowledge, individuals become divided not only from others but also within their own selves. They are divided into the sane and the mad, the law-abiding and the criminal, the healthy and the sick, and are encouraged to identify and separate aspects of their own bodies in exactly the same way. It is through these modes of objectification that individuals are produced and governed.

The third mode of objectification identified by Foucault (1979, 1982) are practices informed by the knowledge of sexuality, which exhort individuals to turn themselves into sexualized subjects. For Foucault the discursive practices that have emerged in the West surrounding the knowledge of sexuality have their roots in the type of power relations that have developed from Christian culture. Of particular interest is the Christian practice of the confession, where individuals are made to tell their sins to a pastor. Here we find the germ of the practice of a science of sexuality, such as psychoanalysis, where a relationship between a patient and therapist is built up in which the former is encouraged to give intimate details to the analyst. The psychoanalyst is trained to decode this information and, through it, establish the truth of the patient's sexuality. Sexuality becomes the hidden secret that holds the key to a person's subjective identity, and which must be deciphered if we are to know the truth of that identity.

Like Lacan, then, Foucault believes that the desires of the individual and their sexual identity are actually constructed by the discourse in which the person objectifies their own self. Foucault differs from Lacan, however, in that he does not believe that psychoanalysis has any privileged access to the secrets of subjectivity, nor does it have an independent object of study in the unconscious. Rather, the unconscious is constructed along with the other aspects of the self in the very discourse on sexuality, and is then exploited as 'the secret'. Psychoanalysis has simply constructed individuals in a new way as the objects of power, only now it is the unconscious which becomes the object of its strategies and techniques. In this sense, Foucault's understanding of the construction of the self is not unlike the 'behavioural' theories of the pragmatists, who see the self developing on the basis of its own discursive practices. However, Foucault attempts to link this insight to the whole realm of power relations.

It is within this realm that we have witnessed the expansion and increased importance of the discourse on sexuality. Far from the common belief that Western society represses and censors this discourse, it in fact encourages its proliferation and induces people to speak the truth of their sexuality through it. Instead of there being a censorship of the discourse on sexuality,

> There was installed rather an apparatus for producing an even greater quantity of discourse about sex, capable of functioning and taking effect in its very economy (Foucault, 1979: 23).

The increasing volume of this discourse is linked to what Foucault calls 'bio-power', which is an intensification of concern with the population as a whole, seeing in it the source of power and wealth. The health and reproduction of the population becomes a central preoccupation, along with the desire to contain and to cure disease, 'abnormality' and perversion. It is in this way that Foucault aims to overcome the macro/micro division in social analysis, by studying the 'micro physics of power' in which knowledge about individuals, and the identities of those individuals, are constructed in local or institutional sites. This micro analysis is then coupled to an understanding of power relations on a global scale, which is made possible by the local generation of knowledge and the government of individualization.

However, like the structuralists before him, Foucault still understands discourse to be the dominant, organizing principle of the social domain. And, as in micro sociology, he sees the social construction of the individual as occurring entirely within discourse. This means that Foucault has great difficulty in resolving any of the problems of anti-humanism. For him, the individual is still a product of power and knowledge and has no other mode of being which is even partially independent of discourse or discursive practices. Yet Foucault also says that the function of power and knowledge, and the object of his entire corpus of works, is the 'government of individualization'. But if the individual is always produced by power and knowledge, and there is no pre-existing individual on whom power works, then what exactly is governed in the process of individualization? If individuals were only the products of the power structure then there would be no need for an apparatus of government.

However, on closer inspection it appears that Foucault has two different theories of the subject within his works. The first is the theory of the subject who is socially constructed by power and knowledge, which we have already looked at in some detail. The second is a more implicit theory of the subject that runs through Foucault's work and which describes a state of individuality not entirely subject to power and knowledge. This is a more existential vision of the spontaneous and active nature of individuals in everyday life, which suggests that the everyday existence of these individuals can never be encapsulated or explained in its entirety by knowledge, nor wholly made subject to power. Something of the existential nature of this existence eludes description by the social sciences and can never be known by them. This is not unlike the approach of the new psychology, which sees that the everyday moral order is only partially recoverable through accounts and theories constructed after the events. In Foucault's work this surfaces as a theory of 'ordinary individuality' which can only partially be described in scientific discourse, although the disciplinary techniques of modern power have lowered the threshold of its description and opened up the 'individual' to power.

> For a long time ordinary individuality — the everyday individuality of everybody — remained below the threshold of description. To be looked at, observed, described in detail, followed from day to day by an uninterrupted writing was a privilege . . . The disciplinary methods reversed this relation, lowered the threshold of describable individuality and made this description a means of control and a method of domination (Foucault, 1977: 191).

So, in total contradiction of what Foucault has said in other places, he is saying here that there *is* an already existing individual on whom power works. Foucault needs this other vision of individuality in his work because, as a Nietzschean, he realizes power needs a recalcitrant object on which to work or it would have no existence. And individuals could never be anything other than the subjects of power unless they were able at some level to resist their subjection to knowledge and discipline. The problem for Foucault is that while he needs this notion of individuality, he cannot describe it. This is because he believes that it is indescribable anyway, but also because to attempt a description would be to create a new object for power. All he can do is to make allusions to the resistances of individuals or of bodies. However, the troubling thing is that these allusions seem to invoke a form of naturalism and, at times, a biological reductionism that Foucault wishes to avoid in his social constructivist theories.

Thus we see Foucault (1979) posing the state of 'pleasure' against the moral norms of 'sexuality, marriage, decency' (1980: 56). Here Foucault appeals to a vision of a more natural or pleasurable way of life, free from the artificial constraints of society, in a way that is almost Rousseauan. And in a unique statement, we can perhaps catch a glimpse into Foucault's vision of the existential nature of everyday life, where some of the characteristics of ordinary individuality are exhibited. In this statement, Foucault comes out against Marx's view that the lives of humans must of necessity be devoted to labour:

> the life and time of man are not *by nature* labour, but pleasure, restlessness, merry-making, rest, needs, accidents, desires, violent acts, robberies etc. (cited in Keat, 1986: 31; my emphasis).

If this is the natural life of humans, then there are bound to be elements in everyday life, in local moral orders and knowledges, that rebel against the power structure. These natural forces are also supported by the nature of the body, for they are more in keeping with its explosive and discontinuous energy which is vividly described in the scenario above. This leads to Foucault's claim that whenever a relation of power is in operation on the body, 'there inevitably emerge the responding claims and affirmations, those of one's own body against power . . . Power, after investing itself in the body, finds itself exposed to a counter-attack in that same body' (1980: 56). At one point in his career, Foucault gave his support to the work of Deleuze and Guattari (1977), who saw the function of all societies as codifying and containing the flows of desire from the human body. However, they believed that capitalism causes such an explosion of desire through its huge productive forces, that desire is turned into a revolutionary force. In this way, the body overthrows the machinery of its government.

The problem for Foucault, however, is that he is now in a position where the natural forces of the body are opposed to the socially constructed edifices of power and subjectivity. Far from this being an advance in the theory of the social construction of the self, it instead perpetuates one of the central problems of the anti-humanist perspective which Shames noted earlier: that of positing the biological body of the individual in an eternally external cultural world. Then there are the two different theories of the self contained in his work, the theory of the socially constructed, describable level of individuality, and that of the natural, everyday character of 'ordinary individuality'. The problem is that these two concepts are incompatible, given that Foucault wishes to claim that individuality is only ever socially constructed.

Increasingly, Foucault moves towards a position where conflict surrounding the government of individualization is seen to be important. These struggles revolve around the question 'who are we?', and assert the rights of each individual to be different: yet at the same time, they also oppose the dividing practices of the apparatuses of government and the social sciences, which aim to separate people into categories where they can be more easily managed. The struggle for and against this totalizing and individualizing power centres around 'the recalcitrance of the will and the intransigence of freedom' (Foucault, 1982: 221–2). However, rather than pose some essential 'will to freedom' in a highly Nietzschean fashion, Foucault wants to talk of a constant 'agonism': that is, a relationship in which two parties constantly provoke the other, and in which conflict and 'struggle' are permanent features.

While Foucault hopes that this relational theory of power and struggle will solve the problem of posing a Nietzschean 'instinct of freedom' (Nietzsche, 1968), it only creates another philosophical difficulty: that conflict is turned into a metaphysics which is abstracted from particular, situated social and historical relations and theorized as an eternal, existential condition of human social being. Power is the attempt to act upon the free actions and wills contained in this existential ferment and to impose some order upon it, governing the individual differences to be found there. But this still leaves the idea of the individual and the conflict of individual wills a problem in Foucault's work. The very idea of such everyday individual differences seems to suggest that difference is somehow integral to a person's own individuality and is resistant at some level to social identity. Yet this is to fall back into precisely that argument we criticized in Chapter One, which claims that individuality is an essence contained within each individual and which no one else can ever know in its essential nature.

It seems that Foucault's continual struggle with incompatible conceptions of individuality and subjectivity revolves around the inability to develop any dialectical theory of social action and identity such as that found in the work of Mead. Instead, Foucault is left with many of the problems of the anti-humanists in his (post-)structural methodology. For example, as Turner (1984) remarks, Foucault creates the view of humans as language receivers but not as language producers. He shows how individuals become the subjects of discourse but cannot demonstrate how social groups of individuals create certain discourses or bodies of knowledge. Nor can Foucault indicate why this knowledge takes the form that it does in different historical epochs, how it is necessarily related to the social experience and relations of individuals of the times.

Thus the practical production of language by humans is ignored, and instead concentration is focused on the discursive production of individuals by language. In that sense there is something akin to Harré's dichotomy of the practical and expressive orders in Foucault's work — except that discourse is not seen as a mode of expression. Nevertheless, there is the idea in Foucault that discourse creates the real within its own domain and there is no real, practical world outside it. However, Foucault (1982) came to admit that there was another sphere of social relations in human life, intertwined with discursive relations and power relations. These are practical relations which transform the real, material world through work. However, Foucault says nothing about the transformation of the real in practice, nor about how this is interrelated with relations of communication and power. Indeed, the bulk of his work is devoted to showing how the world is created primarily in discourse. Yet Foucault is now claiming that there is a practical as well as a discursive mode of transformation of the real, a claim not far removed from the Marxist view that humans are capable of transforming the natural world and their own natures in practical activity. This view also entails, however, that the real world and the body be accorded a materiality to begin with, one that is open to transformation but only within the broad limits that materiality will allow. Reality and the body cannot simply be constructed by discourse in any which way. To say anything meaningful about human life, we need to know about the mode of transformation of the real and the material limits placed upon that transformation.

Such an approach, however, which would constitute a materialist theory, would be totally at odds with the more idealist tenor of Foucault's theories of knowledge and power. Despite the fact that Foucault continues to reproduce many of the dichotomies of the new psychology through an idealist approach, his ideas have been taken up with enthusiasm by many psychologists and social psychologists. The result is that many of the traditional dilemmas are reproduced in social psychology, only in what appears to be a more 'radical' manner.

Structuralism, Post-structuralism and Psychology

The general principles of structuralism and post-structuralism have found favour among more radical social psychologists, and are seen largely as an advance in the social constructivist paradigm. For example, Henriques et al. (1984) aim to extend Lacan's approach into a post-psychoanalytic psychology, by going beyond Althusser's theories through the use of post-structuralist ideas. They think that Foucault's theory of discursive practice overcomes the problem of a division between the symbolic realm and the 'real' that was present in structuralism. The concept of 'reality' is done away with and replaced with the notion of discursive practice, in which the reality of the world and the materiality of practice is always constituted within discourse. Hence, there is no 'reality' of which the symbolic realm is only a reflection, or to which symbols refer as a 'representation'. However, this ignores the fact that discourse is still understood as the dominant and organizing factor within post-structuralist methodology, and its relationship to material practices is never properly worked out — as I showed above. In fact the authors never state what they mean by the term 'material practice' in opposition to the one they more frequently use, that of 'discursive practices'. They appear to conflate the terms, and also the issues connected with them.

At times it appears that the authors use this device as a means to reintroduce the Althusserian notion that individuals are fixed and determined in their actions by the system of signifiers, and are thereby placed in the network of discursive practices. In this light, the practices in which individuals are engaged, which they believe to be freely chosen, and their corresponding capacities for autonomous actions, have very little concrete materiality about them; they are, in fact, culturally based illusions organized by the discursive network of signifiers. Thus, the centred, rational, autonomous subject is 'deconstructed' by this approach: it is shown to be an illusion constructed by the dominant discourse. Through the means of its deconstruction, another type of subjectivity is shown to be possible, a subjectivity which is decentred, desiring and non-individuated, existing in a state of its own difference.

Following a more strict Foucauldian line, psychology can now be seen as part of the disciplines and techniques which fix the centred, ego-bound individual in their socially designated place.

Psychology is part of the knowledge about individuality which creates the 'individual' as an object and subject of government. As Nikolas Rose claims, the mental sciences 'render previously ungraspable facets of human variability and potentiality thinkable'.

> In so doing, they also make new aspects of human reality practicable. As objects of a certain regime of knowledge, we have become possible subjects for a certain system of power, amenable to being calculated about, having things done to us, and doing things to ourselves in the service of our individuality (1989: 130).

Thus social psychology has partly created and supported the image of the isolated, rational individual needed in the calculating social world of capitalism. The individual is objectified in such a way that he or she becomes open to calculation and to techniques of management that will ensure profitability and wealth. The mental sciences are then 'techniques for the disciplining of human difference', in which a type of individuality needed by the social system is produced in the place of natural difference. Rose's position on the mental sciences can be summarized in his belief that,

> They domesticate and discipline subjectivity, transforming the intangible, changeable, apparently free-willed conduct of people into manipulable, coded, materialized, mathematized, two-dimensional traces which may be utilized in any procedure of calculation. The human individual has become calculable and manageable (1989: 129).

Three ramifications then emerge from this general critique of psychology. First of all the possibility is created for social psychology as a subject to be deconstructed by demonstrating how the production of its knowledge is linked to power. Parker (1989) shows how social psychology has always been interested in the management of individuals, and for long periods of its history has been actively involved in creating plans for the management of production processes and workers so that maximum profitability can be ensured. He also claims that general cultural changes currently under way in the Western world, which is shifting from a modern to a post-modern culture, have undermined the traditional technical and managerial role of social psychology. Its objectivity as a 'science' of behaviour has been called into question by linking it to power, and its traditional object of study — the 'individual' placed in a 'social' context — is also undergoing deconstruction.

Leading on from this, the second consequence of the critique of psychology is the deconstruction of the traditional Western notion of the individual subject. This is something which Sampson (1986, 1989), in particular, has been concerned with. Like Henriques et al., he sees the Western subject as the work of ideological practices that repress the fluidity and indeterminacy of the open-ended human subject. Instead of this possible open-ended subject, ideology fixes the individual in place within the structure of social relations and places a controlling ego at the centre of its psyche. This view within psychology of the ego in charge of an otherwise divided personality, has its roots in theories of governance and authority in the Western world. In order to escape this ideological trap, Sampson believes that we need the production of a new type of subjectivity, something which requires both structural and psychological change.

The third ramification of the critique of psychology is that Rose believes that psychology is already beginning to generate such alternative visions of subjectivity. Psychology no longer simply crushes subjectivity but works by 'producing it, shaping it, modelling it, seeking to construct citizens committed to a personal identity, a moral responsibility and a social solidarity' (1989: 130). However, these are still 'regulatory practices', and it is uncertain to what extent they are regarded as more progressive than the conceptions of individuality that went before them in psychology.

However, there are still a number of difficulties stemming from the structuralist and post-structuralist approaches in psychology. These methodologies are treated in an uncritical manner, leaving many of the problems we have already noted in the (post-) structuralist tradition unresolved. A new ingredient is added, however, particularly by Parker and Sampson who follow Derrida in their use of the method of deconstruction. Like the post-structuralists before him, Derrida believes that all meaning is created in language, which has to be seen as a self-supporting text. There is nothing outside of this text — social, psychological or physical — which is the bedrock of meaning and which language expresses. Meaning is created wholly within the text and all forms of social, psychological or physical presences are also created there. Western culture tends to ground meaning upon these presences — society, the self, the body — and make absent all traces of the text which create and support them (just as we privilege the presence of speech and the speaking subject over the written text which is absent). Derrida deconstructs Western ideas by emphasizing the absences over the things we generally regard as present; writing over speech, the fragmentation of different texts which produce the world over the 'reality' of an homogeneous 'society', and the decentred, fluid, processual self over the centred, stable and fixed identity. He therefore stresses the dynamic processes of a contradictory self, one that displays difference both within itself and in comparison with others, above the fixed individual identities and social categories of persons.

Through Derrida's methodology, social psychology would suffer a double deconstruction, because the traditional concept of the 'individual' with which it worked has now been unravelled: and, on top of this, the 'society' in which the individual was placed by social psychologists can also be deconstructed. Following postmodernist theorists like Baudrillard (1983), who clearly draw inspiration from Derrida's work, 'society' is not seen as a given entity but a constant flux between competing texts of reality. Society is simply produced by these competing texts in a domain that is referred to, confusingly, as 'the social'.

However, these theories have a number of implications which I regard as negative. The notion that reality is produced within the text reawakens the spectre of that otiose solipsism that Gergen warned of in respect of social constructivist theories in the new psychology. Are there no material limits that define what can be said and produced within texts? If there are not, the world can simply be rewritten in any way we choose. Similarly, if 'the social' is seen as a fragmentary interplay of different texts, social relations are denied any reality at all in which we could see the competing texts emerging and taking root. To achieve social change all we must try to do is rewrite the texts. And if that state of 'individuality', which is governed and made present by the text of psychology, is actually a constant process behind which lie many unconscious absences, then

> the scientific object is far more concrete, far more real, than its elusive 'real' referent. Persons are ephemeral, shifting; they change before one's eyes and are hard to perceive in any stable manner. The act of scientific observation . . . makes the individual stable through constructing a perceptual system, a way of rendering the mobile and the confusing manifold of the sensible into a cognizable field (Rose, 1989: 124).

But here we see a familiar argument, that the sensible world is ephemeral and in a state of flux which can only be ordered by the categories of knowledge that provide a cognitive grid through which it may be perceived. Furthermore, this method also reopens the dualism in Goffman's work between the phantasmic self, its appearance in the conceptual and cognitive grids provided by the moral order, and the reality of the self as it exists beneath this surface appearance. The only difference between Goffman's approach and post-structuralism, in this respect, is that post-structuralism substitutes scientific knowledge for the moral order as the mode of information in which appearances are constructed. This is the dilemma present in Foucault's confusion over the identity of the individual which is socially constructed within the social sciences, and that quality of individuality, of difference, which has to be governed in the first place. Thus, post-structuralist theories reproduce the dichotomy between the appearance and the real, between the phenomenal world structured by discourse and the real which is always bound to remain entirely elusive.

Worse even than this, the Derridian theory of difference tends towards perspectivism. Once overarching social systems of meaning and identity have been deconstructed, each different consciousness — each processual perspective — looks out upon its own self-determined landscape. As Descombes (1980) points out, Derrida does not actually deny the unity of individual consciousness, but the existence of collective consciousness. Each ego has its own perspective and this is why each must give up the belief that it is the centre of the world, or that its ideas are the true and universal ones. While this truly *post*-structuralism does still reject the centrality of the Cartesian 'I', it welcomes with open arms the whole tenor of Leibnizian monadology.

This creates unbearable tensions in the work of social psychologists like Parker and Sampson who want to align these philosophical perspectives to a practical political and psychological programme to bring about 'structural' social change and a new form of subjectivity. As Parker (1989) says, there has to be a reference to real social structures in order to provide an adequate account of power relations and the political movements needed to change them. Yet post-structuralist and post-modernist theory denies any appeal to a 'reality', a 'society', or any system of independent values which could be used to justify any theory of concrete power relations or a programme of reform generated by it. These visions are simply products of the text, outside of which there is nothing. Therefore all accounts of power and social structure are relative, as are all political ideals.

Ironically, because of the position they now find themselves in, the post-structuralist psychologists and the French philosophers who have influenced them, cannot explain why their vision of the decentralized subject of difference and individual perspectives is more adequate, or is to be preferred, to other theories of the subject. If there is no appeal to reality or to independent criteria of evaluation, how could such a theory recommend itself? The theory of decentred subjectivity would have to be regarded as just another social scientific construction. There is also the danger that far from being a radical conception of individuality, such perspectivism leads instead to a conservative form of individualism, decentralized libertarianism and free competition that some individuals may well find more repressive than the liberal democratic state. (For a related critique from a feminist perspective, which turns deconstruction against itself, see Burman, 1990.)

While many psychologists, post-structuralists and postmodernists struggle in this impasse, Foucault himself moved on in his analysis of subjectivity. His final volumes on sexuality and a paper on the enlightenment provide some surprising twists in his theory of subjectivity, ones which have not yet found their way into social psychology.

Ethics and Mature Subjectivity

In Foucault's final publications there was an attempt to develop an analysis of the ethical formation of the self that in places looked uncannily like Harré's theory of social being. Here Foucault began to study 'technologies of the self' alongside the technologies of power and discipline which subject individuals. Concentration becomes centred on the moral codes through which individuals structure their own conduct, forming practices of the self. As in ethnomethodology, by acting according to explicit or implicit moral prescriptions and expectations, the individual becomes the ethical subject of action. Foucault (1986a, 1988) analysed these changing practices of the self, from the Graeco-Roman ethics of taking care of the self — involving attention to one's sexual activity — to the Christian doctrine of self-renunciation; in particular the renunciation of sexual pleasures.

Despite the difference in moral codes to be observed, the

practices of the self always operate along the same technological lines: they involve techniques through which individuals determine the 'ethical substance' of the self — that part which will be constituted as the material for moral conduct. 'In these conditions', Foucault claims, 'the contradictory movements of the soul . . . will be the prime material of moral practice' (1986a: 26). The formation of the self as an ethical subject is thereby

> a process in which the individual delimits that part of himself that will form the object of his moral practice, defines his position relative to the precept he will follow, and decides on a certain mode of being that will serve his moral goal. And this requires him to act upon himself, to monitor, test, improve, and transform himself. There is no specific moral action that does not refer to a unified moral conduct; no moral conduct that does not call for the forming of oneself as an ethical subject; and no forming of the ethical subject without 'modes of subjectivation' and an 'ascetics' or 'practices of the self' that support them (Foucault, 1986a: 28).

The problem for Foucault in the above is that he must now posit a freely acting agent who decides upon their own 'mode of being' and selects 'that part of himself' that will form the object of moral practice. As in Weber's existentialism, an individual who is already formed and developed to some degree has to be presupposed prior to this process, one who can make fundamental choices and commit themselves to the value of their own choosing. There also remains the problem of the nature of the 'substance', 'material', or 'soul', on which the ethical subject works and delimits. This substance must have some original energy or direction of its own that requires the ethical subject to act upon it. Thus once again we find problems of voluntarism, individualism and naturalism creeping back into an approach which pretends to have done away with such problems.

Also, like Weber, Foucault's understanding of ethics appears to be concerned with the relationship of individuals to a body of codes, dictums or precepts. He never considers, as does Mead, that the ethical relationship might be a relationship *between* social beings, a network of relationships and interactions in which moral codes are not only adhered to but also set and changed in the face of practical problems. Thus, in his ethics as in the theory of discourse, Foucault sees individuals as the receivers and not the producers of ethics. Ethical precepts are just another technique for the self-subjectivation of individuals. This contrasts sharply with

Mead's ethics (see Schwalbe, 1988) where individuals are not determined by moral codes, but can, through their *social* consciousness, act in a manner which is ethical and yet never wholly determined by rules or codes.

Foucault (1986b) did come close to picturing a mature social agent, capable of autonomous activity free from the authority of dominant powers. This is the subject who is the creation of the Enlightenment, endowed by that tradition with the faculties of critical and independent thought. Foucault is no longer saying that this type of subjectivity is simply an illusion, a creation of enlightened discourse behind which lurks power. He now appears to be saying that this is an emergent form of human subjectivity with concrete powers for rationality and autonomy, and as such is a way of escape from traditional modes of subjugation and domination. A subject has developed historically who is capable of putting their socially constructed powers to independent use.

However, Foucault now seems bound to support aspects of Western culture and philosophy that he spent the majority of his career subverting. In the event, he can only bring himself to suggest that we refuse aspects of the social identities offered to us that lead away from maturity and back to domination. Foucault can offer little that is positive to the discourse in which agents transform and reconstruct society and the self, because he cannot contribute to the debate about who we are. His theoretical approach is tied to the belief that all answers to this question are intrinsic to knowledge and therefore to power. Thus, in the end, Foucault can only suggest a refusal of social identity, and a turning inward of individual self-consciousness to create an 'aesthetics of the self', where each individual makes their own personality into a work of art. This is like Nietzsche's call to the 'supermen' to mould their characters into an artistic plan to 'delight the eye' in the face of common values.

Once again in French Nietzscheanism we find a turning away from collective and social consciousness, with a final resort to an ethical and methodological individualism. And all of this from an approach that once promised the 'death of man' and a vision of the social construction of the self.

Conclusion

The structuralist and post-structuralist theory of the social construction of subjectivity is riddled with the type of contradictions and dichotomies that the approach has tried to overcome. The dichotomy between the discursive and material realms, the notion of an everyday individuality opposed to a socially constructed identity, and the vision of a biological body in an eternally external cultural world are all dilemmas the approach has failed to resolve. Added to this, post-structuralism cannot engage in an analysis of concrete social relations, for it understands the social to be synonymous with discourse. In the post-modernist tradition, the whole idea of a society is then called into question and one is faced with the ultimately solipsistic belief that all reality, including the social, is the construct of discourse. Socio-political analysis flounders on these rocks.

To overcome these problems we need to look more closely at Foucault's notion that humans are engaged in three types of social relations — relations that transform the real, relations of communication and relations of power. While this was suggested by Foucault, it was a notion that he — along with the other structuralists and post-structuralists — failed to elaborate in any systematic way. These three types of relations are important because it is within them that social selves are formed. It is these relations, and the way they determine the formation of personality, I will be looking at in the next three chapters in order to gain a better understanding of the formation of personality. Here, I hope to link theories of the formation of social selves with the structure of relations of production, culture and relations of power and interdependence within the social figuration. I will also seek to develop the theory of the social formation of the conscious and unconscious self, begun in structuralism, within a different methodological framework. This framework must allow for a more concrete sociological and social psychological approach to social selves without losing some of the insights gained in theories of discourse, particularly from the work of Mead. This is the synthesis that I believe is needed for the study of social individuals.

PART TWO
Personality in Social Relations and Interdependencies

CHAPTER FIVE
Social Relations and Personality

In Marxist theory, the essential social relations and activities in which humans are engaged are those that transform the real world we live in. For Marx, this is the reason why humans are to be seen as social beings; it would be impossible for people to meet their needs and survive in the world, were it not for the power of transformation generated by social activity, and, more specifically, by social labour. The level of productive power required to change the natural world could never be generated individually. As I showed in Chapter One, for Marx, it is only in capitalist society, where individuals are separated from the means of production when these become owned as private property, that people feel themselves to be 'isolated individuals', alienated from the society they form together. In capitalist society, our interdependence as individuals confronts us like an external force, rather than as internal and necessary social connections. And yet capitalism is a society of the most advanced social relations and socially developed productive forces: it is the *type* of relations that exist in capitalism that make individuals feel isolated and powerless. But the isolated individuals of capitalism are still social beings, their personalities developed within capitalist social relations.

Lucien Sève takes as the starting point for his psychology of personality this notion of humans as necessarily connected through relations that transform the real. For Sève, the development of the personal capacities of each social individual takes place within productive activity organized by the division of labour. Each person can only develop to the level of the productive forces created in society, for these constitute the social heritage which individuals appropriate in their personal development. It is not through the gene that people inherit the talents necessary to the continued existence of humanity; instead, these are handed down and transformed from generation to generation through social relations. What is essential to humans, then, is not located in each separate individual, but in the social relations which form the social and historical heritage through which individuals develop as personalities. Sève, then, takes a decisive step in the direction we are following here, by theorizing social relations as primary in the study of individuals. He inverts the traditional view of the relationship between individuals and society: it is not the individual, but social relations which are the basis for the real life processes in which personalities develop. However, this view has its roots firmly planted in the theories of Marx.

Social Relations, Activity and Social Being

Marx and the Theses on Feuerbach
The genesis of Marx's dialectical theory of the development of social being within activity structured by social relations, can be found in his *Theses on Feuerbach*. In these eleven short theses, Marx mounts a critique of the materialist and idealist philosophy of his day, and creates his own dialectical resolution of these two branches of philosophical thinking. The platform which launches this dialectical regeneration of theory is primarily a critique of the materialist philosophy of Feuerbach. In his work, Feuerbach (1972) attempted to create a materialist anthropology of human nature and activity, by showing that it is the embodied, social activity of individuals which determines their social being and consciousness. Human nature consists of certain inborn needs which can only be satisfied within a community of other individuals, and so leads people into interaction with one another. It is only within this community of active and embodied others, which becomes reflected in consciousness as 'you', that individuals find their own existence reflected back at them so they may become conscious of themselves as an 'I'. Therefore Feuerbach does not understand the human subject — the 'I' — as the essence of humanity which is endowed by God, believing instead that human nature and human society is essential and primary in the formation of the self.

However, Marx (1977) was critical of this understanding of

humanity. For Marx, all that Feuerbach had done was to resolve what philosophers had previously understood as the religious essence into his own abstract notion of the 'human essence'. That is, Feuerbach sees human nature as fundamental, containing all the needs of the human species in an unchanging form, and it simply requires interaction with others to satisfy those needs. Marx thought that Feuerbach had missed the central point: that is, human needs are not satisfied by interaction alone, for in an often hostile environment humans must labour to *produce* the objects to satisfy their needs. This leads to a second mistake in Feuerbach's thinking, for in believing that the needful and sensuous nature of humans is satisfied solely by interaction, sociality is conceived of only as intersubjectivity. It is conceptualized in its mental rather than its practical form, as contemplation rather than activity which can actually change the natural and social world. There occurred as a result of this the division between materialism and idealism, where materialist philosophers such as Feuerbach saw the essence of humanity as contemplation set in a real material and social world, and as governed by that external world. On the other side were the idealist philosophers who believed that humans created the world for themselves, but did so in a boundless way, unfettered by any material or social prerequisites. So for Marx,

> The chief defect of all hitherto existing materialism (that of Feuerbach included) is that the thing, reality, sensuousness, is conceived only in the form of the object or of contemplation, but not as sensuous human activity, practice, not subjectively. Hence, in contradistinction to materialism, the active side was developed abstractly by idealism — which, of course, does not know real, sensuous activity as such. Feuerbach wants sensuous objects, really distinct from the thought objects, but he does not conceive human activity itself as objective activity. Hence . . . he regards the theoretical attitude as the only genuinely human attitude, while practice is conceived and fixed only in its dirty-juridical manifestation (1977: 156).

What Marx is stating here, is that the human subject and their contemplation should be conceived on the basis of practical activity in the world — particularly labour activity — for this is formative of all other experiences. This new conception should no longer be cast in the framework of an anthropological materialism — where human needs are satisfied in the real world but remain basically unchanged — but instead it should be recast as *historical* materialism, where human subjectivity and needs are developed in the concrete, historical activity of human beings. In both the material world and in social history, humans produce their means of subsistence in order to survive. And as they produce, they change not only the natural, material world, but their own nature as well: their needs, their passions and their capacities. Humans appropriate nature through their social relations of production, yet the objects of production emerge from the production process in a changed form, as do the human producers who create them. Not only have the objects that satisfy needs changed, the very needs they are designed to meet have been transformed in the process. Human nature is therefore not a static entity for Marx, and he berates Feuerbach and the other philosophers for conceiving it as such.

Equally, for Marx, the idealist picture of humans making of the world whatever they willed it to be, was inadequate. This philosophy could not conceive of the effort involved in the development of human potentials, that they were not something pregiven, and that history inevitably involved human action and labour. The thing which Marx believed both limited and liberated the creativity of humans, was not an abstract 'spirit' or 'will', nor their human nature, but their inheritance of the social legacy of previous generations.

> Men make their own history, but they do not make it just as they please; they do not make it under circumstances chosen by themselves, but under circumstances directly encountered, given, and transmitted from the past (Marx, 1977: 300).

However, the dichotomy between idealism and materialism is mirrored in the style of discourse theories propagated by Mead and the social constructivists. A theorist like Mead bears striking resemblance to Feuerbach, whose theories are very much a forerunner of interactionism. And as I noted in Chapter Two, Mead, like Feuerbach, has understood the social formation of human consciousness and self within interaction, yet has failed to place both society and personality within a process of historical change. Also, Mead and the French phenomenologist Merleau-Ponty (1963) both realized that meaning had a practical as well as a discursive and mental aspect: indeed, structured physical activity is the basis of meaning. Yet in the work of both theorists, the meanings and objects produced in this activity are still conceived only intersubjectively and not as the objects of practical production.

The perspectives of idealism and materialism become even more jumbled in social constructivism as objects and reality are conceived only in terms of the contemplation made possible by discourse. Like Feuerbach, the social constructivists tend to disregard sensuous human practice. They also tend to resolve the essences constructed in discourse or ideology into the human essence, just as Feuerbach did with the religious essence. In an even more extreme fashion than Feuerbach or Mead, they do not acknowledge the sensuous, physical practice of interaction as a basis for meaning and consciousness. There are seen to be no material or practical limits to the constructions possible in human knowledge.

In these theories, then, what limits and enables humans to act are the boundaries and perspectives of social consciousness, whether this is seen to be based in interaction or in discursive structures. But as Marx indicates above, humans make contact with the world physically in labour as well as mentally through consciousness. What both enables them to act *and* limits their actions is the legacy handed down to them through the ensemble of social relations. Social being is created in human activity as structured by social relations which have a concrete history, and the social being created therein determines the consciousness of individuals. Human ideas are always connected in a complex way to social existence. In this sense, for Marx, human being is always social being, for the individual — their nature and consciousness — can only be understood in the context of the social heritage that has been handed down to them through social relations as they unfold within the historical process:

> the human essence is no abstraction inherent in each single individual. In its reality it is the ensemble of the social relations (1977: 157).

Historical Materialism and the Individual
Lucien Sève believes we must begin to understand individuals from this fundamental lesson contained in the *Theses on Feuerbach*, that the human essence is no abstraction, but is in reality the ensemble of social relations. Marxian theorists must not wipe the slate clean of historical, social relations, or of individual lives, for the core of the problem in the social sciences is the mediation between the general movement of society in history and the lives of individuals. As Marx says, 'the social history of men is never anything but the history of their individual development, whether they are conscious of it or not' (in Sève, 1978: 477).

The development of individuals always takes place within a social logic; this is constituted by the ensemble of social relations which are the matrices of activity within which the personality is constructed. For Sève, the person cannot be detached from their deep sociality and deprived of their historical form, for they are not bodies in an external environment. Rather, humans are always embedded in the material world as active bodies, and are always part of the social relations as a moment and embodiment of the social totality. It must be emphasized that Sève is not arguing that individuals can be reduced to the level of simple products of social structure, as in anti-humanism, and thus deprived of their active role in society and their singularity. This is because he does not believe that individuals arise from the social base as one of its products. Instead, the basis of human life is to be found in the biological constitution of humanity. However, as I have already pointed out, the biological nature of humans cannot be separated out from social history and treated as an independent element, for the logic of human activity, along with needs and capacities, is always determined within social relations.

Sève forces us to think in a dialectical way about human nature, social relations and activity, for the active and needful structure of the organism always lives within, appropriates and expands the social structure. This is to be thought of as a dialectical relation because the two structures — organic and social — are not actually separate, but part of the same unity. Marx understood that individuals were biological beings with needs and passions, who were driven to produce objects in the world which would satisfy their desires. As Agnes Heller (1976) has shown, this means that humans must have original biological needs which historical production transforms. In the process, new historical needs do develop — including the 'radical needs' for self-determination — but these are always built into the framework allowed for by the biological organism. Marx does not deny the existence of a human nature, then, but simply denies that this can be studied independently from the history of the development of social relations. Norman Geras (1983) shows how Marx distinguished between the terms 'human nature', which refers to those tendencies and impulses inherent in the human species at birth, and the 'nature of man', which describes how these basic dispositions develop into full capacities, talents and characteristics in the process of their social and historical development.

Social relations are thus the mode of existence for human bodies, in which the organic structure actively realizes itself. The essence of humanity is therefore excentric; it is not to be found within the body as an essence, for it is established between individuals as social relations and then appropriated by individuals as personality. Thus there is a continual process of elaboration in the dialectical relation between active individuals and the structure of social relations.

Sève uses these insights from Marxism to show that it is not a social science which replaces the investigation of individual lives with that of social relations: rather, it shows the unity between these two investigations. In order to designate this unity, Sève believes that the object of a Marxist theory of personality should be 'social individuality'; that is, the individual who develops socially into a personality. Marxism is thus a humanism, because it refers to the historical development of humanity and to the conditions of the development of individual personalities: yet it is a *scientific humanism* because it understands that individual development can only be studied on the basis of a social science concerning the historical development of society.

Sève attempts to crystallize this relation between the biological organism and social relations — in which the individual develops into a personality — by the term 'juxtastructural relation', a relation which will hopefully avoid either biological or social reductionism. He also wants to argue against the likes of Althusser through this concept, claiming that individuals are not just a *product* of the social base like the 'superstructures' — the ideas and ideologies of the age — but are *part* of the 'social base'. This is the forces and relations of production that produce not only objects for consumption, but also the political relations and ideas in which people in that epoch are enmeshed. Sève is trying to destroy the idea that individuals are produced by ideologies, and instead he hopes to restore Marx's true theoretical intent: that individuals were to be understood as active producers, of their environment, the goods to satisfy their needs, and also the ideas which described their social relations. Thus:

> It is clear for two reasons in particular that even in this broad sense the concrete individual is not a superstructure of the social relations. In the first place, while being radically functionally determined by the social *base, social individuality* does not occupy a superstructural position with regard to it, since it is an *integral part* of this base and its processes

of reproduction; the basic individual life-processes do not appear *on the basis* of social relations, they are part of them. In the second place, social individuality itself develops within biological individuals who as such are not at all the product of the social base and its contradictions but of a quite distinct reality. Thus although they are functionally determined by the social base (and its superstructures) *quite as much* as the superstructures themselves, individuals do not arise *on* this base with superstructural characteristics but are as it were *laterally meshed in* with it and become wholly subordinated to it — although it is not their *actual source*. To designate this specific type of essential connection . . . I suggest the concept *juxtastructure* (1978: 144).

What Sève is trying to show here is that individuals are not products of the social base because they are biological beings who are the main element of both the forces and relations of production. But just as individuals are not produced by the social base, neither are they produced as superstructures, because, as social individuals, they are a fundamental part of both base and super-structure. Sève continues by saying that while social individuality is not a direct product of the social structure, in the end it is wholly dependent on it, for the juxtastructural relation is an 'oriented circularity' in which social relations are always determinate over the biological structures of the individual 'in the last instance'. This is an attempt by Sève to underline the fact that social relations always determine the forms of individuality in society, not vice versa, even though individuals are not the direct product of those relations. While this may be acceptable in terms of the relation between individuals and their society, what is more questionable is Sève's uncritical incorporation of Marx's division of society into a social base and a political and ideological superstructure. I will return to this point in my critique of Sève at the end of this chapter.

For Sève, then, we need concepts located in the historical forms of human activity and relations in order to understand the nature of social individuality. The advantage of this method can clearly be seen in the study of needs. By developing Marx's idea that in producing to meet their needs in social history, humans change them in the process, we begin to understand that an anthropological theory of humanity cannot be based in concepts such as need, instinct or desire, because these things change as the formation of human activity changes. Social sciences should not begin from the speculative notion of needs as they are imagined in some ideal-type model, frozen in time and space; instead they should start out from the concrete investigation of the historical forms of needs and desires as they emerge in social activity. This would be the method of a scientific anthropology, one based in historical materialism rather than speculative philosophy. The investigation would not proceed by studying the structure of human needs or instincts and the activity they give rise to; rather, it would work in the opposite direction, showing how need is based on historically given forms of activity. The formula would not be Need–Activity–Need (N–A–N) but Activity–Need–Activity (A–N–A).

This means that investigations of personality formation must not be based on individualist concepts, but must first study the structure of social activities and relations in which individual lives are embedded. It also means that, unlike most forms of psychology, which begin by studying the activity and psyche of the child — or the mentally ill — Sève proposes instead that we begin investigations from the standpoint of everyday, adult activity.

> Until now psychology has sought above all to understand man by way of the animal, the adult by way of the child, the normal individual by way of the sick, the total system of the personality by way of its isolated functions, and the content of this personality by way of certain forms of activity. We think the time has come to supplement this rather unfruitful effort by a real effort in the opposite direction (1978: 285).

What this real effort at a psychology of personality is concerned with, is the scientific investigation of the social relations that contain the heritage which individuals appropriate in their activity. The human subject therefore becomes a part of the totality of social relations, something which Sève believes we can see the realization of in psychoanalysis, where it is the relation between nature and human cultures which produces the structure of the personality. However, Freud does not realize that this relation involves social relations, which mediate the interchange between individuals and the natural world. It also involves social production, which creates the objects of needs and desires. Psychoanalysis, like interactionism, also understands the world of the child as the forerunner of the adult world, whereas in reality it is the adult world which shapes and guides the activity of children. For example, the key to understanding play, for Sève, is in terms of the re-enactment of adult activity as a preparation for the child in anticipation of their adult social relations and activities.

So in Sève's theory of personality, we must begin from the standpoint of the structure of social relations and activities. Yet how do these translate into the logic of individual lives and what do they actually tell us about individuals? Sève believes that they tell us something about the *general forms of individuality* that develop in each historical epoch on the basis of social relations. For example, categories of individuals such as capitalist and worker are not pregiven types of individuals. Rather, they are categories of individual activity created within capitalist relations, which describe the activities of certain individuals rather than types of personalities. Also, we can understand some of the contradictions inherent in these activities which will translate into personal dilemmas: for example, the capitalist will be torn between their activity of accumulating capital and their desire to spend that capital on their own personal fulfilment, an activity which would cut against the grain of their role as accumulators. Similarly, workers will be divided between their roles in the work process, where their activities are directed by the needs of capital, and the desire to have greater self-determination over their own lives and their own work activities.

For Sève, the study of social relations also shows the true nature of human alienation, which was initially understood by philosophers as the estrangement from the truly human core — the essence — at the centre of our being. What Marx's mature works showed was that alienation was not the estrangement from an inner core, because the human essence was now seen as social relations: rather, alienation was understood as the separation of the vast majority of individuals from the social heritage they have helped to create — the assimilation of which is limited for them, not by their own personal needs, but by the needs of capital. Alienation is not so much a result of the division of labour, as sociologists like Simmel believed, where the collective culture of humanity outgrows what any one individual can hope to assimilate in a lifetime. Rather, alienation occurs because of the particularly limited tasks people perform in the capitalist division of labour. Here, the development of personal capacities is not determined by the individual's need for self-development, but by the need of capitalists to make a profit from the production process so as to accumulate more capital. Sève believes that Marx shows how, in capitalism, there are the highly developed productive forces on the one hand, and yet the impoverishment — and therefore, the alienation — of individuals on the other.

It is this contradiction between the forces and relations of production that is lived out at the centre of the lives of individuals in capitalism. On one side, there are the highly developed forces of production that would allow individuals to develop capacities in a full and all-round way; and yet, on the other, the relations of production prevent the full appropriation of the forces of production, by harnessing their power to the production of greater levels of capital. However, Sève follows Marx in seeing this as the precondition for the transformation of capitalist social relations into socialist and communist relations. For Sève, such a revolution occurs when individuals fully realize the nature of the contradictions which haunt their lives and relate it to their oppression under capitalism. At present people may hide from this contradiction by retreating into their private lives. Eventually, though, people will realize the only way to overcome these contradictions is in political activity, which aims to overturn them and to construct instead a socialist society where the development of individuals will be limited only by their interests, needs and the organic limits to what any one person can appropriate in a lifetime.

It remains to be seen in full what the psychology of personality will be like when informed by this type of Marxian theory. So far, Sève has only outlined a theory of the general forms of individuality. Now he must detail the way in which concrete, singular personalities arise as moments of the logic of social relations in which they are enmeshed, and how the contradictions of capitalist society cut to the heart of peoples' lives.

The Psychology of Personality: the Individual in the Division of Labour

Sève's psychology of personality, then, is not to be a science of a single object — the isolated individual — but a science of relations; in particular, those relations in which the personality develops and which underlie the psychic acts of individuals. The psychology of personality is therefore primarily concerned with the social relations between acts.

> I call this object personality and by this I mean the total system of activity of a given individual, a system which forms and develops throughout his life and the evolution of which constitutes the essential content of his biography (Sève, 1978: 451).

In the system of activity which constitutes each individual

biography, Sève (1978: 299) hopes a Marxist psychology would be capable of understanding 'the whole structure and development of real human personalities' in the context of their lived experience. However, the experience of the lived body in the material world is not conceived of by way of its highly generalized activity, as in Merleau-Ponty's phenomenology. Instead, the lived body is understood in terms of the *productive activity* in which physical and intellectual capacities develop. Sève claims that, 'if a man is a being who produces himself in social labour, it is at once obvious that *the psychology of personality is founded on the analysis of social labour or it does not exist*' (1978: 148). From this position Sève seeks to explain human personality in terms of the whole range of activities structured by the relations of production.

In the psychology of personality, then, the *act* becomes the first basic concept, for it is within activity structured by the ensemble of social relations that individuals appropriate the human essence. Here, I use the term 'appropriation' quite deliberately, for Sève is not arguing that individuals simply 'internalize' their social acts, assimilating them into an already prepared psychological plane: rather, the term appropriation refers to the way individuals 'build by incorporating' (Ollman, 1976: 89) what they produce into their nature as social beings. For Sève, activity is constitutive of the personality, and yet an act is always social because it is locked into the whole system of activity in society which stretches far beyond the conscious reach of any single individual. This is at the very basis of Sève's notion of the unconscious — also elaborated by Smith (1985) — in that individuals are not always fully aware of the networks of social relations and activities which determine their own individual acts. This is because an act goes out into the entire circuit of social activity and returns to itself 'through the vast mediations of social relations' (Sève, 1978: 304). Social relations are always the structured medium through which individuals act, whether they are aware of this or not. And it is through social relations that the consequences of one's actions will return, reshaping the self in the process.

Thus, the characteristic of an act is that it has a consequence within society, producing a result within the social network. This result returns to the individual through the mediations of social relations as a product. It produces in individuals a capacity, which is the knowledge that one's action has had an effect on the world and can be used again in future to produce that same effect. Thus *capacity* becomes Sève's second basic concept in the psychology of personality, for a capacity is the psychological product of an individual's activity. The increased learning of capacities will be the basis, and the motive, for the activity and personal growth of the individual. This insight turns the whole theory of personality around, for as Sève has already shown, the motivation to act no longer has a purely internal, organic source, but depends largely on the product which that activity yields in the social world. So the structure of human motivation is no longer Need/Product, but Product/Need — the actual product the act produces providing the motivation to engage in activity. The *P/N formula* of motivation is Sève's third basic concept in the psychology of personality, and completes the triad of basic concepts he will use.

There is a dialectical relationship which Sève detects between acts and capacities, as the activity of a person always gives rise to the accumulation of capacities which are expressed in current activity. Given this dialectical nature of development, Sève has split acts into two types: 'sector I acts' are those which develop new capacities, while 'sector II acts' use the capacities that have already been learned to carry on activity. In real life processes, these acts will overlap, some acts belonging to both sectors at the same time, as no single act is produced in isolation from those already possessed. Of prime interest to those practising Sève's psychology of personality will be the balance between these two sectors of activity within a person's biography, for this will show how successfully or unsuccessfully that person is developing within the structure of their activity. Those individuals with a high proportion of sector I activity will be appropriating more of the social heritage than those with a low proportion of this type of activity, although individuals need a balance with sector II acts in which they can practise the capacities already gained.

However, what is also important to individuals in the structure of their activity is where they stand in the class hierarchy and within the division of labour. For example, working class people will have in their biographies a high proportion of what Sève calls 'abstract activity', which is activity performed with the sole purpose of creating profit and accumulating capital rather than fulfilling the needs of the worker. It is activity relating to the development of capital, not the self-development of the individual. This type of abstract activity will mean using capacities already learned in work activities that tend to be highly repetitive, thus repeating sector II activities over and over again. Very little time will be given over to learning new capacities which enhance the personality. In general, those in more middle class occupations will escape some of the more soul destroying work, for their position in the division of labour will provide them with occupations in which there may be a higher level of what Sève calls 'concrete activity', which is activity related to the learning of new capacities and the development of the individual. Yet within capitalism, all work will to some extent be abstract activity, as all those who work — even the capitalist — will have the larger proportion of their time governed by the need to accumulate capital, rather than the needs of their own personal development. People then have to look outside of their work activities, to their own leisure time, for activities which are related to their own need for self-development. As I showed in Chapter One, for Marx, the lives of individuals within capitalism are divided between that part determined by some branch of labour and that part which is personal.

Even in personal life, though, individuals find that their own consumption and recreation is geared more to preparing them for the return to the labour process, rather than to the satisfaction of their own needs. Most people, then, will be alienated and stunted in their personal growth, for their talents and needs cannot develop in a full and meaningful way. Abstract and concrete activity is therefore reflected in abstract and concrete aspects of the personality. The degree to which one of these forms of activity is dominant in the personality, will depend on the *use-time* a person has within their biography to give over to one or the other form of activity. Those with a high composition of abstract activity in the use-time of their biography will tend to be more alienated than those with a higher level of concrete activity, for their personalities will be less abstract. The concept of time is therefore important to Sève, because

> What we are looking for . . . is the structure of activity itself, in other words the dialectic of its development in time, which represents the unity of its functioning structure and its laws of historical movement. And in addition, if this dialectical structure, i.e. the *real* activity of the concrete individual, is indeed what we are seeking, it is necessarily a reality which men constantly have to deal with in their life, therefore a *practical* reality, the empirical aspects of which are quite visible even if the elaboration of its theory and the construction of its topology

present great difficulties. I put forward the hypothesis that this reality which is absolutely basic, and in a sense which has always been perfectly familiar, is *use-time (l'emploi du temps)* (1978: 333).

Time is central in Sève's work, therefore, because it structures the field across which the activity of the individual unfolds within their social relations. As these form the basis of a person's biography, so the structure of use-time, as it unfolds, also marks out the 'fundamental law of development' of the personality. Sève attempts to elaborate this in terms of a diagram, reproduced as Figure 1, where the basic divisions and contradictions in a person's biography under capitalism are represented in temporal form. The basic elements of the biography are the acts which constitute what Sève calls the 'infrastructure' of the personality, along with the time the individual has to devote to these different acts. The use-time between acts within a biography can be represented as in Figure 1.

As we can see, the right hand column of the diagram represents the abstract, alienated activity of the person, while the left hand

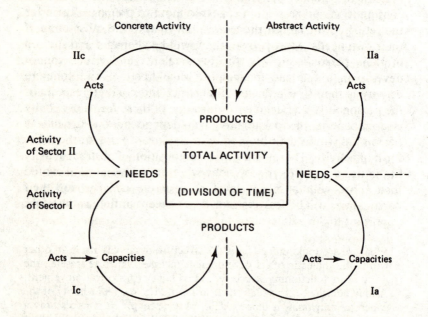

Figure 1 *Use-time within a biography as represented by Sève (1978: 347)*

column represents the concrete activity in the biography. The two columns running horizontally represent sector II acts and sector I acts respectively, and the whole diagram divides into four basic quadrants. Quadrant Ia shows the time spent in sector I activity which produces capacities, yet is abstract activity, performed under alienated conditions. Quadrant IIa shows the amount of time spent practising these capacities. The same formula is repeated in the left hand side of the diagram, but this shows concrete as opposed to abstract activity. Activity in all four quadrants generates products, and these serve as the motives for individuals to engage in these activities, creating in them certain needs.

The diagram of the topology of a biography can be utilized in the case of any particular individual to illustrate the contradictions at the centre of their lives. For example, if we applied the diagrammatic format to the life of a child at school, the largest proportion of their activity would be in quadrants Ic and IIc, as most of the child's activity is spent learning and practising new, personally useful, capacities. Very small amounts of use-time would be spent in sectors Ia or IIa. This could be compared to the biography of an industrial worker which would show the reverse position in the infrastructure of use-time: here, the vast majority of hours in a day would be given over to abstract activity, and within that the largest proportion would be in quadrant IIa, meaning that it would not only be abstract activity but mainly repetitive sector II activity. In this life, there is very little left of a person's use-time for quadrants Ic and IIc of activity, which is the development and practice of new capacities outside of abstract activity; or even for quadrant Ia — the learning of new capacities in abstract activity. The biography of this individual indicates that the personality will have largely stagnated, personal growth having been stifled by the tasks performed within the division of labour, mainly aimed at the development of capital rather than the development of the self.

Apart from abstract and concrete activities, Sève also believes there is a third category of activity which he calls 'intermediary'. These acts are performed for the benefit of other people, but they are not abstract in their character; they are not performed in return for wages, and no individual profits from them in money terms. This category of activity would therefore include all the aspects of social action which concerned the interactionists such as

Mead and Harré, for intermediary acts would include all the face-to-face exchanges that occur between people in their everyday lives. Sève includes these acts in what he refers to as the infrastructure of the personality because they are productive of capacities in the individual, and also because they involve all the facets of a person's sociality. In this category, Sève would place family relationships, interpersonal and communal relationships and love relationships. It is within these relations that the child grows and learns, so that, 'the concrete personality first presents itself as an ensemble of personal, indeed inter-personal, non-alienated activities, unfolding as self-expression' (Sève, 1978: 341). However, this is destroyed as the young adult increasingly becomes occupied with abstract activity.

On the basis of this infrastructure of activity there arises what Sève labels as the 'superstructure' of the personality, which he divides into 'spontaneous' and 'voluntary' controls. These superstructures play an organizational and regulatory role within the personality, but they do not play a productive role, generating new capacities. Spontaneous controls arise on the basis of concrete activity — including intermediary activity — and these controls include the emotional responses to others within interpersonal activity. The structure of the emotions as they develop in interaction would be involved here. However, the voluntary controls are those that arise on the basis of abstract activity, and these include the controls exercised over the personality which are external to its concrete development. In this sense, the abstract rules which govern behaviour, the conduct and decorum that must be adhered to, some of the self-images we feel we must aspire to but do not fit, are all voluntary controls. These controls will feel more alien within the personality, as they are not related directly to concrete personal needs, nor to the individual's everyday interactions.

All these contradictions within personalities under capitalism are seen by Sève as potential forces which might move people *en masse* to overcome them by transcending capitalist social relations and setting up a socialist society. There is no other way for individuals to resolve these personal dichotomies, as they are based in social divisions and inequalities. Any personal solutions, such as a retreat into private life, leisure activities, or interpersonal relations, all of which are more rewarding and more concrete, will only be temporary stop gaps which postpone the resolution of the problem rather than solve it. To be rid of alienation in both society and the personality, Sève believes it is inevitable that individuals must become involved in revolutionary activity. However, there is a danger in this way of looking at individual biographies. That is, Sève appears to be less interested at this point in the concrete individual than in seeing the life of each personality as the means by which the Marxian dialectic of history brings about its final change — the culmination of the process of history in the communist society. This is ultimately a reductionist move, for Sève is theorizing individuals as nothing more than the vessels of teleological historical processes, and this must lead us into a thorough assessment of his entire psychology of personality: just how viable a proposition for psychology is his theoretical hypothesis?

Language, Culture and the 'Social Habitus'

One of the main advantages of Lucien Sève's Marxist approach to the personality over the traditional approaches in the psychology of personality, is that he uses Marx's dialectical approach to show how social relations are fundamental to personality formation. Relations are not external to the self, but are internal, in that they make the personality what it is in each historical epoch (Shames, 1981). It is not natural propensities nor genetically inherited talents which determine the development of each individual, but the relation of each person to the social heritage through the division of labour and the use-time within the person's biography. This determines the structure of the individual's activity and therefore the development of their personality. By making human activity central to the analysis, Sève shows how Marxist theory as he conceives it can correct the mistakes of humanism and anti-humanism, and through its 'scientific humanism' can transcend this debate.

But the main problem with Sève's method is that he sees the appropriation of the social heritage purely in terms of the individual's relation to social labour — in other words, their relation to the production process through the division of labour. This leads Sève to claim that the psychology of personality is founded in the study of social labour or it does not exist. However, as Sève also notes (1978: 98–9), in a study of Marx's *Capital*, it is not human labour in general which is the real human essence, but the 'particular forms of social relations' typical of each historical period. This means that the forms of social relations in a society are more than the relations of production, and are not simply a superstructure of those relations. Even if one wished to follow the arguments of the more traditional historical materialists, and understand all social relations as determined by relations of production, the personality must still be formed in relations other than those of production. The self cannot, therefore, be understood simply on the basis of social labour, or its relations, alone.

Sève realizes this himself, and hopes to forestall charges of economic reductionism by claiming that

> one must consider the system of the division of labour in all its aspects, technical and economic, domestic, political, cultural, etc., as an ensemble of objective social facts indispensable for understanding the temporal topology of concrete personalities in a determinate society (1978: 274).

But the problem is that this is exactly what Sève does not do: he does not consider the division of labour in all its aspects when he studies personality formation, concentrating instead on the technical and economic aspects. Nowhere does he consider the domestic, political or cultural factors mentioned above, instead focusing solely on the division between abstract and concrete labour. This leaves many individuals out of the analysis altogether, such as those who do not work, or who do not work for wages. And as Robert Ashcroft (1982) points out, for many individuals the split between concrete and abstract activity is not as simple as a split between concrete and abstract labour. Many activities which are not done as paid work within capitalism will be experienced as abstract. For example, recent feminist literature shows that duties performed by women in the home, purely for the benefit of their families, can leave women as depressed and unfulfilled as the most mind-numbing factory work (Beechey and Whitelegg, 1986). Here Sève has ignored the division of domestic labour and the entire field of the unequal balance of power between women and men (Elias, 1987a). The vital question for the psychology of personality would then be, how do these relations reflect in the personality development of the sexes?

Perhaps this failing can be traced to Sève's attempt to base personality development in the 'infrastructure' of activity, which in traditional Marxist terms means the economic base of society. Personality development is then determined by one's labour activity and the capacities and skills it demands. But this leads to the mirroring of one of the dichotomies in Marxist theory which I mentioned earlier in this chapter — that between base and superstructure. In some readings of Marx, the economic base and the relations of production are seen as wholly determining the 'superstructure', which is composed of the ideas and the political and cultural relations of the age. Little attention is paid to the superstructure in this version of Marxism, because it can be taken as totally subordinate to the economic base, and therefore the study of the latter is of the greatest importance. I believe we can see this dichotomy reflected clearly in Sève's work, and this is the reason he tends to relegate the study of domestic, political and cultural factors to only minor importance in his psychology of personality.

Another way in which this problem manifests itself is that while Sève is forced to recognize the importance of interpersonal actions in terms of his category of 'intermediary activity', and that this is bound to occupy an infrastructural position in personality formation, this is not accounted for anywhere in his scheme of individual biography. Only abstract and concrete activity is included there, even though interaction must be primary in any life. Again, in the traditional Marxist mentality, such activity is implicitly regarded as only of secondary importance to productive activity.

This leads to a total disregard of communicative interaction and language, in terms of the role they play in personality formation and the development of consciousness. Sève does not bother to consider the effects of culture, which is interposed between material existence and consciousness, and composes the way in which we view ourselves and our experience. As C. Wright Mills expressed the problem:

> men live in a second-hand world . . . The consciousness of men does not determine their existence; nor does their existence determine their consciousness. Between human consciousness and material existence stand communications and designs, patterns and values which influence decisively such consciousness as they have (1963: 375).

This idea is one that I will consider in the next chapter, where the relations of communication will be connected both to material existence and human consciousness, through the work of the cultural-historical school. The point here, however, is that Sève does not give enough consideration to relations of communication in the formation of personality, even though he takes a quotation from Marx's *Grundrisse* which claims that it is 'language by way of which [the] personality constructs itself' (1978: 224); however, this is not followed up anywhere in his own work. Marx and Engels also made other statements linking language to consciousness, and to the necessity of intercourse between humans who must cooperate and produce in order to survive. They claimed that:

> Language is as old as consciousness, language *is* practical consciousness that exists also for other men, and for that reason alone it really exists for me personally as well; language, like consciousness, only arises from the need, the necessity, of intercourse with other men (1970: 51).

Unfortunately, in opposition to this, there are places in his work where Sève (1978: 183, 243–4) suggests that consciousness is not a social formation, but is a biological fact which remains constant throughout the human species: one which can be studied in a very generalized way by neurophysiology. But if we are to take seriously what Marx and Engels are saying above, then not only is language inseparable from consciousness, it is also an essential element in the intercourse between human beings, including that involved in social labour. How could one possibly separate language and consciousness from labour activity and regard them as 'superstructural'? And this applies not only to social activity but to the personality as well. How can an 'infrastructure' of the personality possibly be separated from a 'superstructure', elements of which must be bound together at every moment? For example, while Sève is undoubtedly right to say that humans do appropriate a part of their social heritage as capacities learned in social labour, these capacities must be learned mainly through communication with other generations. And what use would these physical capacities of the body be without language to steer them? While Marx did state in his early writings that it was production that distinguished humans from other animals, in his later works he began to stress how it was the *purposive* character of labour which 'stamps it as exclusively human' and 'distinguishes the worst architect from the best of bees' (in Sayer, 1987: 27–8). And in the *Grundrisse* Marx says:

> Nature builds no machines, no locomotives, railways, electric telegraphs, self-acting mules etc. These are the products of human industry; natural material transformed into organs of the human will over nature, or of human participation in nature. They are *organs of the*

human brain, created by the human hand; the power of knowledge objectified (1973: 706).

Here, Marx is not arguing that the human mind and human knowledge are only of secondary importance in understanding the productive process; instead he is showing 'to what degree general social knowledge has become a *direct force of production*' (1973: 706). Products are therefore just as much a result of the human mind as they are of the human body. What Sève refers to as humanity's 'inorganic body' is not, then, simply a reflection of physical capacities, but conscious ones also. Activity enters the body as capacities, but these would be no use — indeed, they would not arise in a complex form — without the self-consciousness constructed in language and in wider social interaction, which enters the body as self-consciously applied steering media, designing action and directing and applying capacities. There is no infrastructure and superstructure of the personality.

We can see this more clearly when we look closely at Sève's notion of the superstructure of the personality, which he splits into spontaneous and voluntary controls. There is a remarkable parallel here between what Mead labelled as the social instincts and the social consciousness respectively, for Sève claims that the emotions would be included in the category of spontaneous controls and that these are endogenous to the personality: the voluntary controls, however, arise on the basis of abstract activity, and in that sense they are exogenous, being destroyed when abstract activity is abolished by revolution. But again, Sève is drawing a very rigid distinction between abstract and concrete activity and, therefore, also between voluntary and spontaneous controls. He does not realize what Mead saw, that social instincts and social consciousness are *two sides of the same psychic processes*, and that social instincts, or spontaneous controls, are conditioned and organized by social relations through the individual's consciousness of those relations. To put it in Sève's own terms, spontaneous and voluntary controls are part of the same *dialectical unity*.

It therefore seems meaningless to say that voluntary controls will disappear when alienation and abstract activity are abolished. There is always bound to be some aspects of social interaction, some actions or rules, which do not relate directly to each individual's concrete needs or actions. Sève (1978: 110) himself claims that social rules will still exist under communism, only these will be democratically controlled; however, they are still social rules which individuals must obey, and they will reflect to some degree as voluntary controls within the personality. Because the self develops through its sociality, it is inevitable that some degree of voluntary control is necessary within the formation of a self-conscious identity. Indeed, in the development of personality, it becomes extremely difficult to separate spontaneous and voluntary controls, because what is learned socially as capacities, or as restrictions and inhibitions, will come to feel as though they are spontaneous. At the same time, many impulses or reactions which are spontaneous — such as joy or anger — will come under voluntary control, and it may become difficult for individuals to express them spontaneously. In different historical epochs the balance between this socially determined unity may well be different, but we must presume the balance will still exist under socialism.

What Sève has touched upon, though, is that the personality which lives in more equal and democratic conditions will not experience the rules which govern behaviour as such an alien and repressive force. The spontaneous impulses that the voluntary controls move to censure will also be experienced as no longer alien and frightening. Instead they will be experienced as a part of the self, no matter how undesirable they may seem. There would under these circumstances be a greater harmony between spontaneous and voluntary controls. However, at the same time, consciously self-determined activity has increased in power over the preconscious, unreflective impulses: this means that the voluntary control of action has grown in power under democratic conditions, not diminished.

However, the last point I want to deal with in this critique of Sève is the detrimental effect on his work caused by ignoring cultural influences in the formation of personality. At one point in his work, Sève sets as a future task for the psychology of personality the study of why certain people develop the interests they do and are thus directed to specific functions in the division of labour. This problem has been approached by Pierre Bourdieu (1977, 1984) in his work on the 'social habitus', which entails looking at the effects of culture upon a person's life conditions and upon their own self. For Bourdieu, the habitus is a system of dispositions and tastes which are learned from early childhood onwards, through the 'cultural capital' passed down within families, from parents to their children. Different groups and classes within society will each have a different habitus, which predisposes them towards specific types of practices and the development of particular life styles. Thus:

> The structures constitutive of a particular type of environment (e.g. the material conditions of existence characteristic of a class condition) produce *habitus*, systems of durable, transposable *dispositions*, structured structures predisposed to functioning as structuring structures, that is, as principles of the generation and structuring of practices and representations (Bourdieu, 1977: 72).

Before individuals even begin to develop rounded capacities, then, they are influenced in the direction of their activity by the habitus: the dispositions and tastes that are handed down to them through their cultural inheritance. But the habitus also forms a limit for certain groups, which is both material and cultural, on the types of activity they can engage in and the capacities they can develop. For example, Bourdieu shows that the type of abstract learning involved in much higher education, and the type of appreciation that the more abstract forms of representation and art demands, depends on an absence of economic necessity which favours the middle class over the working class in these particular activities. So the material conditions of life and the cultural conditions of a life style go hand-in-hand. This is something which Sève does not recognize, a fact which can be seen in an example which he gives to support his division of the topography of individual biographies. Here, Sève (1978: 348–9) claims that a child at school will have a large proportion of concrete activity in their biography and therefore more room for personal development. Yet Paul Willis (1977), in an ethnographic study of adolescents in school, shows that a large number of young working class people feel their lives at school are highly abstract, with little concrete relevance to the realities they will have to face as workers. Willis finds that the main source of discontent comes from the adolescents' home lives and their general contact with the older generation, where they find little importance placed on education in working class culture. That Sève regards the effect of culture on the personality as only of secondary — superstructural — importance, is much to the detriment of his whole theory of personality formation.

In Bourdieu's theory, the dispositions that develop in people through the inheritance of economic and cultural capital, angles them in a trajectory towards certain positions in the social structure — through the education system and workplace hierarchies, to jobs and social status which reproduce the inequalities in social relations. Indeed, the dispositions in the habitus can be seen as the internalization of social relations, in terms of relations of difference and distinction — marked by tastes and status symbols — between different social classes and groups. The social heritage contained in relations can therefore be assimilated through culture as well as activities. Bourdieu's whole enterprise can be read as an attempt to show the unity between all social practices, economic and cultural.

But this means that for a proper perspective on the problem of personality formation, we have to look on a wider scale at the whole range of social relations and practices in which the self develops. This would include all those relations and activities — between social classes, between the sexes and races, and within culture — in which the personality is constituted, along with those activities and aspects of the self which Sève has relegated as 'superstructural' or 'intermediary'. What has to be rejected is Sève's economic reductionism, his way of understanding the personality in terms of social labour only, and of taking the concepts of Marx's political economy — base, infrastructure, superstructure etc. — wholesale into social-psychological analysis. As I noted earlier, if we stick with Sève's hypotheses we are left with a psychology of personality which views the self as simply a vehicle for the working out of historical and economic contradictions. This simply will not do. However, as Gerhart Neuner says (in Sève, 1978: 484), in a well balanced response to Sève's work, if he does not always put forward solutions to the problem of personality formation which are always convincing, this does not mean his basic thesis is not valuable: rather, 'it is more a matter . . . of working out convincing solutions to the problem of the personality, of its structures and laws of development and of putting them up for debate'.

I believe that in putting forward more convincing solutions to the problem of personality formation, we need to begin to look at the way in which the self is formed through the workings of language and culture, and how this is also a fundamental element of the social relations and practices of everyday life. Bourdieu's work is of importance here, but so is the work of a group of Soviet psychologists and linguists, discussed in the next chapter, which proves that more convincing theories of social selves are possible within a theory inspired by Marxism.

Conclusion

One of the greatest contributions that Sève has made to the debate about the social formation of selves, is demonstrating how the personality is a moment in the totality of social relations. Humans are not the products of social structure, for relations are the medium of their activity. The structure of social relations is therefore generative as far as individuals are concerned, and the contradictions in those relations move humans to transcend them. Also humans have an organic basis which cannot be eradicated in society. However, the organic structure itself is determined by the medium of social relations, and the appearance of its limitations is transcended in historical development. Therefore, individuals become human and develop as personalities through the historical structure of their social relations which carry the human 'essence'. In this way, these relations are not only external to individuals but form the topology of the internal, psychological terrain. This occurs in the activities contained within the use–time of an individual's biography.

However, in studying the learning of capacities within biography, Sève has concentrated only on the capacities learned in social labour. This leaves on one side the capacities developed in individuals through culture, knowledge and interaction. Indeed, from the work of Bourdieu we can understand just how important these cultural capacities are, because they angle people towards positions in the division of labour prior to the formation of the individual's capacities in those positions. Thus the capacities we learn prior to taking up a role in the division of labour are of crucial importance. If we ignore cultural capacities formed in the social habitus as a whole, we tend to reduce human experience to a one-dimensional framework, just like the structuralists and post-structuralists who saw individuals as the product of discursive structures and ignored the social relations and activities of individuals through which the real world is transformed. The real experience of humans in the world is rich and multi-dimensional: it involves not only social labour or culture on their own. Rather, it is composed of social relations which are practical and cultural. I now want to look at the work of Marxist theorists who demonstrate the necessary, dialectical unity between the two, and the role that labour, communication and knowledge play in the formation of personality.

CHAPTER SIX

Social Relations, Culture and the Self

In this chapter I will look at the work of a group of psychologists and linguists from the Soviet Union, generally labelled as the 'cultural-historical' school, whose work is of tremendous importance to the project of developing a theory of social selves. Like Sève, these social scientists are inspired by Marxism, but, unlike Sève, they do not try to reduce human personality to the sphere of social labour alone. Instead, they attempt to formulate theories of personality on the level of social relations based in both labour and language. The cultural-historical setting is of prime importance here, and psychology itself is regarded as a historical science which must understand human capacities as determined by social development. To study something historically means to study its movement and development, and this can apply just as much to an individual as to society: indeed, the study of the development of the two are inseparable. This led one of the founders of this school of psychology, L.S. Vygotsky (1896–1934), to the study of the social development of the child. His work does not make the mistake of mainstream Western child psychology, which views the personality of the child as the basis of adult personality: rather, Vygotsky's work shows the importance of the cultural nature of personality development, with adults being the conductors of the social-historical world through which the child forms its own self.

For Vygotsky, what is most characteristic of humankind is purposive, self-determined activity, which is made possible by the 'higher mental functions' of self-consciousness and the intellect. These higher mental functions are not contained 'inside' the personality as natural pregivens which develop of their own accord, for they are functions which have developed in social history. Therefore:

To find the origins of purposeful action, one must transcend the limitations of the organism. The source of human consciousness and freedom should not be sought in the internal world of the intellect, but in the social history of mankind. To find the soul we must first abandon it (cited in Van der Veer and van IJzendoorn, 1985: 3).

Vygotsky, and others in the cultural-historical school, abandoned the vision of the human soul as biologically or spiritually innate, finding an alternative vision of humanity located in social history and in the cultural development of each individual.

Social History and Personality

For the cultural-historical school, personality not only develops through the socio-historical relation of individuals to the physical world, mediated by the labour process, but also through relations to other human beings which are mediated by language. It is the development of labour and language taken together which marks out the level of cultural-historical development, and in turn this determines the general level at which personalities will develop. Like Sève, these theorists agree that it is activity structured by social relations that is fundamental to the formation of the self. Here, activity gives rise to social being, and it is social being that determines the extent to which consciousness and self-consciousness will develop. To the cultural-historians, the nature of human activity has undergone significant changes, the balance tipping from spontaneous behaviour towards more minded, rational and self-regulated activity. The formation of human consciousness and self-consciousness, which enables individuals to distinguish themselves from others and from other aspects of nature, is the pivot in this change in social activity. The emergence of this type of activity did not simply depend on the fact that humans must produce their means of subsistence, for it was the way in which humans produced that forged the change: humans began to produce consciously, and in this the orientation of their action depended not only on the collective process of labour, but on the way this was directed through language. As A.R. Luria puts it, when distinguishing the cultural-historical style of psychology from that of others:

> The basic difference between our approach and that of traditional psychology will be that we are not seeking the origins of human consciousness in the depths of the 'soul' or in the independently acting mechanisms of the brain (where we shall find nothing). Rather, we are operating in an entirely different sphere — in humans' actual relationship with reality, in their social history, which is closely tied to labour and language (1981: 27–8).

In this school of psychology, then, relations are very much the key to the formation of personality, as they were for Sève; only in the cultural-historical school, relations are mediated by the labour process and by language. As Jerome S. Bruner remarks in his introduction to Vygotsky (1962), in Vygotsky's psychology neither the mind nor the hand amount to much considered in isolation: it is their combination in consciously oriented productive activity which gives human action its unique quality. And while the tools with which people produce are the medium through which they gain mastery over nature, so language is the tool and the medium through which people gain influence over the behaviour of others and over their own actions. Language is therefore the basis on which the higher mental functions develop.

> a tool . . . serves as a conductor of humans' influence on the object of their activity. It is directed towards the external world; it must stimulate some changes in the object; it is a means of humans' external activity, directed toward the subjugation of nature (Vygotsky, in Wertsch, 1985: 78).

However,

> a sign [that is, a psychological tool] changes nothing in the object of a psychological operation. A sign is a means for psychologically influencing behaviour — either the behaviour of another or one's own behaviour; it is a means of internal activity, directed towards the mastery of humans themselves (Vygotsky, in Wertsch, 1985: 78).

Here, in Vygotsky's idea of the sign as a psychological tool, we observe a striking parallel with the work of Mead. Both theorists believe that a sign is the social means of influencing the actions of others and, in the process, the sign also becomes a subjective means of directing one's own actions. So while a sign is developed socially and has primarily a social function, it is also that element of activity which can be turned towards the self as a subjective attitude. However, one must always remember that for both Vygotsky and Mead, all elements of human activity must be objective before they can be made subjective. A.N. Leontyev takes up this theme of the objective and object-oriented nature of human activity. That is to say, activity is primarily an objective social function taking place in the interaction between people, which is oriented to what Mead called 'social objects'. These are objects that are the focus of group activity and which take on a meaning within social relations that becomes subjectified as mental imagery. The difference between the cultural-historical school and Mead, is that they introduce the notion that social objects are *produced*, along with their symbolic and meaningful representation. Thus, tool use and language use are the two mediums of human interaction, and it is through both these mediums that we create and appropriate the social heritage.

A tool mediates activity that connects a person not only with the world of objects but also with other people. This means that a person's activity *assimilates the experience of humanity*. It means that a person's mental processes (the 'higher mental functions') acquire a structure necessarily linked to socio-historically formed means and modes, which are transmitted to him by other people through team-work and social intercourse. But to transmit a means or a mode for carrying out some process can be done only in external form — in the form of action or in the form of external speech. In other words, the higher and specifically human processes can arise only through mutual interaction of person with person, as *interpsychological* processes, which only later come to be carried out by the individual independently. When this happens, some of these processes lose their original, external form, and are converted into *intrapsychological* processes (Leontyev, 1972: 19).

Leontyev is here pointing out the necessary interconnection between practical and mental activity, and that the processes of the mind — facilitated by language — are internalized forms of social activity. He is also showing that culture and the intercommunicative, intrapsychological processes, cannot be divorced from practical activity in the material world, and that team-work, social intercourse, and the higher mental functions, go hand-in-hand. The social heritage which creates individual capacities, abilities, knowledge and self-consciousness, is formed externally in social relations and activities before it is appropriated as psychic activity. As Thorlindsson says, 'the object of consciousness is a product of human activity and is apprehended as such. Knowledge is the knowledge of objects integral to people's relations to the world, and these relations rest on practical human activity' (1983: 291).

In this approach, the development of mind can be described in terms of the development of human practice, where mental reflection is always a component of practice, regulating human interventions in the world. This can still be true in societies such as ours, where knowledge has become highly specialized and is abstracted from everyday activity. Even in these circumstances, knowledge cannot be divorced from the technological relation to reality, either as a cause of technological breakthroughs, or as an effect of them, reflecting the nature of science and technology in its image of the world.

A.N. Leontyev (1981) believes that the connection between the material and the mental, between practice and thought, is to be found in communicative activity, for language originally emerged out of the division of labour. In this division, individuals come to specialize in certain aspects of one overall group activity, and the goal of that activity will not be attained as a direct product of the action of any one individual. Under these conditions, communication becomes necessary to coordinate group activity and to transmit the meaning of the separate tasks to each individual. Because it was soon realized that speech had an effect on the actions of others, it could be separated from tasks which acted on objects alone, and used to act on other people in the whole realm of social intercourse. As language separated from a total dependence on practical activity, verbally communicated meanings also became abstracted from a direct reference to objects, so that their ideal form — or representation — can take on an interdependent existence as an image in consciousness. Consciousness itself is no longer tied directly and immediately to practice, but also has an interdependent life. As A.N. Leontyev (1981: 221) says, 'consciousness is the reflection of reality refracted as it were through the prism of socially developed *linguistic* meanings or concepts'.

Language and signs, then, come to develop beyond the boundaries of practical activity, as a whole realm of cultural existence through which individuals can communicate and appropriate experience and information, beyond that which is necessary for purely practical tasks. Luria (1981: 27) points out how, at first, language was closely connected with practical activity, having a 'sympractical character', but gradually became interdependent with it as a 'system of codes adequate for expressing any information'. For him, this illustrates the fact that, 'if humans had not possessed the capacity for labour and had not had language, they would not have developed abstract, "categorical" thinking' (Luria, 1981: 27).

Furthermore, Luria (1976) gathered evidence to show how the higher mental functions develop along with forms of social labour, by studying the effect of education on agricultural workers in the Soviet Union. He noted that as organized processes of labour are formed and tasks become more highly differentiated and coordinated, the requirement for the learning of literacy skills becomes greater. This is because of the need of each worker to understand the whole field of coordinated activities so that they may better adjust their own actions to those of their fellow workers. The actions of the individual, and their own comprehension of those actions, can no longer be tied to particular situations, but must extend beyond the particular context in which the action is framed. Communication skills are vital if this is to occur. A.N. Leontyev therefore noted that the ability to lift oneself out of a particular viewpoint, so as to take an overview of the situation, is one which is greatly extended by increased linguistic — and therefore conscious — comprehension of the context of action.

Culture and the consciousness of individuals cannot, therefore, be 'superstructures' of a social 'base', for they develop in an interdependent relation with real, material human activities. The primary function of language and consciousness is to steer and direct social practice. Similarly, production is not simply a base on which culture forms, but is wholly integrated with it. As A.A. Leontyev (1981: 243) (A.N. Leontyev's son) explains, language is a system of ideal objects or quasi-objects — linguistic signs — which 'emerges in social activity as the converted form of actual connections and [social] relations'. However, the symbolic system which arises from social relations does not remain as a superstructure to a social base, but is re-integrated with social relations and practices to form a new functional whole.

Human cognition therefore develops as part of a wider system of social experience constituted by the whole realm of practical and cultural relations. Acts are not simply appropriated by the personality, which forms itself as Sève believed, as an exchange between acts: rather, practical and cultural relations are appropriated as an internal *conversation* which forms what we have come to call the 'mind'. There is agreement again with Mead on this point, in that the cultural-historical school see consciousness as an internal dialogue which reflects the social relations between individuals, and will also reflect within the consciousness of particular individuals their own place within those relations. As Vygotsky says,

> the very mechanism underlying higher mental functions is a copy from social interaction; all higher mental functions are internalized social relationships. These higher mental functions are the basis of the individual's social structure. Their composition, genetic structure, and

means of action — in a word, their whole nature — is social. Even when we turn to mental processes, their nature remains quasi-social. In their own private sphere, human beings retain the functions of social interaction (1981: 164).

We can see here a reflection of Mead's idea, that even when individuals are alone, they still think using truncated forms of their social conversations and the pattern of their social vocabulary. Similarly, for the cultural-historical school, the self and the mind is a dialogical structure which mirrors the type of conversations occurring in society. It is important to stress here the difference between this approach and the type of structural linguistics which has informed much social scientific work in the West. The cultural-historical school do not place primary importance on the grammatical structures which underlie language, but as Wertsch (1987) shows, they emphasize the determinate role of everyday speech in the structuring of language and thought. This means that the self is not constructed according to a pre-structured discourse or language, for the self is a dialogue which reflects and refracts concrete social interactions in which it plays a part. These dialogues are always incomplete and in a state of continuation, and the dialogical self is always an active part of these ongoing processes. The personality is not a product of social discourse, but is a self-created aspect of concrete social dialogue.

This also has consequences for structuration theories within the social sciences, like Giddens's, which tend to see the social situation, and the self that acts within it, as a product of the social rules which structure the exchanges between individuals. For the cultural-historical school, neither social nor linguistic rules are the medium of social action or the psychological processes of the self. What mediates human activity are tools and signs, and these are an essential part of the concrete relation between humans and their material environment, and between individual humans themselves. These real relations and the form of their mediation are determined as functional wholes which then shape and define human activity. As Wertsch says,

> The fundamental claim here is that human activity (both on the interpsychological and intrapsychological planes) can be understood only if we take into consideration the 'technical tools' and 'psychological tools', or 'signs' that mediate this activity. These forms of mediation, which are products of the sociocultural milieu in which they exist, are not viewed as simply facilitating activity that would otherwise take

place. Instead, they are viewed as fundamentally shaping and defining it (1987: 7–8).

However, the forms of mediation, the technical and psychological tools, not only determine the shape of social activity but also the shape and structure of the personality. I now wish to turn to Vygotsky's theories of psychological development to see exactly how the socio-historically formed mediators of activity are fundamental in the creation of the personality.

The History of Personality Development in Ontogeny

Vygotsky sees the development of the personality occurring in relations, particularly the *active* relation of the child to its environment of objects and to the humans who compose its social world. This does not mean that Vygotsky theorizes the influence of the individual on the one side and that of the 'environment' or social world on the other. Because this is a dialectical and developmental approach, the personality develops *within* these relations, not externally to them. The child is not on the one side with the world on the other, for the child's experience and personality is constituted in its active relationship to its world. It is this relationship that will become internal to the child and shape the psychological plane and the structure of the self. Vygotsky identifies the misrecognition of the child's relation to its social world as one of the fundamental problems of psychology, in that:

> We have inadequately studied the internal relationship of the child to the people around him . . . We have recognized in words that we need to study the child's personality and environment as a unity. It is incorrect, however, to represent this problem in such a way that on one side we have the influence of personality while on the other we have the influence of the environment. Though the problem is frequently represented in precisely this way, it is incorrect to represent the two as external forces acting on one another. In the attempt to study the unity, the two are initially torn apart. The attempt is then made to unite them (1987: 32).

But this attempt is bound to fail, as we saw in Chapter One, because the problem has been stated incorrectly, creating a dichotomy between the personality and the social world where there should be a unity. Vygotsky continues by trying to set the problem right about the central importance of relations in creating the child's experience and personality.

> The child's experience is the kind of simple unit of which it is impossible to say that it is the influence of the environment on the child or a characteristic of the child himself. Experience is a unit of personality and environment as they exist in development . . . Experience must be understood as the internal relationship of the child as an individual to a given aspect of reality (Vygotsky, 1987: 32).

Vygotsky's entire corpus of works aims to show that the relation between the child and its environment does not unfold spontaneously from the child's own activity considered in isolation from others. Rather, the child must always be considered in an interdependent relation to those around him or her, who instruct the child in its activities using the materials and the knowledge of the day. As Valsiner (1988) points out, the interdependent relation between children and adults may not always imply conscious instruction in modes of activity, because the child may implicitly learn from elders by using their behaviour as a model. Equally, the child may use social objects within the socially structured environment to solve problems independently of adults, in which case the guidance of the adult social world is still a factor in this mode of learning.

It is on points such as these that Vygotsky disagreed with the developmental psychologist Jean Piaget. Piaget (1926) believed that it was the problem solving activity of the child which determined the development of the logical processes of the mind and of consciousness. For Vygotsky, however, Piaget never considered problem solving activity in the context of a social world, and ignored the crucial relation between the child and the adults who guide its development. The child rarely acts alone, always actively solving problems and developing the self-conscious ability to guide its own actions in an interdependent relation with an adult or more able peer. While the relationship of instruction is an interdependent one, the more able partner usually will have the more dominant role.

This means that children begin to master functions in interaction before they are capable of using them self-consciously, at a more advanced level. Vygotsky called this gap between what is learned and what is independently mastered the 'Zone of Proximal Development'. This he defined as: 'the distance between the actual development level as determined by independent problem solving and the level of potential development as determined through problem solving under adult guidance or in collaboration with more capable peers' (in Wertsch, 1979: 2). Thus, under adult guidance, children will begin to engage in types of activity that they are not yet capable of engaging in of their own volition. They learn these functions before they self-consciously master them. Vygotsky says that, 'consciousness and control appear only at a late stage in the development of a function, after it has been used and practiced unconsciously and spontaneously. In order to subject a function to intellectual and volitional control, we must first possess it' (1962: 90–1). Once such a function is possessed and can be used independently by the child, it becomes the basis on which the child moves on to learn and eventually master new functions and problem solving activities.

Vygotsky believes that the biology of the developing child is important in determining what skills or ideas it can begin to learn at certain stages of its life. Humans could not develop capacities or perform acts they were not biologically able or adapted to. However, biology does not lead the process of personality development; rather, cultural instruction determines the level to which people will develop psychologically. This is because what is learned is not given in biology, but developed in cultural history and transmitted to the child in learning.

For Vygotsky, speech is a key element in the transmission of the cultural heritage to the child. Again he disagreed with Piaget on the function of speech in the activity of children. In their empirical studies both Vygotsky and Piaget had noted that young children tend to talk themselves through their actions, speaking aloud to themselves as if they were talking to another person. For Piaget, this was evidence of the fundamentally egocentric nature of childhood speech, which only becomes used socially to communicate with others as the child matures. For Vygotsky, this could not possibly be the case, for the child must have learned its language from its elders in interaction with them. Only after this stage does the child begin to speak to itself as an accompaniment to its own activity. Unlike Piaget, Vygotsky does not believe that the child speaking aloud to itself is a passing phase, which is part of the overall transition from egocentredness to social awareness in children. Instead he thinks that this is an important stage in the development of inner speech and therefore of subjective thought.

Vygotsky's own studies uncovered three stages in the development of speech and thought in the child. First of all there is 'social speech' where the child is introduced to the speech content of the adult world — initially by its parents — and taught how to use words. Then, secondly, there is 'egocentric speech', in which the child will use words to guide its own behaviour by talking aloud to itself as an adult would who was giving the child instructions. In this phase the child commands its own actions in the style of adults who have been guiding its activity in the past. The third and final stage of this development Vygotsky calls 'inner speech', for the child no longer continues to speak out loud to itself to command and regulate its activity, instead having internalized the social form of communication as a way of autonomously regulating its own actions. At this stage, speech 'centres' itself in the personality as a conscious ego — the 'I' — which creates the internal plane of self-consciousness.

In Vygotsky's work, therefore, psychological functions develop firstly on the social level, as relations between humans, before they develop at the psychological level. He claims that every process in the development of the higher mental functions appears twice:

> first, on the social level, and later, on the individual level; first, *between* people (*interpsychological*), and then *inside* the child (*intrapsychological*). This applies equally to voluntary attention, to logical memory, and to the formation of concepts. All the higher functions originate as actual relations between human individuals (1978: 57).

But this means that, as Vygotsky pointed out earlier, the child masters activities practically, in its interactions with adults, before it masters them intellectually and can use them autonomously. At the earliest stages of child development, before the child begins to master speech between the ages of two to three years, mental functions and intelligence are closely tied to the sensori-motor functions. The child's thinking is closely bound to its practical activity and to its socio-emotional attachments to its carers, which form the relationships where needs can be expressed and met, and the wishes and desires are created. At this stage in development, thinking is totally encapsulated in the child's activity and emotional responses, and has not yet developed as self-consciousness which can regulate and direct actions. This level of mental functioning never disappears, for Vygotsky understands that desires and emotions remain the forces that motivate thought and action throughout life. He says:

> Thought itself is engendered by motivation, i.e., by our desires and

needs, our interests and emotions. Behind every thought there is an affective-volitional tendency, which holds the answer to the last 'why' in the analysis of thinking (1962: 150).

What is transformed, however, as children begin to master language, is the actual thought processes themselves. If emotion and desire remain the motivating forces behind thought, then in language these thoughts find a new medium for formulating themselves and a totally new structure. For Vygotsky, 'speech does not merely serve as the expression of developed thought. Thought is restructured as it is transformed into speech. It is not expressed but completed in the word' (1987: 251). Speech is therefore a key to the development of thought rather than being an advanced form for its articulation. Vygotsky draws a distinction in this manner between the 'lower mental functions', which are closely tied to the emotional and active responses of the body, and the 'higher mental functions', which emerge with the learning of language and the development of self-conscious, self-regulating thought processes. For Vygotsky, then, thinking is initially a bodily process, for the higher mental functions only emerge with language, which creates a new medium and structure for thought.

From his empirical studies into the development of children, Vygotsky detected that the curves of development of thought and speech are separate until the child is about two years of age. At this stage, thought and speech join together to initiate new forms of thinking and acting. In its activity, the child becomes curious about the names of things, and as a result, there is a rapid increase in vocabulary. But more importantly, the child is learning the signs which represent objects and has discovered the symbolic function of words: the child is learning to place objects, including its own self, in a system of social meanings, and is thereby becoming an object to itself. At this juncture the self begins to emerge in awareness and the inner conversation is begun with that self. As Mead would put it, self-consciousness is being forged out of the consciousness of experience within communicative interaction. Vygotsky outlines this process, in which, 'schematically, we may imagine thought and speech as two intersecting circles. In their overlapping parts thought and speech coincide to produce what is called verbal thought' (1962: 47). Thus we see how thought and speech are joined in communicative interaction to develop the higher mental functions.

In this process of verbal thinking, the unit of analysis for

Vygotsky is what he calls 'word meaning'. That is, once language is fully internalized when a child has passed the phase of 'egocentric speech', the word no longer appears in its fully articulated form in order to command our actions: in fact, the vocalization of inner speech dies out and we operate 'not with the word itself but with its image' (Vygotsky, 1987: 262). We operate with the *sense* of a word, rather than with its full verbal expression, so that in thought 'we know our own phrase before we pronounce it' (Vygotsky, 1987: 261). The sense of a word is all the psychological events aroused in consciousness by the word, rather than its precise meaning in a particular context. Because of this, speech for oneself is very different in its structure from speech for others, for inner speech is mute, silent speech. Also, the syntax of inner speech has its own structure, for we do not need to fully express a sentence to understand our own meaning. Instead, we can understand ourselves through hints and allusions, thus expressing our thoughts without putting them into precise words.

> In inner speech, the syntax and phonetic aspects of speech are reduced to a minimum. They are maximally simplified and condensed. Word meaning advances to the forefront. Thus, in inner speech, the relative independence of word meaning and sound is graphically illustrated (Vygotsky, 1987: 275).

Consciousness therefore develops within the personality as a whole — in its bodily, emotional/volitional aspects — and with each stage in the development of consciousness there is a transformation in its internal structure. Initially, self-awareness is absent from mental activity, which remains purely on the level of what Giddens (1984) calls 'practical consciousness', where there is a non-reflective understanding of how to perform an action. Later, as thought and speech begin to merge, there appears what Giddens has termed 'discursive consciousness', where thoughts can be articulated in words — both socially and psychologically — and there is self-conscious awareness and control over thought and action. The primary unit in this discursive consciousness, which mediates between internal thoughts and social speech, is 'word meaning'. This is the form of mediation by which practical consciousness can be translated into discursive consciousness, and if so desired, expressed to others in external speech. But social speech remains the foundation on which this whole process rests, for individuals would not be able to think and act in such a way were it not for the social conversation between them occurring within joint activities.

However, it is not only consciousness but the whole of the personality which is transformed through these processes. In recently translated lecture notes, Vygotsky (1987) shows how the emotions, memory, imagination and the will are created as consciousness — and the whole of the personality — becomes centred around word meaning. Emotions, for example, are developed through the social and self-conscious moulding of impulses and affects, which lose their automatic character and take on a more voluntary function in the personality. In the mature self, the emotions play a subordinate and supporting role in thought, prompting and motivating, but not controlling thinking. It is only in pathological thought processes, such as schizophrenia, where emotions begin to control thought — resuming their dominant and automatic character at the periphery of the self, rather than in relation to the self-conscious centre.

The stages in this development of personality and consciousness are followed up by Bozhovich (1979, 1980), who shows how, at about the age of three years, the child begins to recognize itself as the subject or initiator of its own acts. This coincides with Vygotsky's findings on the development of thought and speech. At this stage, involuntary motivation no longer remains the driving force in the personality, as the cognitive and affective processes are brought into balance by the self-conscious personality — the 'I'. The 'I' itself is the product of speech, the linguistic reference point that the child uses to identify its new found sense of its own self as a subject and initiator of action. This only occurs, though, in interaction with others, for the child's action is orientated within its social relationships: these determine the instruments that mediate its activity, as well as the changing needs which are the foundation of the child's capacity for action at each stage of development. There is, then, a gradual transformation of motives in the maturation of the child, which are created along with the different forms of activity the child is engaged in during the stages of its social development.

However, despite attempts to update and extend Vygotsky's theories, they have come in for a number of criticisms in recent years, even among those generally sympathetic to his approach. Van der Veer and van IJzendoorn (1985) are critical of Vygotsky's rigid separation of the lower and higher mental functions, whereby he appears to claim that the lower mental processes are automatic and therefore innate within the personality. They claim that research has now shown that what Vygotsky referred to as the lower mental functions are also created in the early social development of the child, a suggestion I will follow up in the next section of this chapter. Vygotsky has also been criticized for concentrating almost exclusively on communicative interaction and the development of thought in the mastery of speech, thus recognizing yet leaving aside the role played by practical activity in the formation of conscious personality.

This has led to some debate about the extent to which Vygotsky's theories are actually Marxist. Kozulin (1990), for example, has recently stated that Vygotsky's style of Marxism belongs to the European cultural tradition rather than the Soviet varieties of Leninism and Stalinism. For Kozulin, this means that Vygotsky's work can now be put back into the European tradition of thought, exemplified today by philosophical hermeneutics and the theory of communicative interaction. While I agree that Vygotsky was highly influenced by European philosophy, we must not forget that Marx was a key element of this tradition which was of such influence on Vygotsky. Why then compare him only with those Western thinkers who are not Marxists? Surely, more suitable comparisons can be made between Vygotsky and other cultural Marxists from a Western European background, such as Lukács, Gramsci and Althusser. Not to do so appears to be an attempt to play down Vygotsky's Marxism and blandly to absorb all that is special about his unique attempt to create a Marxist psychology into a position not unlike ethogenic social science. (Harré et al. (1985) now try to claim that ethogenics is inspired by Vygotsky.) Other scholars, such as Wertsch (1985) and Lee (1985) keep Vygotsky firmly in the full spectrum of his intellectual background, of which Marxism is undoubtedly the mainstay. As Valsiner (1988: 125) says of Vygotsky, 'he relied seriously but intelligently on the Marxist philosophical background which considers human beings to be active participants in their interaction with the environment'. It is this emphasis on human *activity* and its necessary relation to consciousness that marks Vygotsky's psychology as Marxist, along with his strong historical approach.

I will address this question of activity within the cultural-historical school in the last section of this chapter, where Leontyev's work will be considered. Suffice to say for the moment that I feel Leontyev's focus on practical activity is not a contradiction of Vygotsky's work, but a different emphasis within the same tradition of thought. What I have already said in the earlier part of this chapter, about the link between practical and communicative activity within the cultural-historical school as a whole, is justification for this approach. However, before considering Leontyev's work, I wish to turn to theories of the formation of the self prior to the acquisition of speech.

Formation of the Pre-linguistic Self

Contrary to many of Vygotsky's statements about the lower mental functions, there is now evidence to suggest that children actively begin to appropriate the social heritage, and to construct their personality under the influence of their culture, before they have acquired linguistic competence. Indeed, it is claimed that the pre-linguistic interactions with adults and the adult world, lays the foundation on which the child acquires language, along with other more specific dispositions. These findings do not contradict anything in Vygotsky's main documentation of the development of the higher mental functions, in fact they complement his work and extend the spirit of his enquiries to the pre-linguistic stage of childhood. They show how social history affects the development of the child, by determining the foundation of dispositions on which future capacities and activities will be based, long before the child is aware of the influences upon it.

Recent work in the early stages of child development has stressed how early activities are set in what Clark (1978: 235) calls a 'social/communicative structure' which is determined by the structure of the adult world. It is within this structure that children act and adults interpret their actions as containing specific meanings. Carers and their children therefore co-ordinate their activities in a socially defined way, the adult taking the leading role in this process, interpreting and facilitating the actions of the child. As Clark (1978: 237) notes, 'in this way the child can do things and intend to do them before he is physically capable of success on his own: social activity precedes individual capacity'. Initially it is the adult who does most of the work in this interaction; but gradually the child is expected to do more for itself, the adult holding back before intervening to help the child complete an action successfully. In this situation, the adult and the child develop expectations about how each will respond and behave, which leads to co-ordinated interactions.

The child is not simply learning how to respond to a stimulus in this early interaction, but is learning a whole pattern of behaviour in a social setting, as well as expectations of the likely outcome of activities in particular situations. The child is learning a repertoire of social behaviour which will be called upon throughout life. This is achieved only in a socially structured setting, as Ferrier (1978) shows, where the repeated pattern of child care events — such as feeding, bathing, changing clothes and bed-times — along with the ritualized use of language, are the means through which children originally orient themselves in the social world and develop a basis on which they can learn language. Shotter (1978: 65–6) remarks that this is not the imposition of a structure upon children by adults, but is more a question of adults finding the structure within the child's activities and facilitating it, or drawing it out, in a socially prescribed way. Important here is the rhythm of interactions between the child and its carers.

Central to all this work is Mead's insight that social meanings are implicit in actions which are then expressed in words. The formation of children's meaningful activity and their communication through gestures, is therefore a precondition for the learning of language. As Bradley (1989: 128) points out, body language has a grammar of its own which reflects that of speech. Lock (1978) also traces this idea in Vygotsky's work, through the notion that symbolic systems are rooted in social transactions, and that for infants these are primarily emotively based. Gestures are originally the main currency in the interaction between parent and child, along with emotive signals such as crying. In the same volume of studies, Edwards (1978) shows that as verbal expressions are gradually mastered by the child, they do not displace non-verbal forms of communication; rather, words are integrated into a sequence of looks and gestures which form the pattern of an overall communicative setting. Social meanings therefore pattern the child's communicative actions and structure their intentions before they have mastered language.

Similarly, as Shotter (1978: 68) demonstrates, the way that parents interpret the actions of the infant as having an intention, and act in order to help them fulfil it, also creates a situation in which the satisfaction of needs is negotiated with the child. Given what Sève had to say in the last chapter about the formation of human needs within social activity, we can see here how the needs of the child are socially developed in the active relationship between the parents and the infant. And if, as Vygotsky thought, behind the process of thinking there is always the emotional/volitional sphere — the needs and desires of the individual — then it is the early formation of needs and emotions which is crucial to the development of thought in the child. This early formation of emotions and needs in interaction prepares the ground for children to develop linguistic competence and learn to express certain feelings or desires in the appropriate social symbols or words. However, in this activity, and in the preparation for it, needs and emotions are socially moulded in specific ways so that the human community has the means by which to express them to others.

Thus human infants move from the social shaping of their sensori-motor activity, to the expression of needs and wants in social gestures, to social activity which is mediated by speech. In another important investigation which links practical and verbal activity, Patricia Marks Greenfield (1978) draws out the parallel between action mediated by language and the constructive element in practical activity itself. Construction activity involves building objects into physical structures, in the same way that words are combined to form the structure of language. Just as objects are agents to the very young child, used because of their size or shape, words are used in what seems like the appropriate context, with little grasp of their overall meaning. Later in development, objects and words are used as instruments for a particular purpose in activity; a finding which backs up the cultural-historical school's linkage between tools and signs as practical and psychological instruments for changing the environment, or influencing the actions of others. Practical and linguistic activity therefore have a similar structure and are linked in the development of mental capacities.

This is explored further by Edwards (1978: 466) in his concept of the 'Original Word Game'. Through this concept, Edwards demonstrates that while caretakers are explicitly teaching children the names of objects in language use, they are implicitly teaching children to locate objects in space, to synchronize dialogue with the others with whom they are communicating and to co-ordinate joint activity through the use of language and gesture. There is, then, an intimate link between the structuring of practical activity in time and space, and the learning of language.

We can see from this that what Vygotsky referred to as the lower mental functions are also developed in the child's social interaction with adults, for these functions are gradually being created within the zone of proximal development. But we can also see the beginnings of the formation of what Bourdieu referred to as the 'social habitus', which is the basic dispositions fundamental to individuals within a particular social group or class. Dispositions and inclinations are formed in the earliest years through the child's interdependence with adults, which will later incline the person towards the development of certain capacities, and will orientate them within social practice as a whole. A repertoire of what Bourdieu calls 'strategies' will be passed on to the child which will enable or limit their social activities in later years. What none of the theorists of child development have considered so far, is the way that the social class of the child will influence the process and affect the dispositions they acquire, or do not acquire, in early pre-linguistic learning.

Also, many of the dispositions and inclinations formed in the habitus from the earliest years of infancy may not be dialogically articulated as part of discursive consciousness, and will continue to operate within the personality as an unconscious force. They interact with the self-conscious 'I' as a silent partner in a conversation without words, motivating or restricting the activities we engage in without ever revealing themselves to our conscious awareness and therefore to our control. Motives and restrictions can be constituted as part of the personality within the structure of our social action, without us ever becoming entirely aware of their operation and their influence. As Leontyev showed within the cultural-historical school, practical activity is still an important aspect in the understanding of human action as a whole, including communicative activity, for it is practice which is the basis for communication, as well as being the foundation of practical consciousness. It is to the exploration of the development of the structure of personality in social activity that I now turn.

The Unconscious Personality: Conversation with a Silent Partner

So far in this chapter I have concentrated mainly on the development of the conscious personality and the higher mental functions in social history, largely through the work of the cultural-historical school. They place importance on both practical activity and activity mediated through language in the formation of the conscious self. However, in the previous section it was shown how important practical activity is in the development of personality, as a basis for communicative interaction and the dialogical structure of the mind. Not all of practical consciousness — the knowing *how* to do things and the motivation to do them — is reflected discursively as self-consciousness, and therefore unconscious aspects of the personality will also be created in social activity. I want to suggest that just as there is not only one level of consciousness, but many — a fact I pointed to through the work of Mead — similarly there is not only one level of the unconscious. The different levels of the unconscious are created in the same way as consciousness — through the activity of the individual.

Leontyev spells out just how important practical activity is in the formation of personality, explaining that activity is 'non-additive' in human life. I take this to mean that one cannot add and subtract activity from humanity, for humanity *is* its activity. One cannot separate the individual or their consciousness from activity as a whole, for these phenomena develop within activity.

> Activity is a molar and non-additive unit of a material subject's life. In a narrower and more psychological sense, activity is a unit of life mediated by mental reflection whose real function is to orient the subject to the world of objects. Activity is thus not a reaction or a totality of reactions, but rather a system possessing structure, inner transformations, conversions and development (Leontyev, 1972: 10).

To analyse exactly what gives activity this character of inner transformation, Leontyev suggests we look at three 'macrostructures' of activity. The first is the pattern of *activity* in society as a whole, of which we are a part and which forms the basis of our motivation to act. The second is the specific *actions* of persons which the structure of activity motivates and the specific goals at which these actions are aimed. The third macrostructure is the *operations*, or the means and methods of action, the *way* in which actions are performed and the conditions which structure it – e.g. habits, customs, accepted practices etc. These three macrostructures are transforming, because activity creates motives which emerge as individual actions. In turn, these actions — once learned — can become operations; that is, practical knowledge about the way to act in certain situations which remains unconscious: it is never articulated discursively in the mind and is purely a background condition for the seemingly spontaneous production of an act.

This means, however, that another characteristic of activity is that actions and goals are separable, for once an activity has been mastered — like driving a car — the goal of 'driving' becomes less important and the action is undertaken unthinkingly. It becomes part of the general operations that form the unconscious, taken-for-granted conditions of action. Thus, a car driver may have the goal of getting in the car to visit a friend, but need no longer think of how to drive the car. These macrostructures are therefore not separate aspects of activity but are inner relations within its overall flow. But the macrostructures will be in very different relations to the consciously acting personality, because they occupy different — albeit related — levels within the structure of activity. Some of the macrostructures we will be aware of, such as the actions we perform; yet we may remain oblivious to others even though they structure our actions. We may not be consciously aware of the operations which form the practical knowledge of how to do something, nor may we always be aware of the structures of social activity which provide our motives to act. While we may be aware of the goals towards which we strive, we may not always be sure of the nature of our motivation.

For Leontyev, this helps to explain the phenomenon of unconscious motivation in human beings. It is not that the unconscious lies deep in some hidden realm of a pregiven self — in fact, exactly the opposite: it is because motivation develops within activity, and is therefore objective, that people often fail to see clearly the way in which motives are subjectively reflected as the propelling force behind actions. To understand motives clearly, one would have to undertake a study of a person's objective activity and not their inner feelings, needs and desires. These are only the psychological signals which direct actions and are themselves phenomena created in social activity. Despite this, the goals, or the signs which represent them, are felt by individuals to rise up internally within their bodies and minds, when in fact they are a creation of the social world. The insight here, brought about by Leontyev's dialectical method, is that consciousness and unconsciousness are not two distinct entities within the personality, but are part of the same unity. Whether the motive for an act becomes conscious or not depends on the place that the action occupies in the system of social activity. When an act belongs to the system of social relations in general, which stretch far beyond the realm of individual action, then the motive for that action may be more psychologically obscure. As Leontyev explains:

> The fact of the existence of actually unconscious motives does not in itself express a special beginning hidden in the depths of the psyche. Unconscious motives have the same determination as all psychic reflection: a real existence, activity of man in an objective world. Unconscious and conscious do not oppose one another; they are only different forms and levels of psychic reflection found in strict relation to the place that that which is reflected occupies in the structure of activity, in the movement of its system (Leontyev, 1978: 124).

So the system of social activity and relations creates motives in the personality to act in a certain way and to strive for certain goals. Leontyev (1978: 117) is in agreement with Sève in this respect, that it is activity which creates human needs and desires. However, these reflect in the personality as internal signals, as signs, through which the motive expresses itself: the particular macrostructure of activity in which the motive is created will determine whether it reaches full conscious awareness or whether the motive and its signals remain unconscious. Many of the motives created in social activity will be unconscious to individuals, because the wider system of social activity itself remains opaque.

A link can be created here between the theories of Leontyev and those of Richard Lichtman, whose notion of the 'structural unconscious' parallels that in the cultural-historical school. Lichtman takes a Marxist foundation as the starting point for his theories, believing that psychoanalysis tends towards an individualistic perspective on human beings. He then aims to integrate insights taken from Freudian theory into a Marxist framework, providing a more adequate analysis of the social production of personality. For example, Lichtman believes that the Marxist theory of the unconscious is similar to Freud's, for both theorists saw that women and men are driven by forces they do not fully comprehend and cannot adequately control. These are powerful forces which cannot be properly represented in consciousness. However, from Lichtman's Marxist perspective, the unconscious is not an inner universe of biologically given drives, but arises from the fact that individuals are generally not aware that their motives and their actions appropriate the logic of the social system as a whole. People are unaware that the source of their motivation is to be found in extended patterns of social activities (hence the term 'structural unconscious').

Lichtman believes this is especially so in a capitalist society, where individuals see themselves as isolated from others. This occurs through ideology, which is an expression of capitalist social relations and the conditions individuals experience therein, which leads people to view themselves through symbolically constructed consciousness as self-sufficient and divorced from others. Thus, symbolic consciousness stands between social beings and their social reality. This reality consists of the extensive network of social relations that is the basis upon which individuals act — a fact now confined to the unconscious, along with our need for other human beings (which is now seen as a weakness to be denied, rather than a basic condition of our existence). This means that within capitalist society, individuals take their own self-interest as the basic motive for action and believe that this is the most fundamental and unchangeable motive of the human character. Yet for Lichtman,

> self-interest and social competitiveness depend upon a general [social] structure which gives meaning to the individual acts of self-aggrandizement and which must be implicitly understood and acknowledged by the actors (1982: 232).

However, individuals do not realize that the source of their motivation to act in this way is social, that the acts they feel impelled to engage in do not well up from inside them, but only find their sense, meaning and motive within the overall structure of social activity and relations.

Besides the structural unconscious, Lichtman detects another level of unconsciousness that he calls the 'repressed unconscious', which, through its defence mechanisms, further distorts and obscures the motives that appear in consciousness. The defence mechanisms which censor certain motives are not organically constituted within the body to resist biological drives that provoke anxiety. Rather, defence mechanisms are socially produced to resist certain motives which are 'constituted-as-unrealizable'. Therefore, for Lichtman, 'motive and countermotive have no existence independent of each other. Both are socially constructed out of a process which construes each only in contrast with the other' (1982: 192).

This theory is illustrated with a re-reading of the Freudian idea of the Oedipus complex, in which repression is created in children by the social restrictions imposed on their sexual desire for the parent of the opposite sex. Through this mechanism the incest taboo is installed in the self as the most primary form of repression. In Lichtman's version of the Oedipal drama, the roles of the protagonists are reversed in truly Vygotskian fashion. It is no longer the forbidden desires of the child for its mother or father which create the need for repression, but instead it is the parents that project their erotic desires on to the child: desires which are, at every moment, surrounded by a taboo. This occurs because, in capitalist society, such idealized expectations of happiness and personal fulfilment are promised within marriage that they can never be realistically achieved. The parents' disappointed illusions are then directed at the child, whereby the parents effectively turn themselves into the objects of the child's desire. Yet the erotic fantasy induced in the child, in which the parent of the opposite sex becomes their fantasy lover, cannot be satisfied because of the taboo against incest, thus creating in the infant the first 'aim-inhibited need'. These needs do not disappear as the person develops but become part of the repressed unconscious: an aspect of our own self which must be denied and cut off from the continued growth of the conscious personality.

This new vision of the repressed unconscious is backed up by the work of the psychoanalyst Jean Laplanche (1989), who believes that it is the unconscious desire of the parents which is codified in language and which acts as an 'enigmatic signifier' towards the child. That is, a signifier which represents adult sexuality, which the child cannot decode. Such a signifier is enigmatic to the child and therefore has a seductive effect upon it, luring the child into a dialogue it does not understand. In the process, the enigmatic signifiers act to create the child's own repressed unconscious — that which is an active force of desire in the personality, but which cannot be consciously articulated. As Lichtman notes, part of the self is then cut off from the growth of the conscious agent and becomes id-like. It continues to exist in a state of what Habermas (1972) calls 'paleosymbolic prelinguisticality', or in his later work, as a 'delinguistified steering media', which directs the personality in its actions while remaining mute — inarticulated and unconscious.

There is also a parallel to this vision of the repressed unconscious in the cultural-historical school and in the work of Mead. In the chapter on Mead it became clear that he saw the 'generalized other' in the psyche, which monitors and censors thoughts, as reflecting the laws and axioms of the universe of discourse, determining what responses and what imagery is permitted or impermissible. As in Lichtman's work, what is accepted and what is taboo is created in the same moment by the same social and psychological processes. In the cultural-historical school, these ideas are explored by Vološinov, who claims that the conflict Freud noted between the psychological forces, such as ego and id, involving two psychic agencies in mutual deception and non-recognition, is not possible between two natural forces which are socially unmediated. As a linguist, Vološinov recognized this process as the interplay of ideological signs which represent socially active people and groups who are in conflict. The conflict between different motives in the psyche, then, is not fundamentally an intrapsychological process but an interpsychological one.

> The content of the human psyche — a content consisting of thoughts, feelings, desires — is given in a formulation made by consciousness and, consequently, in the formulation of human verbal discourse. Verbal discourse, not in its narrow linguistic sense, but in its broad and concrete sociological sense — *that* is the *objective milieu* in which the psyche is presented. It is here that motives of behaviour, arguments, goals, evaluations are composed and given external expression. It is here, too, that arise the conflicts among them (Vološinov, 1976: 83).

Vološinov (1976: 89) links internal conflicts not only to psychological repression, but shows how conflict and repression in the personality arises through the social conflicts between different groups that reflect in ideology (Vološinov, 1973). Social and psychological repression cannot be separated precisely because the conflicts of the psyche are ideological conflicts, which in turn represent social conflict. It is for this reason that both Lichtman (1982: 277) and Vološinov (1973: 37) argue that orientation in one's own self, without the distorting influence of ideology and repression, is inseparable from orientation and greater conscious control of the social situation. Only when this is achieved by collective engagement in political democracy can a truly social self be created, with a clear consciousness of his or her own goals and ideals, and the social power to make them effective. As Lichtman says of Mead's view of the democratic society and self, his 'insight into the reciprocity of selfhood needs to be realized through political transformation' (1982: 277). Thus, we not only need a new theory which captures the social nature of the self, but also the social and political transformations that would make possible the development of more truly social individuals.

Conclusion

In this chapter, I have attempted to show that a more rounded theory of social selves can be developed from theories influenced by Marxism. This involves not only the consideration of the effects of labour and practical activity on humans, but also the cultural and linguistic elements which shape the personality. Labour and language mediate the relation of individuals to the natural world as well as their relations to one another. These forms of mediation enter the personality as new structures of thought and self, which are appropriated in the activity of the person as it is structured by social relations. This happens from the earliest days of infancy and continues throughout the life of the individual. Not only is consciousness structured in this process; so too are the different levels of the unconscious self, whether it be the structural unconscious which forms the basis of our social habitus — the social origin of which remains obscure to people in their everyday lives — or the repressed unconscious, which is that part of our own self which is delinguistified and denied. The whole structure of the personality is therefore formed in social relations and activities.

I will spell out in greater detail the structure of the social self in my conclusion in Chapter Eight, along with the need for greater democratic control of social processes that such a personality structure necessitates. Before that, I wish to explore the theories of Norbert Elias, who has also studied the socio- and psycho-genesis of the personality in a historical fashion. Many of the findings of his sociological and historical studies are pertinent to the knowledge of the cultural-historical development of the self, as well as to the social formation of the emotions and the personality structure of individuals in the Western world. It is to his work I now turn to further explore some of the ideas developed here.

CHAPTER SEVEN
Power Relations, Interdependencies and the Civilized Personality

From our studies of Marxist theories of the self, we have gained an insight into the historical development of humanity as a whole and the personalities of individuals in particular. However, the historical perspective on the development of humankind and their individual powers is not limited to Marxism alone. It is also the central theme running through Norbert Elias's theory of the 'civilizing process' in the West, and the socio- and psycho-genesis of personalities within this process, which complements and extends the insights from Marxian cultural theory. For Elias, humans can never be considered as separate from the figuration of social relations they form between themselves, a figuration that is bonded and changed by varying balances of power between the different groups and individuals within it. We are always locked into figurational relations with others, so that the actions we undertake, and the personalities we develop, are dependent on the processes within those figurations. Furthermore, these processes are formed by the changing historical network of interdependencies between individuals, which, in turn, is influenced by the fluctuating balances of power within the figuration over time. To see this more clearly, I propose to investigate Elias's work in more detail, beginning with the methods of figurational sociology itself, drawing out from this the relevance to the theory of social selves which I am developing here.

The Figurations and Interdependencies of Individuals

One of Elias's central analogies when describing the figurations of individuals is that of the game. For him, being a member of a figuration is like taking part in a game, where the actions of the individuals involved are influenced by the moves being made by their fellow players and adversaries. In a figuration, as in a game, people are enmeshed in relations where they form alliances with some, or engage in hostilities with others, so that the changing pattern and formation of the figuration is influenced by a mobile balance of tension between the players. These alliances and oppositions between individuals or groups form the interdependencies which make up the figuration itself. As Elias says,

> By figuration we mean the changing pattern created by the players as a whole — not only by their intellects but by their whole selves, the totality of their dealings in their relationships with each other. It can be seen that this figuration forms a flexible lattice-work of tensions. The interdependence of the players, which is a prerequisite of their forming a figuration, may be an interdependence of allies or of opponents (1978a: 130).

Interdependence is also, therefore, a central element in Elias's sociology, for as he indicates above, the interdependencies between individuals are the framework of the figuration. The concept indicates the way in which humans within a group or a society are bound by mutual dependence on each other. This is increasingly so in modern societies, where the division of labour has advanced to such a degree of specialization that we are reliant on each other for the functions we perform in the figuration. However, this type of dependence is only one aspect of a figuration. As Elias mentions above, not only allies but opponents are dependent on one another. Just as a game of football requires two teams pitched against one another to make a match, so enemies in the figuration are dependent on one another to continue — with the desired outcome of winning — their particular conflict.

This is of importance to the concept of power that Elias develops through the figurational model. For him power is not a property owned by one group, which is inflicted or imposed on others. Instead, power is a relation between individuals or groups, and this always comes in the form of a balance. Only in very rare circumstances do we find an individual or group with no power or influence over others. Power relations are a balance within the figuration because the changing network of relations may allow one group to increase their power chances and gain a relative dominance over others. Yet this is unlikely to be a complete dominance, for the most powerful groups will still be interdependent to some degree with the groups who they dominate, so that the oppressed will have some measure of influence which limits the manoeuvres of those in ascendancy. For Elias, then, 'power is not an amulet possessed by one person and not by another; it is a structural characteristic of human relationships — of *all* human relationships' (1978a: 74). It should not be thought of as 'a thing that one can put in one's pocket like a key' (1984: 251). Thus,

> the concept of power has been transformed from a concept of substance to a concept of relationship. At the core of changing figurations — indeed the very hub of the figuration process — is a fluctuating, tensile equilibrium, a balance of power moving to and fro, inclining first to one side and then to the other. This kind of fluctuating balance of power is a structural characteristic of the flow of every figuration (Elias, 1978a: 131).

This is why Elias claims that there are constraints upon individual actions within the figuration. It is because people are part of this tensile equilibrium of power that they find the possibilities for action both limited and enabled by the figuration as a whole. Like Foucault, then, Elias shows how the field of possible actions is structured by relations of power. However, he understands that the freedom of individuals to act in certain ways, and the restriction of their manoeuvres in other respects, are an element of the chain of interdependencies that link them to others. It is always tempting when Elias talks of the constraining effect of figurations to begin thinking in terms of the Hobbesian problem of order, or Durkheim's theory of the *sui generis* authority of social rules. This, however, would be a grave mistake. Unlike Hobbes or Durkheim, Elias is not proposing that humans have a nature which is essentially destructive or egoistic, and which must be constrained by social regulations: rather, he is simply pointing out that, in a figuration, our actions are always tied to, and limited by, the actions of all those with whom we are interdependent. As in a game of chess, no single player is able to play without regard to the rules of the game or the moves of their opponent. One move is always followed by a counter-move, which in turn will inspire the next move from the appropriate player. The impulse to act and the constraint upon action is thus part of any figuration, be it a game or a set of social interdependencies.

Similarly, in games and social figurations, no single person controls the process of the game itself. Everybody involved in the figuration attempts to influence the outcome, but this always remains uncertain. Together, people form an interlocking network of relations, and the result of their reciprocal actions within these relations will never be what any one person intended. Those for whom the changing balance of power has moved in their favour will still be unable to entirely control the processes within the figuration, even though they may have the greatest influence or the most ability to protect themselves from unfavourable consequences. The outcome of many people acting together in a figuration will be to produce a result that no single person or group had intended. In this way, the figuration has a dynamic all of its own, even though it cannot be separated from the actions and interrelations of the individuals who compose it.

This is one of Elias's main reasons for developing the concept of figuration. It is to show that behind the processes that sociologists have called 'social structures' or 'social systems', there are individuals involved in reciprocal actions and relations — a multitude of social interdependencies. It is therefore wrong to separate 'social facts' from facts about individuals, for the two are not separate entities, but simply different perspectives on the same figurational process. However, it also follows from this that individuals can never be treated as separate from their societies, because from the moment we are born we are always in a figuration of interdependencies with other people. The figuration is therefore the unit of analysis, and it is only within it that the different perspectives of 'I' and 'we' — the individual and the group as a whole — develop. In fact, as Mead pointed out, the personal pronoun 'I' only emerges in terms of relationships, for

> one cannot imagine an 'I' without a 'he' or a 'she', a 'we', 'you' (singular and plural) or 'they' (Elias, 1978a: 123).

Elias is showing here how these are not pregiven entities, but reference points within a figuration. They indicate the positions held by people in their relationships to one another. It becomes misleading to use concepts such as 'I' independently of their position within the figuration, in which the rest of the pronouns have a reference point, for it makes it appear that these pronouns have a natural existence in themselves (such as an 'ego' for example). Like the psychologists we have looked at earlier, Elias is aware that the experience of oneself as an 'I' only develops along with the recognition of the separateness of others.

This means, for Elias, that we must make a fundamental transformation in our image of human individuals, away from the traditional notion of 'homo clausus', which sees the individual as a self-contained entity — a world within themselves — and towards the notion of individuals as 'homines aperti': that is, individuals who are bound together in the historical processes of the figuration and who are open to mutual determination (Arnason, 1987). And, as Elias also says, the concept of 'homines aperti' 'also helps us to understand something else — that the concept "individual" refers to interdependent people in the singular, and the concept "society" to interdependent people in the plural' (1978a: 125). It may also help 'to achieve a degree of detachment from the feeling that one exists as a person "within", and all other people exist "outside" ' (1978a: 125).

However, only changes in the balance of power can describe the dynamic of figurational processes, and these are not the direct result of any single individual. Rather, the plans and the moves of the players are influenced by the course of the game, a fact which necessitates that we always view social processes through a 'they' perspective — studying long term figurational processes and dynamics — as well as adopting an 'I' and 'we' perspective, showing how participants experience the figurational influences on them and the way they respond to these. For individuals, relations within the figuration are historically variable, changing as the balance of power and the nature of interdependencies alter. This necessitates the changing of individual strategies of action within the figuration, which also creates a different structure of personality formation: a change not only in the patterns of activity, but also in feeling and thinking. In this process the entire structure of social being is recast. It is this process of socio- and psycho-genesis which is at the heart of Elias's investigations into the 'civilizing process'.

The Socio- and Psycho-genesis of the 'Civilized' Personality

In his work on the 'civilizing process', Elias aims to show how changes in modern societies that we have come to regard as 'civilizing' — the internal pacification of the population and the resolution of conflicts through non-violent means — depend upon the competition between different groups for social power. He is therefore going against the traditional view that civilization is the removal of conflict from society, showing instead how the process is one of the transformation of conflicts. Unlike Freud (1930), who thought that civilization amounted to the increased repression of humans' innate aggressive and sexual drives, Elias shows how civilizing processes emerge from the changing balances of power in society and involve the transformation of the structure of human personality as a whole — including the balance of emotional inclinations. It is the changing forms of human feeling and thinking with which Elias begins his study of the civilizing process.

Elias steps on to the moving platform of this historical process as the balance of power in society begins to tip towards the nobility and their courts, and away from the Roman Catholic church, in the late Middle Ages. In accordance with a rebalancing of the scales of social power, Elias discerns a change in the code of values against which individuals measure and devise their own actions. In this period, there is a move away from chivalrous standards of behaviour towards a concept of *civilité*, through which the self-image of people in the West became expressed. Elias believes that the finest example of the changing sensibilities of the times is Erasmus's treatise *On Civility in Children*, published in 1530, and intended to instruct the sons of the nobility in polite behaviour. The popularity of the book in its own times is an indication to Elias that it catered for some deep seated needs of the people in that age — the need to know what was expected of a person of the upper classes in order to maintain, or advance, their position in the social ranks. But behind the advice given to the nobility on what is the new standard of behaviour expected of people of good breeding, we catch a glimpse of the world of the Middle Ages, the standards and habits of conduct which one must change in order to develop new strategies of action, adapted to a transformed socio-political network of relations.

What Elias shows us through Erasmus's writings, is a human figuration which is not unrecognizable, yet one where there are many gestures and aspects of behaviour which now seem strange or bizarre to us. For example, people greet each other standing on one leg. Medieval paintings and statues present the odd movements of walkers and dancers. These seemingly incidental details are crucial for Elias, for they 'not only represent the "manner" of the painter or sculptor but also preserve actual gestures and movements that have grown strange to us, *embodiments of a different mental and emotional structure*' (1978b: 56; my emphasis). It is this changing mental and emotional structure of personalities which is a key focus of Elias's work. He finds more evidence of it in the changing manners of the period, where people are instructed by the likes of Erasmus on the 'polite' way to behave in public, especially when eating. People are advised not to blow their noses into the table cloth when assembled for a meal, nor to gnaw at bones and put them back into the communal dish. Boys are also taught how to fart silently in public and how to behave correctly on entering a brothel.

While the type of polite behaviour that Erasmus counsels is no surprise to us, for our manners and conduct today are still modelled to a large extent along these lines, what is surprising is that adults had to be instructed through books that these were the correct ways in which children should behave. It illustrates for us that these strategies of social action had still not stabilized into a definite pattern, and were in the process of being established and learned. Also it shows us something of the standards of behaviour in the Middle Ages, standards that would soon become regarded among the members of the nobles' courts as 'uncivilized' or 'barbaric'. However, Elias does not record this behaviour so that we can celebrate the values of our civility, but wants us to regard the behaviour of the Middle Ages as a part of the social figuration of the times; in this sense, it fitted the needs of the people in this period, and was meaningful and necessary for them because it was in accord with the nature of the social relations in which they lived.

In the Middle Ages, violence and severe external restrictions and punishments for breaches of rules were more common in everyday life. Elias looks at a tapestry from the Bodleian library in Oxford, depicting some scenes from the life of a knight (Elias, 1978b; Dunning, 1987), and notes how the artist does not bother to remove from the panorama of everyday life scenes that today people may find disturbing or repugnant. People are robbed openly in the street, and poverty is depicted in graphic detail. The gallows stand in full view. Nudity and sexual relations are also more openly on show and are not removed from the tapestry by acts of self-censorship on the part of the artist. Aggression and violence, perpetrated by the ruling group and by the ruled, is also depicted with total candour, suggesting that this was a common-place part of everyday life. The enjoyment that humans took in acts of violence could also be more openly expressed, as we can see in the reproduction by Elias of the battle hymn of the troubadour Bertran de Born.

I tell you that I find no such savor in eating, drinking, or sleeping as in hearing men shout 'Get them!' from both sides, hearing the neighing of horses that have lost their riders, hearing the cries 'Help! Help!', and in seeing men great and small go down on the grass beyond the fosses, and the dead with their sides ripped open by the pennoned stumps of lances (1978c: 231).

What is unusual in this, for Elias, is not the scenes of battle and destruction, for they are common enough in the twentieth century. Rather, it is the way that de Born feels no compulsion to hide his open enjoyment of the battle and the scenes of carnage. This can also be seen in the record of a cleric which has survived from a medieval monastery, describing the activities of one particular knight, who, 'takes particular pleasure in mutilating the innocent. In a single monastery . . . there are 150 men and women whose hands he has cut off or whose eyes he has pulled out'. And we learn that his wife is just as cruel; 'it even gives her pleasure to torture the poor women. She had their breasts hacked off or their nails torn off so they were incapable of work' (Elias, 1978b: 194). Again, it is not the acts of cruelty that are of note, more the open way they are enjoyed and inflicted. This is still more evidence of a different mental and emotional structure of the people of these times, for unlike the people of today, their acts of violence were fused with a greater proportion of excitement and enjoyment than with repugnance and shame, and therefore their relish could be more openly indulged.

In Elias's reading of the changing times, however, these acts of openly enjoyed violence began to be expunged from the courts of the nobility. There, aggression and conflict became expressed through increasingly non-violent means, in competitive strategies and stratagems, all laced with the spice of wit, intrigue and scandal. Here we see the disappearance of battle and violence as a means of social advancement, and instead there is the constant jockeying for social power by winning the favour of the nobles. In court society the major route for advancement in the social hierarchy is through the display of pleasing manners, which show a person to be of good breeding and not of lowly stock. Those who showed by their manners that they were well bred and of refined conduct, won the respect of others within the social ranks. Here we see the careful management of self-identity and the gaining of respect through expressive behaviour, that Harré talked about in his theories, which is inimical to a successful social and moral career. Only now we can see that the Renaissance person who plans his or her behaviour to elicit the respect of others, is not a universal model of human personality, but is a type of person who develops within a particular figuration of social interdependencies. The refined manners which gained a person respect were a mark of distinction for the nobility — and later, the aristocracy — who used their conduct to maintain their dominance over the lower classes.

The careful control of the display of emotion to the point of hiding one's 'innermost' feelings, along with the careful management of 'outward' identity and the cultivation of rational modes of thought — involving long-term planning and greater degrees of foresight — are all linked to the development of the social figuration and its balance of power. As this began to coalesce around the monarch and his or her court during the period of the Renaissance, this type of 'civilized' conduct and personality became more firmly established as the norm. It also spread rapidly to the middle class of tradesmen, merchants and intellectuals — who were the main purchasers of the books on manners — who hoped to use a display of good conduct to gain access to the court. This jostling for power and favour between the social classes created more pressure on the aristocracy to refine their behaviour to even greater degrees, so they could maintain a symbol of their distinction. As the embellishments of their behaviour grew more intricate, the thresholds of shame and embarrassment were also increased — the thresholds one could not cross without making a *faux pas*, offending social conventions, and disgracing oneself in public. This created greater pressures towards the management of public identity, as the 'correct' standards of conduct were raised, demanding even greater control of the emotions and bodily functions.

This everyday social conduct, however, must be understood as part of the wider social formation where power is becoming centralized around the courts of the aristocracy and the institutions of the state. This creates a link in Elias's theory between the macro social processes occurring over a long range time span, such as the power balances that surround the formation of the state, and the micro processes of everyday social behaviour. As power balances, rivalries and interdependencies are spread over wider areas, Elias argues that the networks that bind individuals together become longer, more differentiated and more complex. Within the more closely interwoven fabric of the figuration, the pressure towards increased restraint on behaviour is heightened, so that actions can be moulded to create the desired effect on another person and, at least, not to cause them offence. These changing self-restraints create a new basis for the formation of the personality and for the emotions and their expression. New ways of thinking and feeling come to remould human impulses which were forged in an earlier age with different social requirements.

As Chartier (1988) points out, because new modes of etiquette, which created transformed structures of thinking and feeling, are dependent on figurational changes in the wider society, etiquette is only one of the instruments through which court society gained and reproduced its domination. The other, perhaps more important, changes which created power chances for the nobility and, later, for the aristocracy, were the monopoly of the means of violence in the hands of fewer nobles and the fiscal monopoly of the monarchy. The monopoly of the means of violence occurred as the feudal lords gradually eliminated one another from the military conflicts which raged around the estates in the Middle Ages. This internal conflict in society is reduced as fewer, more powerful feudal lords gained a greater monopoly on the means of violence. Gradually, even they were eliminated in this growing monopoly as the kings and queens reaped financial rewards from a period of economic inflation. They were in a position to benefit from this because they gained their direct incomes from taxes, which not only left their profits undiminished by inflation, but boosted them. On the contrary, the feudal lords found their financial power greatly reduced by rising prices as their incomes were fixed to land rents.

This left the monarchy in a position to hire the largest armies and to bring the nobility and war lords into their service as courtiers. There were still great tensions within this balance of power, not only between the aristocracy and the nobility, but also between these groups and the church. However, after the period of the Renaissance when court society was finally established around the absolute rule of the monarch, Elias shows (1982, 1983) how the monarchy were in the most advantageous position to play upon and exploit the tensions between the different groups in the figuration. The factionalism between different nobles and their plays for social power, alongside the competition for favour from the church, divided the opposition and left the absolute ruler in a dominant position. They were still reliant for their relative power on the figurational network as a whole and the balance of power within it, yet they were in a position where the dynamic of the figuration was working in their favour. It was a situation no single social group had designed nor could control, and yet the unintended consequences of the actions of many groups and individuals over a period of time had produced an outcome favourable to the power chances of the monarchy.

The domination of the aristocracy revolved around a tripartite constellation of the monopoly of the means of violence, a fiscal monopoly and the acceptance of standards of etiquette which served to mark as a distinction the aristocratic standards of behaviour that developed in the court. Although military battles still raged between nations competing for power, society became internally pacified as the figuration stabilized around a new, centralized state structure with a monopoly on the means of violence. It was in such a figuration that the pacified, yet none the less aggressive, competition between courtiers took place for the favours of the king and queen. It was in court society that standards of 'civility' came to be used to measure the actions of individuals, and aggression towards others was to be hidden behind the outward display of polite manners.

There are a number of points that need to be made at this juncture if one is to understand Elias properly. First of all, Elias is not making a value judgement at this stage; he is not claiming that this type of polite behaviour is actually more civilized than that which went before in the Middle Ages. As Mennell (1989: 30) points out, Elias uses the term 'civilization' in its everyday, value laden sense, to denote that we in the West — not only in absolutist times, but also in the contemporary age — do pride ourselves on our polite and well regulated behaviour, and generally believe that it is superior to that of people of other places and times. Elias does not fall into the trap of accepting this judgement at face value, instead showing how 'civilized' standards of behaviour emerged from a long battle for power and depend for their continued existence upon a balance of tensions in society. Within this balance, the notions of 'civilized' behaviour are used as a mark of distinction to reinforce the adherence to the standards of conduct of the ruling group. Yet, despite this, Elias also uses the term civilization in a social scientific sense, to refer to the actual historical evidence of a lessening of violent tensions within nation states in the West, and the externalization of those violent tensions into the relations between different nations. These are now marked by the violent conflicts, alliances and oppositions that once marked the internal relations within nation states in the feudal era. The term civilization therefore does have an empirical, sociological referent — the internal pacification of society and the greater self-regulation practised by individuals over their own behaviour.

Furthermore, Elias is not making a value judgement when it comes to the behaviour of individuals within civilizing processes. He is not claiming that human nature remains basically unchanged, wherein the violent and aggressive impulses of humans simply become better hidden by outward displays of polite civility. Such an image would portray individuals in the modern age as simply more accomplished liars, hypocrites who hide behind a pretence of civility while desiring to plunge the knife into someone's back. Rather, what Elias wants us to contemplate is the entire restructuring of the personality and psychic economy in the process of historical change. To designate this level of the psychic economy and personality structure, Elias uses a German term which is common to that used by Bourdieu — the social 'habitus'. That is, the characteristics and psychological dispositions shared by groups of people in a particular historical configuration, and in a particular position within their own social hierarchy. What has changed in the civilizing process is not the degree of people's honesty, but the entire structure of their thinking and feeling.

Elias's theory of the personality is therefore a holistic one which, like that of the cultural-historical school, draws heavily on gestalt psychology for its inspiration. As in the gestalt model, the rational and emotional aspects of the self are not separated and, instead, there is an effort to show how rationality and the emotions are developed together as part of the overall formation of the personality structure within the social process.

For example, in the West, the tightening and lengthening chains of interdependencies and the internal pacification of social bonds, has created a new habitus of personal dispositions and a new personality structure. Where people have carefully to manage their identities and practise greater self-control over the expression of emotion, there is a greater differentiation between the drives — the feelings and emotions inspired by social life — and the drive controls — the forward planning of the conscious self and the restrictions and taboos placed upon the display of feelings in social life. The personality structure is therefore not compartmentalized in its nature, because the psychic economy develops as a whole within social life — its functions become remoulded and differentiated in the social process. Equally, the emotions are not given in an unchanging form by nature, and therefore the affective structure of humans should be regarded as a whole: it is shaped in its entirety within the social figuration. Elias says:

> Though particular instinctual manifestations may be indicated by different names according to their various directions and functions — we may speak of hunger and the urge to spit, of the sexual instinct and aggressive impulses — in life these are no more separable than the heart from the stomach or the blood in the brain from blood in the genitals. They complement and partly supersede one another, transform themselves within certain limits and neutralize one another; a disturbance here makes itself felt there. Thus they form a sort of circuit in a person, a partial totality within the totality of the organism, whose structure is still opaque in many ways, but whose form, whose social stamp is in any case of decisive significance for the dynamic of a particular society as much as for any individual within it (1978c: 229).

For Elias, then, the biological determinants of the human organism are not of decisive importance in governing the conduct of the individual, for what is of greater importance is the social figurations which place their 'stamp' upon human impulses, remoulding them in the process. Human inclinations are, to use Elias's term, 'malleable', which is to say they are plastic and open to reshaping within different social configurations. In showing how the drives of individuals are reshaped in the social process, Elias is historicizing Freud's (1930) notion of the 'cultural super-ego', which was a super-ego of values and prohibitions established within the entire community by its leaders. Without the correspondence between the cultural and individual super-ego, the moral development of individuals would never match that within social life. This is something expressed in Elias's (1978b: xiii) work, through his 'socio-genetic law', which states that each individual must go through their own civilizing process in their development. This does not mean that each person literally goes through all the historical phases of civilization in miniature, but that the personality of each child and young adult is moulded in relation to its parents, who themselves display aspects of the moral outlook of their culture.

While Elias would disagree with Freud, that the cultural super-ego simply reflects the standards imposed by great leaders, he does recognize that there are standards of behaviour that are common throughout a culture and which emerge in its history. What became taboo in the society of the Middle Ages is now taken-for-granted as being taboo, because it is indelibly carved into our super-egos through the habitus of civilization. In the Western civilizing process, the emotional structure of individuals is rebalanced so that greater repugnance and guilt attaches itself to acts of violence against fellow citizens, displacing the more pleasurable aspects of violence that could be openly indulged in the Middle Ages. Indeed, the affective structure of that age was also socially moulded, for it was necessary within the feudal social structure for individuals to be prepared and ready to use violence; to protect their land, their possessions and their own person. In the Renaissance, with the centralization of the state and the monopoly of the means of violence, the affective structure of humans changes again, shifting toward an increased sensibility to acts and objects which are deemed to be offensive.

These changes in the habitus go hand-in-hand with a new social geography, where what is judged socially offensive is hidden from sight in private spaces and removed from public view. Certain bodily functions, nakedness, sexual relations, violence, the slaughter of animals, poverty, all these became subject to greater social taboos and hidden in private spaces. We can see in this process the demarcation between the public and private realms, and the formation of the collective and individual spheres of social life, that was the centrepiece of Harré's theories. Only now, we can see that they are not givens of social and psychological life, but are the products of a long-term process of socio- and psycho-genesis. However, we can also see that the categories of modern psychological theories, such as Freud's categories of the ego, super-ego and id, can also be placed within the historical framework. It is the greater constraints upon social actions that are part of the figuration of court society — and later, of bourgeois society — which create the increased compartmentalization of consciousness, conscience and the affective drives. None of these functions can, in actual fact, be separated from one another and, as we have already seen, even the more automatic impulses of humans are open to remoulding as the personality structure as a whole changes within its social relations. For Elias, then, the emotions are always socially formed.

The libidinal energies which one encounters in any living human being are always already socially processed; they are, in other words, socio-genetically transformed in their function and structure, and can in no way be separated from the corresponding ego and super-ego structures. The more animalic and automatic levels of men's personality are neither more nor less significant for the understanding of human conduct than their controls. What matters, what determines conduct, are the balances and conflicts between men's malleable drives and the built-in drive-controls (Elias, 1982: 285).

What counts, then, to Elias, is the actual relationship and the balance between the psychic functions and the affective structure. Together these form the personality structure itself, and they are forged together in a process of socio- and psycho-genesis. As the cultural-historical school showed, in the modern age the emotional/volitional sphere tends to be subordinated to the rational thought processes, which are engaged in planning and consciously regulating actions. Elias is showing the socio-historical processes behind this psychic economy, linking it to the figurational economy of power balances and tensions. It is only where these create a high level of social constraint and a demand for greater degrees of self-regulation, that we find greater barriers between the different psychic functions. As Elias explains:

The pronounced division in the 'ego' or consciousness characteristic of man in our phase of civilization, which finds expression in such terms as 'super-ego' and 'unconscious', corresponds to the specific split in the behaviour which civilized society demands of its members. It matches the degree of regulation and restraint imposed on the expression of drives and impulses. Tendencies in this direction may develop in any form of human society, even in those we call 'primitive'. But the strength attained in societies such as ours by this differentiation and the form in which it appears are reflections of a particular historical development, the results of a civilizing process (1978b: 190–1).

There is an idea here in Elias's work that is not unlike Lichtman's concept of the structural unconscious, in that the whole psychic structure, and the motives and drives created within it, are moulded in a social process of which the individual is not necessarily aware, as its networks stretch far beyond individual horizons. This also encapsulates the theory of the repressed unconscious, for Elias is also showing how the feelings which can be expressed in public and those which must be hidden in private — in a special place, or kept within the self — are created in one and the same social process. He is also putting into historical perspective some of Mead's discoveries, for the theory of the civilizing process shows the particular point in history where there appeared a more marked division between the 'I' — the 'inner' sense of a true self — and the 'me' — the public roles and functions that the individual adopts.

This is the source of the feeling that people in the modern age have of being a homo clausus, a little world in themselves that no one else can ever really know. It is the sense that we have come to call — with many different connotations — 'alienation'. The feeling expresses the greater division in the self between conscious, rational and self-regulating psychic processes, and the emotions that they have moulded. People feel that their true self is locked deep inside them, with their wishes and fantasies, and that their rationality is a separate entity which is only the surface manifestation of their personality. While Elias does not believe, as would Marx, that this alienation has a purely economic origin, there is something in his vision that is akin to Sève's description of the voluntary controls in the personality and the way individuals find these alienating. That is, Elias recognizes that many of the controls that constrain the feelings and actions of individuals are internalized social restraints, and that they reflect the power balance of which individuals are a part within their figuration. For example, the powerful social restraints that formed an external pressure for individuals to conform, and which were symbolized by the gallows in the Middle Ages, have now become internal, psychological modes of social control.

In this sense their is something in Elias's theory which is similar to Marcuse's (1970) notion of 'surplus repression'. Through this concept, Marcuse claimed that in society there is repression over and above what is required for a well regulated social existence, and that surplus repression exists simply to keep ruling groups in power and maintain their domination. While Elias (1970: 136) has declined any relationship here, there are many similarities, as well as differences, between his work and that of the philosophers and psychoanalysts of the Frankfurt School (Bogner, 1987). Elias does, however, come close to Marcuse's theory of surplus repression when he distinguishes between necessary and unnecessary social restraints. These are, on the one hand, the necessary restraints needed to maintain a social figuration through the constraints that members inevitably place upon one another and, on the other hand, the restraints that are deployed to reproduce the power of ruling groups. Elias hopes that his model of the civilizing process will help people in the future, so that 'we may be able to judge more closely what kind of restraints are required for complicated societies to function and what type of restraints have been merely built into us to bolster up the authority of certain ruling groups' (1970: 136). Should we ever manage to rid ourselves entirely of unnecessary restraints (something Elias believes is a highly unlikely scenario) then the constraint of the figuration will not be experienced as so negatively alienating as it is today (Elias, 1987b: 76).

The elaboration of Elias's work in this respect has been under-taken by Wouters (1977, 1986) who shows that societies go through formalizing and informalizing processes. In formalization, the figurational balance of power is consolidated in favour of ruling groups, while in informalization, the balance of power moves towards less established groups. During such periods, there is a change in the standards that govern behaviour, and a realignment of the personality structure through the social habitus, where it is possible to create a 'controlled decontrolling of emotional controls' (Wouters, 1986: 3). In such a process, while the limits on conduct imposed by society are not abandoned, nor the constraints required for civilized behaviour overturned, there is a shifting outwards of the limits on behaviour, a pushing back of the boundaries that limit public and private expression, with the corresponding move towards the more open display of feelings that previously had to be kept hidden. However, Elias and Wouters are at pains to emphasize that this is a continuation of the civilizing process and not the subversion of it, for internally pacified social relations are still maintained.

A link can be made here with Vološinov's concepts of 'official' and 'behavioural' ideology, the former being the ideas and standards of conduct of the ruling classes, while the latter is the everyday ideas and conduct of individuals who belong to other social groups. Using these concepts we may begin to think of how people develop their emotional feelings within the behavioural, or perhaps even the private, interchanges of everyday life, while the official ideology of the age creates a limit to their public expression. Examples of this can be found in the research of Peter Gay (1984, 1986), who — using published and unpublished diaries and letters — shows how the Victorian middle class enjoyed passionate sexual relations, both inside and outside of marriage, while at the same time having to construct 'fortifications of the self', that is, fortifications of public reticence and reserve, behind which a private space could be maintained for the expression of certain feelings. Similarly, lesbians and gay men sheltered behind a 'facade of discretion', until it was shattered by some very public court cases involving 'homosexuals'. Nevertheless, we can see that what is accepted and what is taboo in any era depends on the relation between different groups and classes in society, and the way in which this relation demarcates the barriers between the public and the private. In the late twentieth century, many of the Victorian standards of behaviour have been relaxed as the balance of power and the structure of social authority has slightly altered. With it has changed many of the official responses to certain human emotions and impulses, with a resulting effect on their psychic economy.

In the theory of the civilizing process, then, Elias is demonstrating how the whole personality structure is forged within chains of social interdependencies which stretch far beyond individuals themselves. The social dynamic of the figuration which intersects and shapes our personalities began to reach dominance centuries ago, and is sustained today by a whole network of interdependencies involving a certain balance of power between groups and individuals. Elias is also showing how relations and interdependencies are fundamental to the structure of the personality, for they are mirrored in the internal relations between different psychic functions and the unity or conflict between them. Socio- and psycho-genesis are therefore two processes which are inextricably linked within social history, with the result that conflicts which exist within society are, in the contemporary period, largely psychologized.

Before moving on to look at the figurational theory of the personality in more detail, I want briefly to deal with some criticisms of Elias's theory of the civilizing process.

Conceptual Problems in the Theory of the
Civilizing Process
One of the main criticisms of Elias's work from a psychological perspective has come from Christopher Lasch (1985), who believes that the proposed formula of a progressive intensification of self-restraint since the Middle Ages is too simple. Lasch also

believes that while Elias has mentioned the psychological scars that the process of civilization inflicts upon people, he has not detailed these scars, nor the depth of the psychological damage they inflict. In this respect, Elias's work does not present the challenge to the civilizing process that is present in Freud's work or that of the Frankfurt School. For Lasch, this is because Elias concentrates on the sublimation of the instincts and emotions — that is, their remoulding and redirection toward different aims and objects — rather than their repression. In so doing he conflates the functions of the ego (consciousness) and super-ego (the internalized social rules).

However, I feel that Elias does not detail the injuries of the civilizing process because in all forms of social life damage can be done to individuals in the process of their upbringing and their interaction with others. This is not just a problem in the Western world, but one that exists in all societies whether or not they have gone through a long civilizing process. It is interesting in this light to look at Lasch's own reaction to the way that societies must all solve the problem of reconciling individuals to some form of social rules which place constraints upon them. He says:

> the manner in which it [society] deals with these psychic events produces a characteristic form of personality, a characteristic form of psychological *deformation*, by means of which the individual reconciles himself to the instinctual deprivation and submits to the requirements of social existence (1979: 34; my emphasis).

But here we see reproduced all the dichotomies that Elias's work tries to avoid, most notably that society is a thing which confronts individuals rather than involves them, and that this confrontation does some damage to an individual who seemingly exists prior to 'socialization'. It deforms an instinctual structure which already gives form to a pregiven individual nature, one which would grow healthy and strong if only society did not spoil it. This is the very dichotomy Elias is trying to escape by showing how individuals are always part of a figuration, and that some constraints are always inevitable within them. As the personality structure is moulded by social relations, its structure is always socially stamped; this process is just as likely to produce well balanced individuals, who can reconcile conflicting emotions and find an outlet for repressed feelings (perhaps in private, or through fantasy and art), as it is likely to produce damaged individuals who cannot help inflicting their pain and suffering on others. Elias's model is therefore well able to deal with these criticisms. Furthermore, with regard to Lasch's point that the formula of a progressive intensification of self-restraint in recent history is too simple, I hope already to have shown that Lasch's reading of Elias is not too accurate in this respect. Elias can account for the changing nature of restraint, including the relaxation of social and personal controls on behaviour, as well as their intensification. Also Elias is claiming that internalized restraints have become more *even*, exerting a more constant pressure on behaviour, rather than becoming more severe.

Another common misconception of Elias's theories is expressed by Giddens (1984: 242), who believes that the theory of the civilizing process does an injustice to other societies — those in the past or across the globe — by suggesting they are less 'civilized' than ours. This tends to conflate the issue we have already dealt with, of Elias's distinction between a value laden use of the term 'civilization' and its social scientific use. This is a problem Elias has created for himself by not making this distinction clear enough in the two volumes on the civilizing process. However, Elias also answers these charges in those same volumes, saying that even societies that we regard in value laden terms as 'primitive' have probably gone through a civilizing process and are internally pacified. What he is concerned with is the civilizing process that occurred in the West after the decentralized and conflictual figurational groupings of the Middle Ages.

From my own perspective, I find two weaknesses in Elias's work. First of all, there is something unconvincing in his account of how self-restraints have to be built into the personality before they can be relaxed, although I find this unconvincing for reasons different from those expressed by Lasch. The problem is that Elias offers conflicting evidence that increased self-restraint over the emotions is necessary before social rules can become more permissive. Below, he applies this idea to the more revealing bathing costumes and sportswear that became fashionable in the 1920s.

> Only in a society in which a high degree of restraint is taken for granted, and in which women are, like men, absolutely sure that each individual is curbed by self-control and a strict code of etiquette, can bathing and sporting customs having this relative degree of freedom develop (1978b: 187).

Yet Elias has shown us that this is not necessarily true. The mixed bathing he reports from the Middle Ages, where individuals were not only scantily clad but in most cases naked, seems to have passed off without any grave sexual threat to women. In fact, people treat nudity as an unexceptional part of everyday life. Thus, it does not necessarily follow that a high level of self-restraint, of the type we know today, had to be in-built before mixed bathing in revealing costumes could safely be introduced. Here, Elias appears to fall into the trap he has so carefully avoided in other respects, by posing an unchanging level of sexual desire which must be restrained by social and, later, self-controls. Rather, we can look at this problem in terms of the production of certain types of sexual desire, and ask to what extent did the privatization of certain social spaces and parts of the body create around them more mystique and eroticism as objects of fantasy and wish fulfilment. In other words, their very repression through social and self-restraints created them as a type of desire qualitatively (if not quantitatively) different from before. This would be in line with Lichtman's work on the creation of certain emotions as repressed and also, paradoxically, with Elias's reassessment of Freud's theory of the personality structure that I have already dealt with in this chapter. It would involve seeing repression and the production of certain types of desire as part of the same social process.

My second criticism involves a reconsideration of Elias's theory of the transformation of aggressiveness, one which is also touched upon by Honneth and Joas (1988: 127). In this we can use a comparison between the work of Elias and Mead, who both understand the social function of aggression in creating internal unity within groups. This is done by setting up external enemies against whom the group must fight, thus creating an 'insider' against 'outsider' type of social solidarity. However, whereas Elias sees the restraint of aggressiveness exclusively in terms of social and psychological controls, Mead believes it can also be achieved by opening up discursive channels through which violent feelings can be dissipated and collective agreements reached. Aggression can be better regulated in internally pacified societies, not just by increasing restrictions on violent behaviour, but by opening up other channels for expression. This prevents society, or certain sections of it, from coalescing into integrated but insularly hostile social units. It also means that social regulation is not the only way to create more pacified societies.

However, my two main criticisms of Elias's work involve modifying some of its claims rather than rejecting its general framework. It is infinitely preferable to many attempts to reconcile sociology and psychoanalysis, for it does not lapse into the dichotomy of society versus the individual. It also has presented us with a more enriched insight into the nature of the social self. It is to a more detailed study of the personality within Elias's theory I would now like to turn.

Human Personality: the Relation between the Learned and the Unlearned

In his later work, Elias (1987c) has posed the question of the social formation of the personality in terms of learned and unlearned responses of the individual. As we have already seen, he believes that humans are born with a nature, albeit one that is flexible and open to reshaping. However, he now believes that this reshaping not only occurs through the learning of social constraints, for the whole symbolic realm of human cultures plays a part in the formation of the self. This was always a latent element of Elias's work, for after all, the ideology of 'civilized' behaviour was to some extent a sign and a symbol of social distinction. Now, though, Elias wishes to place a theory of symbolic learning at the centre of his sociology and social psychology.

Human personalities, like the individuals in other animal communities, are born with a certain species-specific set of reactions and symbols. These are the instincts and the instinctual reactions that Freud, in the realm of psychoanalysis, and ethologists in the study of non-human species, have concentrated upon. For Elias, though, humans are marked by their unusually large capacity for learning, which tips the balance in human behaviour away from fixed patterns of action and reaction, towards learned activities within social life. The main vehicle for learning within the human community is the symbolic system which is developed within figurations. This produces a number of effects, most notably a blurring of the distinction between learned and unlearned aspects of human behaviour. For example, Elias shows how smiling is an unlearned sign employed by humans all over the world to signify friendly intent. And yet the learning of the more expanded system of signs and language, which is not species-specific but group-specific, actually allows humans greater control over, and elaboration of, their natural repertoire. We can now control smiling so that it is not a simple reaction, but an intentionally deployed symbol. We have also developed different types of smiles within our cultures that communicate different meanings and are not part of our natural, species-specific symbols. In this respect we can distinguish between friendly smiles, sarcastic smiles, triumphant smiles, and so on.

This example of smiling is simply one among many which illustrates the increased control of species-specific symbols used by humans. Besides this, there is the whole realm of cultural symbols which are socially developed and learned. The mastery of these symbols involves the development of the whole personality, a fact which the cultural-historical school so clearly indicated. While these symbols are learned, they will none the less become part of the personality structure as a whole, so that the individual is capable of using them spontaneously, as part of what we commonly call our 'second nature'. That is, they will develop in our psychic economy propensities towards actions that are socially learned, yet feel to be so natural to us that we perform them without thinking. What is learned and unlearned, then, comes to blend together in a personality structure where some of our actions are performed unthinkingly, while others will come under our conscious control.

Human groups therefore live within what Elias (1989a: 199) calls the 'fifth dimension' of symbols. That is to say, we live not only in the four dimensions that the philosopher of relativity, A.N. Whitehead (1920), described. For him, the first two dimensions were those of time and space — which mark out the duration of human lives and the boundaries of our activities — and, within these, the third and fourth dimensions which were particular moments and points where we interact with one another and (in Mead's phrase) 'slice' the world from our own perspective. Besides Whitehead's four dimensions, Elias discerns a fifth, the symbolic dimension in which humans live, through which we struggle to orient ourselves to each other in the figuration, and struggle for conscious control over our actions. It is this need for orientation in the human community, one never completely fulfilled by our automatic instincts, that drives people to develop group-specific symbols to better attune their actions within and between social groups. The system of symbols also becomes the means through which we aim to master our fixed, instinctual responses, and bring them under conscious control.

Through his multi-dimensional approach to orientation, knowledge and the self, Elias is acknowledging the reality of both the human body and the natural and social world in which people act. Our symbols do not 'represent' the world, for they are the medium of social orientation within the world and within our own selves. Knowledge can therefore differ from reality and can never totally approximate it. However, knowledge always refers in some way to the other dimensions of experience in which human selves and minds also develop. This means that while knowledge can never totally capture the material reality of the other dimensions, some knowledge can be highly object-orientated, providing humans with a more adequate means of adjusting to and changing the conditions of existence. Such knowledge also enables us to take a more distantiated, emotionally detached view of the world, one which is invested with less of our fears and anxieties. Experience is therefore multi-dimensional and cannot be reduced to the symbolic realm alone.

Through the symbol theory, Elias employs arguments that at times sound as though they have been entirely borrowed from the cultural-historical school, even though there is no evidence he is familiar with their work. Perhaps Mead has been an influence although, again, we are given no indication of this. Nevertheless, given what Elias says above regarding the social and personal function of symbols, he develops a theory in which what we have so far referred to as the human 'mind', in fact indicates 'the human capacity for putting through their paces symbols anticipating a sequence of possible future actions without performing any action' (1989b: 343). In this sense, Elias believes that the term 'mind' is very much like the term 'soul' — or in the German *Geist*, which translates literally as 'ghost' or 'spirit' — in that it refers to actual functions of human psychology and personality, which can be explained in terms of social action within figurations, but instead have been given a metaphysical explanation. It is the duty of present day social scientists to devise more adequate, non-metaphysical explanations of personality.

Like the cultural-historical school, then, Elias believes that the mind is a function in the orientation of human social action, and also a means of orientation in one's own self. What we still regard as the unknown substance which is the seat of our thoughts and feelings, is in fact the human ability to reflect on the world and one's own self using symbols. Like Vygotsky, Elias therefore believes that thought is the soundless manipulation of symbols which have been developed in social communication. The symbolic dimension also mediates between consciousness and foresight, and the fixed impulses of the species which form the realm of the unconscious. It therefore shapes this realm in a specific way by expressing certain impulses as psychic drives through symbolic means. What is often referred to as 'instinct' is not the property of some primary, undiscovered region, but is a concrete element of everyday life which is part of the innate orientating equipment of humans, extended and elaborated by symbols. Through his psychoanalytic work in group therapy, Elias (1969), and others who have used his ideas (Foulkes and Anthony, 1957), have drawn on this notion to see psychoanalysis as a reorientating device, which allows individuals to redirect their blocked impulses through readjusted symbolic devices.

However, the theories which Elias has begun to develop in respect of the symbolic construction of the personality are largely incomplete. These were begun in his later years and, as I have already said, there is no indication that he was aware of the work of the cultural-historical school whose ideas could profitably be drawn upon to extend the penetration of Elias's insights. This is a task that I intend to undertake in the conclusion to this work. Drawing together many of the key insights we have gained throughout this study, I hope to offer a new model of social selves for the social sciences. In this task, Elias's work has set us further down the road.

Conclusion

Elias's figurational model of sociology has many advantages over other methodologies, most notably because of its refusal to separate society and the individual. To this end, it is a sociological model which attempts to show how even large-scale, macro social processes — stretching back over a long-term historical period — are connected to the actions and intentions of human beings, even if the outcome of these actions is, in the final analysis, that which no single person intended it to be. In this way, Elias looks at the civilizing process in the West in order to understand the socio-genesis of our societies, as well as the psycho-genesis of the individual persons who are formed in this process. Equally, Elias does not separate the formation of rational consciousness from that of the emotions, instead seeing the personality structure as a totality, each part of which changes in unison with the others. A transformation in one aspect of the personality causes all its other aspects to change as well. Furthermore, these changes in the personality structure are brought on by transformations in the socio-historical processes in which each one of us, as social beings, is embedded. At no single point is personality formation separated from social formation in the work of Elias.

Because of this, there are also aspects of Elias's psycho-genetic theories which can be profitably compared and criticized using the concepts developed by Richard Lichtman, for Elias also has similar notions of the structural and repressed unconscious. That is, our personalities are formed within social structures, the dynamics of which are not totally revealed to our consciousness. Also, the repressed elements of our personalities are formed in the same social processes as those elements of which we are consciously aware. Involved in these social processes that are formative of the personality, is the symbolic system and its role in structuring the psychic functions, a role so clearly described by Elias and the cultural-historical school. This takes us much nearer to the synthesis of social scientific theories that I develop in the conclusion, which describes the make-up of the social self.

CHAPTER EIGHT
Conclusion: The Formation and Reconstruction of Social Selves

The general argument of this study has been that the image of humans as monads, as isolated and self-contained individuals, is totally inappropriate for the study of personality. In order to truly understand the human self, the vision of humans as monads must be dispensed with. Instead, I have shown there is an alternative understanding of people within the social sciences, one based on the notion that humans are social selves. Involved in this is the basic insight that everything which is unique and personal about our identity does not radiate from within the self as something pregiven or innate. Rather, the basis of human difference and individual identity is to be found within society, in the social relations that exist between individuals. It is only in relation to others and to the material world in which we live, that humans come to realize their separateness from all that surrounds them. Furthermore, it is only in realizing this separateness in relation to the others and the objects of our world, that we see ourselves mirrored in the ways in which we affect them or in how they respond to our actions. Human individuals can only make themselves into a subject to the extent to which they have become an object: that is to say, to the extent they have realized their own existence through the effect their actions have had in the world around them, or by making them into a distinct entity in the eyes of others.

This makes the idea that there is a basic division between society and the individual into a nonsense. All efforts to find the 'relationship' between the 'two' are wasted, for when we look at society and the individual we are viewing exactly the same thing — social being — from two different angles. Any understanding of the social nature of the self must therefore be a dialectical understanding. By this I do not mean a circular mode of theorizing, wherein society affects the individual in some respects while the individual affects society in others. A dialectical relationship is one in which a new dimension is created by the reciprocal relations and effects of objects or humans. In this respect, the self is the new dimension which is created in the active relationship between human bodies in their material environment. Originally in these relations there is no self: just the bodies of human animals who seek to satisfy their needs and protect themselves socially. As the group becomes more organized in methods of production and communication, basic instinctive reactions and needs are brought more into the scope of social organization and conscious reflection. The state of self-conscious 'individuality', where each individual takes on their own identity, is not innate or prior to society but only comes into existence *through* social relations. It is only in the social relations and objective activities between human beings, and between humans and their environment, that we find the birth and sustenance of the self.

In this conclusion, I will trace the contours of the dialectic of social selves, arguing that the self is formed within social relations. Of prime importance in the formation of personality are relations that transform the real, relations of communication, and relations of power. It is within these relations that the whole of the personality is developed — self-consciousness, needs, emotions and drives, along with the barriers we believe exist between them. The origin of the differentiation and compartmentalization of different aspects of the self will be traced to its essentially social roots, which are often hidden or obscured from our vision. Finally, a model of social selves will be constructed by synthesizing many of the insights drawn from this study, putting the model forward for further debate and for future use in the social sciences. In all that follows, two central concepts stand out in the theory of social selves: these are the concepts of social relations and of social activity, which create a foundation for the vision of human individuality as socially based.

The Dialectic of Social Selves

The Self as Discourse

One of the central insights gained in the first part of this work was that the consciousness of self and the awareness of one's own identity is achieved through the discourse taking place in the social group. George Herbert Mead argued that the self was not a fixed entity but was a process arising out of the relations and activities —

the 'interactions' — between social beings. In particular, he concentrated on the symbolic nature of interaction and how this becomes the foundation for the creation of meaning. For Mead, the most developed form of symbolic interchange was language, through which individuals could converse and orientate their activities in a more complex fashion. It is only on a social basis organized through symbols and language that a sense of individual self is possible, as humans see the effects of their actions reflected back at them through the responses and attitudes communicated by others. Rather than the human self existing as a monad, for Mead, the very state of human individuality and difference is only possible on the basis of social interaction and the meaningful discourse between people. Self-awareness and self-identity is only formed in society. The social group is not a creation of pregiven individuals; rather, the very state of self-conscious individuality and personal difference is based on the prior existence of society and the efforts of humans to co-ordinate their actions and, thus, to communicate within the group. As Mead said so clearly, it is society which is the basis for the self.

This insight is continued to some extent in the work of the ethogenic school, although here we begin to find the emergence of an analytical distinction between practical and expressive activity, with concentration becoming focused on the expressive order. The self is still understood as a social creation, being formed in the discourse of the social group, but now that discourse is not seen to relate directly to the practical concerns and activities of social selves. Expressive concerns and needs take pride of place in the organization of the social group. While Harré, for example, does insist that there is a relation between the practical and expressive orders, for what is practical can always become expressive, this makes the distinction between two theoretical 'orders' extremely unhelpful. It obscures Mead's understanding that symbols, signs and language only become meaningful because they are lodged in the practical, social activity of the group. Activity is therefore the bedrock of meaning and, thus, the practical and the expressive cannot be separated. What is lost in the ethogenic approach is the practical and, therefore, *objective* origin of meaning. Once this foundation has become undermined, activity loses its central importance and there are many relapses into subjectivism, where the origin of meaning and the powers of the self are sought within the nature of each singular, isolated, architectonic person.

The problem of the origin of meaning and the self becomes even more exaggerated in contemporary French philosophy. Theorists from this tradition base their understanding of discourse and meaning on the linguistics of de Saussure. Here, the meaning of a discursive or linguistic system arises from within the system itself, derived from the rules and regularities that govern the internal relationship between the symbols and signs. Meaning is determined by the relationships and binary oppositions between these symbols and signs. Hence, we know what the word 'cold' means and the concept of coldness that lies behind it, because we also have the word and the concept of 'warmth', the two terms being defined over and against one another. However, once again, the role of human activity within the social group is missing from this understanding of discourse and meaning, even though it was something to which de Saussure constantly referred. The origin of meaning and the instruments for its reproduction are seen to be the universe of signs, discourse and meaning itself. Language, rather than activity, becomes the foundation of the social world and the well-spring of meaning.

This notion is taken to its logical conclusion in structuralist and post-structuralist theory, where language becomes the organizing principle of social life. Language has the power to 'place' individuals in the social system it has carved out by constructing their personalities, creating meaning and, thus, determining their life-course. Divorced from human activity, the linguistic and cultural system becomes the organizing principle of social life and of the 'illusion' of 'individuality'; a state in which humans supposedly can exercise their own free choices and determine their own actions. Yet this is simply an illusion, for individuals are determined in every fibre of their being by the cultural system and the symbolic realm it generates.

At this point in the analysis, we find ourselves stuck firmly in the humanist and anti-humanist impasse. Most of the insights from Mead's theory of symbolic interaction and the self have been lost. Instead we are faced with, on the one hand, a humanist relapse into monadology and subjectivism in the ethogenic school and, on the other hand, an almost absurd anti-humanist reification of the cultural system, in which human activity appears to play only a contingent part in social life. Discourse has been elevated above its human subjects, who are only the places in its conversation or the vehicles for its expression. What has been lost is that which I feel to be most important in understanding the nature of humans as social selves — the social relations and activities between people. It is the concept of relations and activities that was rediscovered in Sève's reading of Marxism as a 'scientific humanism'.

Beyond Humanism and Anti-Humanism: Marxism as Scientific Humanism

In Marxist theory, social relations are essential in understanding social life and the capacities of individuals, because humans must enter into relations in order to transform the real world in which they live and satisfy their needs. The structure and organization of social relations, such as the division of labour, also shapes the labour activity of each individual — the activity humans must engage in so as to transform the real. Social relations were for Marx what philosophers had previously referred to as the 'human essence', for in any epoch the social relations between people embody the productive power and, thus, the character of humanity. Only through these relations are the tools, skills and knowledge handed down from generation to generation which allows humans to practise and to develop their productive power and control of the natural world.

Marx argued, in the *Theses on Feuerbach*, that it was not the structure of the natural world or human nature that governed people's mental reflection upon the world, nor was it mental activity conceived in isolation which determined human consciousness. Mind does not determine the process of thinking. Instead, it is sensuous activity in the world, or practice, which determines our consciousness of the reality that surrounds us and of our own selves. Just as in the pragmatist philosophy that inspired Mead and which he sought to extend, it is the way we act upon the world that determines our consciousness of it. Only Marx saw this activity as labour activity rather than symbolic activity. By acting on reality in order to produce the objects to satisfy need, humans become profoundly conscious of that world in ways that could not be achieved through mental activity alone. Human being is then largely determined through social relations and the way in which people act upon the world, in social labour, to produce objects for consumption and to satisfy need.

Both Marx and Mead are therefore in agreement upon the notion that it is the way people act within the world that determines human consciousness. However, Marx is providing the historical perspective on the macro-structure of social relations that Mead lacked, also showing how it is these relations that structure social activity and the consciousness generated by it. Sève rightly labels this as 'scientific humanism', for Marx is not doing away with the idea that humans create their social world in relations and activities: however, neither is Marx arguing that humans can simply create or recreate society and nature in any which way they choose, or simply alter their consciousness to suit some preconceived purpose. To paraphrase Marx, humans make their own history but they do not make it in conditions of their own choosing: they make it under conditions handed down from previous generations, in the form of the mode of production and its dynamics. In this effort, the means of acting upon the world will be expanded, but under conditions inherited from the past.

Human activity can never be considered outside of the framework of social relations and their history, which provide the logic of social activity — its rhyme and reason. The meaning of activity cannot, therefore, be considered purely in terms of symbolically constructed meaning, nor with reference only to activity: the meaning of activity must also be viewed in the context of its history and within the framework of social relations. Again, I feel Marxism has a vital role to play in helping us to understand that we cannot interpret the actions or the motives of individuals simply by seeking out the meaning that has inspired their activity. Rather, we must set activity and the individual accounts given of actions and motives in the context of their social logic: that is, of social relations and social activity as a whole.

While Sève has gone some way towards demonstrating how such an understanding of individuals and their activity could be worked out, by seeing the biography of the person as structured in social relations, his approach has been limited in its almost exclusive focus on the relations of production and the capacities learned in social labour. A fully rounded psychology of personality would have to extend beyond this to include not only what Foucault called relations that transform the real, but also relations of communication and power. This is the sociological basis for the understanding of personality that I have sought in the second part of this study, seeing personality in social relations and interdependencies that are involved in transforming the real, communicating with others and exercising power. It is in this overall context we must devise a psychology of personality.

*Personality in Relations of Production, Communication
and Power*

Scientific humanism, then, involves seeing the logic of individual
lives and selves in terms of social relations and activities. Sève
constructs a psychology of personality upon this basic insight, in
which a person's activity within the relations of production is
essential in the formation of capacities which mark their development as social individuals. Through social labour and the construction of personal capacities, individuals appropriate their social
heritage, building into their personalities aspects of the productive
and cultural power created in social history. Appropriation of the
social heritage is the process by which individuals come to embody
the level of social development as capacities — physical and
mental abilities that mark out the level of their own development
as personalities.

However, in capitalism, individuals find that they embody the
contradictions within the social relations of this particular society.
Ownership of the means of production by the capitalist class
creates alienation from the social heritage for the mass of people
and, therefore, lack of opportunity for the social development of
the personality. The stunting of personal growth is a psychological
scar inflicted by capitalist relations. This is because the whole
system of production is geared to the development of capital and
not the individual. Capacities are only developed in people if they
are needed for the accumulation of capital, not for the benefit of
the development of human potential. People are therefore alienated in this society, being developed to a certain degree, yet
limited and stunted in their overall growth. Sève therefore shows
how social relations are not just external to individuals but are
internal elements of the self, determining personal growth.

In this way, Sève clearly illustrates what is often obscured from
our vision: how personality is developed in social relations that
transform the real world. Yet he has analysed these relations to
the total exclusion of relations of communication and power. This
means that while Sève has accounted for part of the social heritage
and the development of personality within it, he has not studied
the relations of communication and the cultural heritage in which
consciousness develops. As C. Wright Mills said, Marx was right
to say that consciousness does not determine existence: however,
Marxists are wrong if they believe that existence simply determines consciousness in a direct and unproblematic way. Between

196 Personality in Social Relations

consciousness and material existence are communications, symbols, language, culture and values, which influence human consciousness and, therefore, social action. In any theory of social selves we must have a clearly worked out understanding of communication, culture and consciousness.

This was provided in the work of the cultural-historical school, who argued that communication and culture is not separate from material existence and human practice but an integral part of it. Both language and labour are necessary for a historical understanding of the development of human powers, because it is within relations of communication as well as relations that transform the real that we find the development of humanity. Without relations of communication humans could not co-ordinate and organize the practical process of material production, nor could they store and hand down to future generations the technical ability to transform the real. Conscious powers such as the rational control of behaviour and development of the intellect — which the cultural-historical school refer to as the 'higher mental functions' — are not given in nature but only emerge when humans act to transform the real through labour and language. Labour provides the physical tools with which to work to transform reality, while language provides what Vygotsky called the psychological tools to influence the behaviour of others through communication and to influence one's own behaviour through conscious thinking and control. Tools and instruments work on the natural world to transform it, while symbols and words, which are psychological tools, work upon human nature and change it.

Psychologically, the symbolic tools we use to reflect upon and to steer our actions, form an inner conversation which is an internalization of the communicative processes taking place in society. Mead, Vygotsky and Elias all agree that this inner conversation forms the activity that we have labelled as 'thinking', its dialogical structure creating what we call the 'mind'. As Elias remarked, the concept of the 'mind' refers to the soundless manipulation of symbols constantly occurring in the inner dialogue we hold with our own selves. At this point we can integrate Mead's insight that consciousness is symbolically formed in relations of communication, with the analysis of the cultural-historical school, which shows that these relations also have a history and a macrostructure which is tied to relations that transform the real. Material and cultural existence, and the social and cultural heritage they create, cannot be considered separately. They form two of the unifying threads running through social history, marking out the level of the practical and conscious capacities of humans within the world.

However, a third element that runs through human sociality, the relations of power, is missing from this analysis. Mead and Vygotsky tend to see the growing powers of rational conscious thought and control of behaviour progressing in a linear fashion without warps or distortions in this process. They do not analyse the inequalities and conflicts in society resulting from the domination of powerful groups, which can undercut the rational, minded control individuals have over their own actions. Such an understanding was part of Sève's Marxist vision, illustrating how personality is alienated and stunted in capitalist relations of power. The question now is how do relations of power translate to relations of communication and affect these processes?

The Soviet linguist, Vološinov, addressed himself to this problem, arguing that relations of power distort the communicative process because there are different 'accents' within the social conversation which reflect different ideological positions in the class structure. Communication is therefore infused with these different accents and ideological positions in society. Social psychologists who are interested in discourse and rhetoric are currently taking a similar stance, analysing how human thought processes are saturated by ideological styles of arguing and thinking (Billig, 1987; Billig et al., 1988). While these social psychologists see ideological dilemmas as a way of thinking through social problems and conflicts, Vološinov also points out that ideology often obscures the social context in which its meaning is produced, undermining the ability of individuals properly to orientate themselves to problems and conflicts — both socially and psychologically. Lichtman referred to this as the creation of a 'structural unconscious', where the social context of the production of meaning is obscured to individuals and the power relations in which the ideology is generated are hidden from consciousness. These social contexts and power relations continue to dominate people's lives and activities, but they do so outside of their awareness and, thus, weaken the ability of individuals to control their own destiny. Rational, conscious control of action is therefore limited in relations of power.

Many of these insights are extended within the work of Elias, who argues that power and inequality is not just economically based on the ownership of means of production, but is also centred on the monopolization of means of violence and control of knowledge. The ascendancy of a particular social class, or religious or ethnic group, depends upon the command and control of economic and military forces, but also brings with it the ascendancy of the group's culture and the establishment of its intrinsic modes of acting and thinking. This is how hegemony and legitimacy are created around the domination of ruling groups. The social power behind ideas to which people aspire is often obscured, just as the power which established the notion of 'civilized' manners and modes of behaviour is hidden. Elias's social scientific analysis has traced the origin of the term 'civilization' to the domination of particular social classes. In everyday terms, however, the notion that people in the West are 'civilized' is often taken by members of this society to be a self-evident fact. 'Polite' manners and 'civilized' modes of behaviour are produced and reproduced without individuals properly understanding the social origin and the nature of the power structure which lies behind their socio-genesis.

In Elias's work, therefore, we can also see the notion that structural aspects of social life are hidden from symbolically constructed consciousness. We think in ways that are determined by the symbolic and linguistic dialogues of our culture, which reflect the forms of behaviour, life-styles, ideas and values of different religious, ethnic and class groups. The dominance of certain ideas reflects the position of these groups in the social hierarchy and their degree of influence. Yet the fact that the figuration of power balances and tensions lies behind the dialogues and dilemmas of symbolically formed consciousness, is often obscured by the very hegemonic nature of ruling ideas and the role they play in forming conscious awareness. Equally, ruling groups also represent and enforce certain modes and standards of behaviour through their value systems and ideas. Not only do we find a structural unconscious developing in the power balances and tensions of the figuration of social relations, but also a repressed unconscious, to which the behaviour and expressions of other social groups — their standards of conduct and the feelings they mould — are relegated. Behind the dispositions that have been internalized in the personality from the earliest years of our social learning, are inclinations and inhibitions which structure acting, feeling and thinking. Such dispositions structure our actions and personalities, and they, too, reflect the standards of behaviour of ruling groups; something of which we are not consciously aware.

I wish to come back to this point in the model of social selves described later in this chapter. Suffice to say for the moment that Elias has a vision of a repressed unconscious within the personality that is not unlike that in the analysis of Richard Lichtman, where feelings and the behaviours they motivate are constituted as unrealizable within the power structure and the social sanctions of particular societies. Both these agencies within the personality, the structural and repressed unconscious, operate in blind and mechanical ways as dispositions over which we have little control. They often undermine symbolic consciousness, taking control away from the self in the production of activity and undermining the conscious, rational control of behaviour. This too is a form of alienation from which individuals suffer psychologically. Elias therefore sees individuals as alienated and isolated in society not only by their separation from the means of production — from social labour and thus from one's fellow social beings (something of which Elias does not speak) — but also by the emotional controls that surround individuals in the modern age, which inhibit our responses to others and separate us from them. While Elias thinks that in all societies there have to be necessary restraints that exist simply because individuals act within a figuration, there are, nevertheless, many unnecessary restraints in most societies which exist simply to shore up the domination of ruling groups. It is these unnecessary restraints that interfere with the rational organization of conduct in society and within the self.

Relations of power come to intersect and structure the dynamic processes of personality in this way. They do so by establishing dispositions; that is, complexes of emotional controls and the impulses they structure, which operate within the personality to mould responses and actions. What becomes important at this stage of the analysis is the second problem we have faced in this study, which is the demarcation of emotions from the structure of rational consciousness. Elias shows how this is dependent on the social relations and type of emotional controls established in Western societies, where we feel ourselves separated from the emotions by the controls that structure them. The question now arises within the theory of social selves, of exactly how emotions are socially structured and what is their relationship to consciousness?

A Holistic View of Social Selves: Consciousness and Emotion

Along with the dichotomy between individual and society, I also began a critique in Chapter One of the dualism that exists in Western social science and philosophy between consciousness and the emotions. The Cartesian view of personality, prevalent in the West, often makes it appear as if consciousness and emotion are diametrically opposed. Indeed, Descartes's own philosophy suggested this, for he saw the emotions as a property of humans' earthly bodies whereas the conscious, rational mind was an appropriation of the divine: something which raised humans above the animal and elevated us closer to the heavenly.

Most of the theories considered here have questioned this view. Few have denied the reality of human nature; yet interactionism, ethogenics, Marxism and the sociology of Elias have all theorized the genesis of consciousness as a social process, and have understood the development and differentiation of emotions and needs to be part of that same process. Another factor these theories have in common is that they do not see the various emotions as compartmentalized and given in nature. Originally, human nature is seen to be undifferentiated and generic, with the various emotions being defined and separated in the historical process. Emotion is therefore socially created and historically variable.

Mead, for example, allowed for the existence of human nature in terms of the responses of the body to stimuli in the environment. Both he and Elias analyse the natural, unlearned responses and behaviours of humans in the same way: as innate devices which orientate us to the reality of the world in which we live. As I have already stated, changes in the nature of human being occur as individuals begin to act in order to *transform* the real. For Mead, this happens within the process of symbolic interaction and the development of cognition. The function of the mind is not to replace noncognitive factors of the body, but to mould and organize them so as to increase the possibility of their satisfaction. Mead used the term 'social instincts' because human nature is not set in a fixed pattern, instead being conditioned by the experience of the social group and the formation of consciousness that occurs within it. As consciousness is developed through the symbolic communication of the group, new modes and methods for the satisfaction of needs and impulses are created. In this process, the whole nature of need and impulse is transformed.

This was illustrated particularly with reference to the role that the mind plays in determining behaviour. According to Mead, behaviour is originally composed by the reciprocal responses of the individuals involved in social activities. With the development of communication and the formation of the self-conscious mind, there is now a mediating agency between the social stimulus and the response of the human body. The mediation is performed by self-consciousness, which now acts to interpret the stimulus from the environment and to mould the response according to the store of social knowledge in which it has been constructed. Emotion is not pregiven in this theory, for emotion does not exist where there is a direct causation between a stimulus in the environment and the response of an organism. In this case, there is simply an impulse within the body which is directly carried out in action. An emotion only arises when self-consciousness is developed to the point where an interpretation of the response occurs through the framework of social meanings. The response is delayed and re-routed through mental activity, which seeks to interpret the response and forms it as a meaningfully recognized emotion. Such a theory of emotion is similar to that in the ethogenic school, where Harré (1986) and others see emotion developing according to 'emotion vocabularies' which are part of the general linguistic framework in the local moral order.

However, the theorist who comes closest to Mead on this issue is Vygotsky, whose theory of signs as psychological tools with which to refashion human nature, is close to Mead's conception. Vygotsky believed that the 'lower mental functions', which are innate within the human species, are transformed as they are culturally developed into the 'higher mental functions'. Thus the lower mental functions as they appear in very young children — such as sensori-motor responses and actions, along with basic mental processes like involuntary memory — are fashioned and developed through the cultural activity of the child and its appropriation of the higher mental functions. Through this process, involuntary functions and sensori-motor actions become open to voluntary control through consciousness. Development of the emotions occurs as bodily states and the involuntary preparation for activity become interpreted through the mind in terms of word meanings, and are subordinated and controlled by the mental functions. Personality develops as a whole in such a way, with the emotions developing alongside and under the control of cognitive processes. Once again, for Vygotsky, the key element is word meaning and the inner conversation derived from society, through which the entire structure of personality is developed within the cultural heritage. Behind every thought may well lie the emotional-volitional sphere, as Vygotsky suggests; but it is equally true to say that, within his psychology, without word meaning and the thoughts they make possible, there would be no awareness of a bodily or mental state as an 'emotion'.

Consciousness and emotion are not two separate and opposing states, then, but develop together as part of the whole personality. As in Freudian theory, emotions and drives are not to be confused with natural instincts, for the former develop as part of the psychic structure as a whole which is not given in nature. This view of the development of the emotions as part of the more general structure of personality is also present in Elias's theories. However, Elias connects the relations of communication and culture in which emotion vocabularies and moral regulations develop to the figuration of power balances. For example, in court society where the interdependencies between people grew much stronger and became more pacified, aristocratic codes of behaviour became more complex. Under these conditions, a new social habitus of personal dispositions was created which forged a different psychic economy to the one established in the Middle Ages. It is not just the meaning of emotion in particular contexts, and the greater care and attention people had to display to their own feelings and those of others, it is also the more even and regular rules that govern the display of emotions in particular contexts which develop and differentiate the nuances of feelings and sensibilities. Elias understands this psychic economy as a circuit which is socially balanced: changes in the pattern of social activity cause changes in the entire structure of the personality complex, including the emotions.

What is most important for Elias in terms of the emotions and their expression, is the social habitus in which humans develop certain dispositions by learning what actions and emotions are appropriate in which contexts. Thus, in the Middle Ages, actions and feelings that we now regard as abhorrent, such as openly enjoyed acts of cruelty or blood lust, could be indulged because they had a meaning within the social structure of the times: they were necessary for people to survive in these eras and they befitted the actions of certain ranks within the power networks of the figuration. Through the learning of social meanings and constraints, humans develop dispositions and emotions which always bear their social 'stamp'. Human nature is malleable and the emotions and inclinations are socially developed in the historical configuration of power relations.

It is within these relations that we also find the separation and compartmentalization of the different aspects of the personality. It was in court society that less flexible barriers were erected in the self between the drives and drive controls, on the one hand, and consciousness on the other. Rational, self-reflexive control now becomes undermined by fears and anxieties of the powers and sanctions possessed by dominant social groups. In these social contexts, power relations are internalized as a semi-permeable barrier between emotions and consciousness. Here, the emotions and their controls are often placed outside the boundary of rational self-conscious control by socially structured fears, such as levels of shame and embarrassment over infringing social rules governing 'good' conduct. The emotions are still socially structured by the fears and anxieties that surround them, but they are not shaped by the individuals' own conscious choices. Instead, they exist in what we have come to call the 'unconscious' — an aspect of personality which is not given in nature but is socio-historically created. It is in this way that relations of power are internal to the self and demarcate the different aspects of the personality within specific historical periods.

However, as Marx showed, human nature is also restructured within relations that transform the real, as people act collectively to change the natural world. In the process of producing to satisfy needs, humans transform the basic biological needs that are given in the species. The need for new objects that satisfy historically created desires is built into the personality through relations that transform the real. Within these relations and activities biological need is transformed into historical need through the productive activity of the social group. Sève showed how this insight can turn the whole theory of personality and motivation around, so we can understand that it is not biological needs that well up inside us which provide the motivation for activity. Rather, it is the activity we are engaged in, structured by social relations, through which we build into our personalities certain needs and desires typical of the historical period in which we live. (The need for certain types of food and clothing, for cars or television sets, is not universal.) To understand the motives behind our actions, the way in which we work or behave in order to satisfy desires, we need to realize that the dynamic of activity and motive does not unfold in the commonly accepted pattern. Here, a need occurs which gives rise to an action which satisfies the need (Need–Activity–Need). Instead, action and motivation unfold in the opposite way, where social activities provide the basis for the creation of historical needs which are satisfied through forms of established activities (Activity–Need–Activity).

This general formula was also taken on board by Leontyev, who extended it by showing how all human needs and feelings are locked into the social activity which makes up existence. The needs which motivate activity are socially and historically created, along with the emotions which accompany our actions and 'colour' them. Emotion, for Leontyev, is not so much a basic impulse, more of a vital force which results from and colours activity. An emotion cannot be understood, then, if it is isolated from the chain of relations and activities in which the individual is engaged, and which inspire and motivate actions and feelings. This led Leontyev into a new angle on the question of conscious and unconscious motivation, for conscious motivation is that of which we are aware within the immediate circle of our activity, which we can bring into symbolically or discursively formulated consciousness. Unconscious motivation, on the other hand, is created through socially structured activities in which we are engaged, the social origin of which we may be unaware, it being outside discursive consciousness. For example, Lichtman has shown how motives of greed and self-aggrandizement are lodged in the capitalist system of social relations; yet this is a fact people often misrecognize, believing such behaviour to be part of human nature. The system of capitalist relations thereby remains an unconscious source for motivation for particular types of behaviour.

The question now, however, is can all these insights be worked out into a new theory of social selves, which would create a model of personality for use within the social sciences?

A Model of Social Selves

One of the main themes of this study has been the identification of social relations as fundamental to the formation of personality. It is the ensemble of social relations that form what Sève called the matrices of activity, which both structure activity and are restructured by it. Relations of production, communication and power are all intertwined and form the basis of the lives of individuals who are part of these relations. In this view, social relations are not so much a fixed structure, bound and governed by fundamental rules; they are what Bourdieu calls a 'generative structure' or what Elias refers to as a 'figuration' — a network of patterned relational changes which have a logic: the logic of social practice. It is in this arena that all aspects of the personality first appear — the mental and the emotional — within objective social activity structured by social relations. Consciousness develops within activity as a more complex means of orientation to others and to reality, and is dependent on the communication and cultural knowledge within the social group. Not only does consciousness develop in this process but also the entire structure of the personality, including the emotions and the unconscious sources of motivation.

It was demonstrated clearly by Leontyev that the emotions as well as consciousness are crystallized in the activity of the group. Also the formation and location of motivation within the self — whether this is conscious or unconscious — depends upon the place the activity which creates it occupies within the network of social relations. The different aspects of the self are not regions that exist within us, but the places that our acts occupy within the social relations and activities which become internal to the self. Thus the movements or contradictions within social relations that exist on a historical or international scale are not necessarily realized within discursive consciousness. They form what Lichtman calls the structural unconscious, which consists of the motives appropriated by individuals within the network of social relations and activities, the source of which is obscured to people by the nature of discursive consciousness. For example, Billig et al. (1988) have shown how ideological dilemmas reflect in individual consciousness and in the attempts of individuals to resolve these dilemmas. However, these are often seen as personal or moral dilemmas and the power structure which lies behind them is not consciously confronted.

The structural unconscious, though, is only one level of the unconscious processes within the self. There is also the level of the repressed unconscious, to which realm the social acts, bodily functions or emotional states that are regarded as taboo are banished, removing them from conscious presence. Forbidden acts or emotions are denied expression in the social spaces and discourses of everyday life, instead being confined to private places which are specially designated, or are denied and repressed within the self. They become hidden from consciousness and cloaked by delinguistification. Like the hidden spaces in social life, they continue to exert an influence over people's behaviour but one of which no one will — or can — speak. Barriers of socially induced fear and anxiety surround these acts and emotions in social life, just as they surround their symbolic or discursive representation in the mind. It is not, therefore, the nature of the act which marks it as conscious or unconscious, but the place occupied by the act in the structure of social relations and in the network of power balances in society. However, what is repressed and inhibited by dispositions which move to prevent the expression of certain acts or emotions, often comes back to disrupt conscious behaviour, for these are agencies in the psyche which, being unconscious, we cannot control. An illustration of this will be given shortly.

Along with the structural and repressed unconscious, there is also a third level of unconsciousness in the personality that Leontyev has called 'operations' or others have referred to as 'habits'. These are learned aspects of behaviour which become so ingrained in the personality that we need not think about how to perform them. The things we learn such as driving a car, finding our way to work, playing a piano, certain attitudes or emotional responses, all become deeply ingrained within the self as implicit knowledge or capacities. They form what Giddens has referred to as 'practical consciousness', as distinct from discursive consciousness. There are also innumerable habits we learn from birth onwards, that seem so right and proper to us we forget they were learned and instead accept them as part of our 'nature'. These habits or dispositions are likely to be common to the social class or religious or ethnic group in which we were reared, as part of the social habitus of that group. Our tastes and distastes, the things we find acceptable or unacceptable, attractive or repulsive, are formed within this social habitus. The marks of distinction we display that unconsciously signal our social status, and which we irradiate with the unconscious ease of people who do not realize what they are doing, are appropriated from the cultural environment at the early stages of learning. Here we find the development and mastery of certain dispositions that we will carry as part of our personality for the rest of our lives and which will determine our life's course to a large degree.

In the social habitus of the self we encounter once again the importance of social relations, for tastes and distastes are not given naturally to some and not to others. Tastes and distastes are defined against one another and reflect the power relations of different groups. For example, both Bourdieu and Elias show how the likes and dislikes of social classes are part of the power relations between them in which they display their status and distinction in the social ranks. What individuals come to find attractive or repulsive depends upon their own position, and the position of the object or behaviour in question, within the network of relations and symbols of power.

Besides these dispositions, however, there exist the capacities that individuals possess which, as Sève showed, will also mark their place in the social hierarchy. The capacities people have learned depend on where they stand in the class structure and the division of labour. These capacities are created by people appropriating their social heritage, not only through work, as Sève has claimed, but also through culture and communication as illustrated by Bourdieu and Elias. Capacities can be distinguished from dispositions or operations in that they are consciously possessed and applied. They refer to the individuals' ability to do something, to make a mark upon and to transform the social or natural world. Like operations, aspects of capacities may slip out of consciousness and become automatic ways of acting, yet, in general, capacities are abilities to do things and change things of which we are consciously aware and which we consciously apply. They bridge the conscious and unconscious levels of the personality, belonging to both levels at the same time.

The capacities to act in certain ways are very close to the aspect of the self labelled by Mead as the 'I'. Capacities indicate the ability and the readiness to act in particular ways within social situations. However, Mead meant much more than this with the concept of the 'I'. It also indicates the individuals' active openness to new situations and the preparedness not only to change social life according to already acquired capacities, but to be adaptive and to learn from experience. Only later is that active experience reflected upon and incorporated into the self as a new capacity, as part of the 'me'. Again, it must be emphasized that the 'I' and the 'me', which form the conscious aspects of the self, are not given regions or fixed functions within the personality. They are, as we have already seen, moments in social action that occur in the network of social relations. It is only in social relations and symbolic interaction that the inner psychological terrain is created. Self-consciousness is a creation of the discourse between social selves, for it is only in communication we can begin to think of ourselves as 'I' and 'me'. These are discursive positions in communicative interaction and not given elements of the self. Subjective positions can therefore only emerge in objective social relations and activities.

From this theory we can now begin to understand what was once referred to as the 'mind' as an inner conversation that we hold with our objective self-image, which is drawn from the social conversation around us. This discursive consciousness does not reflect all aspects of social activity, nor does it reflect every aspect of the personality which is forged in activity as a whole. However, it does reflect some elements of our social and natural world, for discourse itself is bound to the relations and activities — of production and power — which involve all the other levels of our being. Considering all that I have said so far, it is interesting to look at the relationship between the conscious and unconscious levels of activity and the self in the terms of both Mead and Freud. Mead has given the labels 'I' and 'me' to the two sides of the social self which develop in symbolic interaction. The 'I' represents the ability and readiness to act in its symbolic form, while the 'me' represents the self-image people form in activity, seeing themselves reflected in the actions and reactions of others toward them. As I showed in Chapter One, Bettelheim (1985) claims that in the original German editions of Freud's works, his term for the ego was also the 'I'. The difference between the two theorists is that Mead shows how the 'I' is symbolically formed over and against the image of the 'me'. However, this terminology, and the likenesses between Mead and Freud in this respect, may help us to outline more clearly the dynamic functioning of the social self.

For example, Freud also had another aspect of the self in his theories that Mead did not consider, which Bettelheim translates as the 'it'. This represents the repressed drives and emotions of the self, which form alien and unknown forces within the personality that compel the individual to act in ways that he or she cannot control. I suggested in Chapter Two that interactionism lacked such a concept, to its detriment. However, we can now begin to think of such an agency in the self, which, like the others, is based in social relations and activity, but is a repressed force in the dynamics of the personality. It is constituted as Lichtman suggested, as a structural and repressed unconscious consisting of those drives which are socially developed as 'aim inhibited' or which are 'constituted as unrealizable'. This denied or repressed aspect of the self, along with the fear and anxiety which surround its silent strivings, becomes an alien force acting within the personality as an 'it'. This unconscious propulsion interacts with the other psychic agencies and creates a disturbing force whose motive and goal is unacceptable and must be blocked.

In an empirical study of the phenomenon of stuttering, Petrunik and Shearing (1988) have used Mead's concept of the self in a similar way, integrating this with the Freudian notion of an alien locus of agency and motivation within the personality which is outside of conscious control. They also apply the term 'it' to this agency, saying that:

> By noting that people can and do *experience* an interior source of action and locus of control that is 'not I' and that is in conflict with the 'I' we seek to expand on Mead's experiential analysis. The 'It' is given a conceptual status similar to the 'I'. Both are viewed as sources of action. What differentiates the 'I' and the 'It' is the experience of the 'It' as an alien source of action that struggles with the 'I' (Petrunik and Shearing, 1988: 437).

What they show in their research is the way that stutterers experience their stutter as an alien agency — an 'imp' as the people interviewed so commonly describe it — inside the self which interferes with the smooth functioning of interaction, taking the initiative away from the 'I'. The stutter is then experienced as 'it'. However, Petrunik and Shearing do not give any indication as to how the 'it' might have been socially constituted along with the 'I'. There are some clues to this, though, within their work. For example, what comes across strongly from the interviews in the study is the degree of anxiety that the stutterers feel in their encounters with others. The end product of a failed encounter, where the stutter has intervened to foil conversation, is shame and embarrassment. In a society such as ours, where goals and self-interests are achieved through successful encounters — as Elias and Goffman clearly showed — there is a great deal of tension around the success of interaction and much fear and anxiety over the possibility of making a *faux pas*.

Such fear and anxiety over breaching social convention is created because, in our society, the way that one conducts oneself in public is a mark of one's status and distinction. To foul up an encounter is instantly to demean oneself in public and to lower one's status position in the eyes of others. This would account for the fact Petrunik and Shearing note, that most stutterers suffer more in front of people they perceive to have a higher status or more authority than themselves. Most are fluent when speaking aloud to themselves, or to animals and children. From this we can see that fear and anxiety over failed encounters is both linked to the premium placed on successful encounters in our society and, more importantly, to the power structure that lies behind this within which status and distinction is allocated to individuals. As Elias (1982: 292) says, the feeling of shame or embarrassment is 'a specific excitation, a kind of anxiety which is *automatically* reproduced in the individual on certain occasions by force of habit' (my emphasis): it is fear of the other's superiority, of the power they possess in the social hierarchy, but also the paralysing fear of one's own inferiority, one's helplessness before such a person in averting the embarrassing situation. A person is then totally exposed without any means of defending themselves against the power and privileged position of the other.

In such a situation a person has lost control of the management of the situation, of their own identity, and of their body, with the result that a learned response of helplessness, which has become automatic, can take control of behaviour producing a 'socio-motor' disorder. This happens in a disorder such as stuttering, where a person's fear of an embarrassing situation and their feelings of inadequacy in front of powerful others, leads to a breakdown of control over the body and the fluency of one's actions. Here the fear and anxiety about losing control and of the learned reactions of helplessness taking over, come to function mechanically in certain situations when they are triggered. We then feel the sense of what R.D. Laing (1965) defined as alienation: the condition in which part of our personality and body begins to function like a machine, outside of the control of the 'I'. Instead, it operates as an 'it' — an alien force we are helpless in commanding.

However, there is a psychological mechanism behind the automatic responses of shame and the loss of control by the 'I' over the individual's actions. This occurs because there is an element of the personality which mirrors the values of society as a whole and, within this, the dominant values of ruling groups. The element of the self that undertakes this function was labelled by Mead as the 'generalized other', or in Bettelheim's translation of Freud it is referred to as the 'over-I' (this could also be translated as 'above-I' or 'upper-I', but I will refer to the 'over-I' here). The 'over-I' exists as a monitor and censor within the personality that attempts to control behaviour in ways that are socially acceptable. Each one of us has internalized this aspect of our personality in relation to our parents, who reflect the dominant values of the wider society. Shame or embarrassment takes its coloration as an emotion from the fact that as an 'I' and 'me' we have done, or are about to do, something which comes into contradiction with social values and is in contradiction with that part of the personality which represents these values. If we hold in any way to dominant social values, then the internal contradiction and conflict will cause tension and anxiety and the possibility of embarrassment. That is because in breaching these values, *we recognize ourselves as inferior*, with the result that we may feel self-loathing and shame. This is what renders us defenceless against the superiority of others and sets off automatic responses of embarrassment.

Thus we can see that behind even the most personal of actions and emotions there stands social relations and the power structure. As we saw from Elias's work in Chapter Seven, this creates the whole structure of the personality and its dynamic responses. It creates the conscious as well as the repressed, unconscious aspects of the self, along with the internalized values of society which create dispositions towards certain types of social behaviour in groups or classes of individuals. The dispositions and restraints, and the emotions they develop and structure, can exist as a repressed unconscious within the self, functioning automatically but in ways that are socially learned. Behind this stands the structural unconscious, the social relations and power structure of which we are not constantly aware, yet which we reproduce in our everyday behaviour. For example, in much psychological literature and in everyday thinking about social behaviour, the maintenance of socially correct conduct is seen as a matter of personal abilities and individual self-esteem (or a lack of such things). The social production and reproduction of this type of behaviour is obscured from our communication and our consciousness.

All aspects of the self, then, are socially formed. They are not regions within separate and self-contained personalities, but are moments in the network of social relations and activities. The 'I' which is formed in communicative interaction consciously plans action in relation to the 'me', which is the self-image we have gained from past interactions. Part of the 'me' acts against the 'I' as an 'over-I' which embodies and attempts to enforce the morality of the social group. The constitution of action occurs within this tripartite relationship between the 'I', the 'me' and the 'over-I'. However, behind this discursive and active consciousness, there exist the social relations and power structure of the group in which the whole of the personality is forged. Not all aspects of this network of power relations are represented in discursive consciousness and may be cloaked by ideology and the contradictions and dilemmas within it. The fundamental influence of social relations exists as a structural unconscious of which people are not necessarily aware. Alongside this there is also the repressed unconscious, which is formed by motives or emotions being constituted as unrealizable by the 'over-I' and thus effectively blocked. They continue to exist as aim-inhibited needs, denied and delinguistified, their energy manifesting itself as an 'it' — a silent agency which interacts with consciousness as a blind and automatically operating disposition, undermining the individual's ability for conscious control. Many other learned actions also slip out of consciousness and become operations, which are so ingrained in the personality they are performed unthinkingly. However, they can also form as practical capacities which are consciously possessed and applied.

The social world of activity and the inner world of the self are, in this way, emergent processes which cannot be separated. There is no division between the individual and the social. We cannot say that the boundary of the personality is the skin, or any other membrane — physical or psychological — which acts as a barrier within which to contain individuality. Indeed, the whole concept of 'individuality' as a self-contained and pregiven entity is now undermined. We must begin to see personality as social in all its aspects and understand individuals as social selves.

Nevertheless it remains true that individuals feel themselves to be separate from others and isolated in their own individuality. This alienation occurs because, as Sève claimed, people are separated from their social heritage within capitalism. However, the picture is more complex than this. Vološinov points to the lack of communicative clarity within the ideology that emerges from class conflict, and Elias has shown that there are unnecessary social restraints that divide people through rigid emotional controls. All these things undermine the ability of individuals to control their collective existence within the social group, and to achieve the degree of knowledge and understanding necessary for greater self-reflexive control over their individual destiny. The question remains as to whether these contradictions and conflicts in the social network can move people to overturn them through a reconstruction of society and personality.

The Reconstruction of Society and Social Selves

I have already identified some of the social contradictions and conflicts that form the basis of individual selves and their inherent dilemmas. There is, for example, the problem of alienation, in the Marxist sense of individuals becoming separated from the means of production and, thus, their social heritage. In this situation, people lose control of the appropriation of their heritage and, therefore, the means of their own personal development. In the Marxist solution to this problem, individuals must unite to overturn alienating social conditions and, in the process, form the basis of a socialist society, in which there will be the all-round development of individual abilities. However, we need to be wary of too simplistic a solution to alienation in the modern world. As the lessons from Eastern Europe and China teach us, the communist societies that are currently in existence have not provided a better basis for the development of personalities than the capitalist societies of the West. At the same time, the inequalities in capitalism cause misery to millions of people and alienate them within their own societies.

It seems that inequality in the ownership of the means of production and the distribution of wealth is only one aspect of alienation that people need to tackle. There is also a need for genuine communication between individuals, undistorted by ideology, and for collective control of existence within more democratic systems of self-government. Under such conditions individuals may find the rational control of social and individual existence, that Vygotsky saw emerging in history, more of a reality than it is at present. We would also experience more fully the democratic, cultural transparency that Mead envisaged as the basis for the social self. Democratic conditions would provide the basis for the greater orientation of individuals in their social life and also, as society reveals itself more to individuals, the basis for greater orientation within the self. However, Dewey's (1951) ideal of democracy as a way of personal as well as public life still seems a long way off. Social inequalities and the unnecessary controls on behaviour which keep ruling groups in power, still divide us.

In these conditions, the structure of the personality is created more through external forces or internalized unnecessary restraints than through the rational, self-conscious agency of the individual. The contours of the personality are marked out by relations of power, and there are many wasteful controls and disruptive unconscious forces created through repression, which take the initiatives and motives for action away from rational conscious control. This leaves the individual feeling that they are compelled by forces and drives outside of their volition. However, Elias is surely right to say that there are some forms of alienation that are integral to all social groups, stemming from the necessary restraints involved in group organization. These may always cause certain problems, but can be minimized only by overcoming the unnecessary restraints that serve to bolster the continued domination of particular social groups.

Until such restraints have been replaced in a society where there could be mutual recognition between fully humanized individuals, the rational and self-governing personality will not reach its maturity. There are still many barriers to the reconstruction of society and the creation of more fully developed selves. These may exist in the form of the resurgence of nationalism and fundamentalism, or in the continued existence (and current worsening) of economic inequality in the West. Here we see just some of the social divisions which are barriers to the social transformation necessary for the development of truly social selves.

Conclusion

I have argued throughout this study and, particularly, in this last chapter, that there are many different levels of dynamic agency within the personality, both conscious and unconscious. These different levels are always interwoven with and determined by social relations and activities of production, communication and power. The place and function within the personality of conscious or unconscious processes, motives or emotions, depend upon their place in the network of related, active and communicating individuals. There is, then, no division between society and the individual, nor between the mental functions and the emotions, the mind and the body, or conscious and unconscious processes. What divisions and barriers there are between the different psychic functions are created within the matrices of social relations, reflecting the divisions and barriers within those relations. We are in every respect social selves. Even our psychological conflicts and dilemmas are a reflection of social conflicts and hostilities.

While this study has drawn on insights from across the social scientific disciplines, I hope to have developed from these a unified theory of social selves which resists dichotomy and dualism. In doing so, I have attempted to seek out the essential social relations that lie behind the conscious awareness of our existence as individual personalities, and show how the self is social in its entirety. Only if we begin from the study of social relations and activities can we truly understand how individuals are social selves.

We can therefore no longer rest happy with the dichotomies between society and individuality, rationality and emotion, or mind and body. Social life is the source of individuality and human beings only develop as truly human within a social context. Certain types of social organization can restrict the development of individuals through structural inequalities, ideological misunderstanding and wasteful social controls. However, these have to be set against the possibility of greater equality, communicative clarity and democratic institutions developing in social life. It is within the scope of the social sciences to identify these limits as well as possibilities for social change. And it is also within the realm of the social sciences to build a unified theory of personality formation; of the personality under present social conditions and of the selves we have the potential to become. These are the tasks of a theory of social selves: and they are tasks which are still largely before us.

References

Allport, Gordon W. (1937a) *Personality: A Psychological Interpretation*. London: Constable.

Allport, Gordon W. (1937b) *Personality, Character and Temperament*. New York: Holt, Rinehart and Winston.

Allport, Gordon W. (1955) *Becoming*. New Haven, Conn.: Yale University Press.

Althusser, Louis (1971) *Lenin and Philosophy and Other Essays*. London: New Left Books.

Althusser, L. and Balibar, E. (1970) *Reading Capital*. London: New Left Books.

Archard, David (1984) *Consciousness and the Unconscious*. London: Hutchinson.

Arnason, Johann (1987) Figurational Sociology as Counter-Paradigm. *Theory, Culture and Society* 4 (2–3), 429–56.

Ashcroft, Robert (1982) *Conceptions of the Individual and the Client in Social Science and Social Work*. Bradford University: unpublished paper.

Bandura, Albert (1977) *Social Learning Theory*. Englewood Cliffs, N.J.: Prentice-Hall.

Baudrillard, Jean (1983) *In the Shadow of the Silent Majorities . . . or The End of the Social and Other Essays*. New York: Semiotext(e).

Bauman, Zygmunt (1978) *Hermeneutics and Social Science*. London: Hutchinson.

Beechey, V. and Whitelegg, E. (1986) *Women in Britain Today*. Milton Keynes: Open University Press.

Bettelheim, Bruno (1985) *Freud and Man's Soul*. London: Flamingo.

Billig, Michael (1987) *Arguing and Thinking: A Rhetorical Approach to Social Psychology*. Cambridge: Cambridge University Press.

Billig, M., Condor, S., Edwards, D., Gane, M., Middleton, D. and Radley, A. (1988) *Ideological Dilemmas: A Social Psychology of Everyday Thinking*. London and Newbury Park: Sage.

Blumer, Herbert (1969) *Symbolic Interactionism: Perspective and Method*. Englewood Cliffs, N.J.: Prentice-Hall.

Bogner, Artur (1987) Elias and the Frankfurt School. *Theory, Culture and Society* 4 (2–3), 249–85.

Bourdieu, Pierre (1977) *Outline of a Theory of Practice*. Cambridge: Cambridge University Press.

Bourdieu, Pierre (1984) *Distinction: A Social Critique of the Judgment of Taste*. London: Routledge and Kegan Paul.

Bozhovich, L.I. (1979) Stages in the Formation of the Personality in Ontogeny: Part I. *Soviet Psychology* 17, 3–24.

Bozhovich, L.I. (1980) Stages in the Formation of the Personality in Ontogeny: Part II. *Soviet Psychology* 18, 36–52.

Bradley, Ben S. (1989) *Visions of Infancy: A Critical Introduction to Child Psychology*. Cambridge: Polity Press.

Broad, C.D. (1975) *Leibniz: An Introduction.* Cambridge: Cambridge University Press.

Burman, Erica (1990) Differing with Deconstruction: A Feminist Critique. In I. Parker and J. Shotter (eds.), *Deconstructing Social Psychology.* London and New York: Routledge.

Cattell, Raymond B. (1979) *Personality and Learning Theory.* New York: Springer.

Chartier, Roger (1988) Social Figuration and Habitus: Reading Elias. In Roger Chartier, *Cultural History: Between Practices and Representations.* Oxford: Polity Press.

Clark, Roger A. (1978) The Transition from Action to Gesture. In Andrew Lock (ed.), *Action, Gesture and Symbol: The Emergence of Language.* London: Academic Press.

Croce, Benedetto (1913) *The Philosophy of the Practical: Economic and Ethic.* London: Macmillan.

Deleuze, G. and Guattari, F. (1977) *Anti-Oedipus: Capitalism and Schizophrenia.* New York: Viking.

Descombes, Vincent (1980) *Modern French Philosophy.* Cambridge: Cambridge University Press.

De Waele, J-P. and Harré, R. (1976) The Personality of Individuals. In Rom Harré (ed.), *Personality.* Oxford: Basil Blackwell.

Dewey, John (1922) *Human Nature and Conduct.* New York: Holt.

Dewey, John (1951) Creative Democracy: The Task Before Us. In Max H. Fisch (ed.), *Classic American Philosophers.* New York: Appleton–Century–Crofts.

Dreyfus, H.L. and Rabinow, P. (1982) *Michel Foucault: Beyond Structuralism and Hermeneutics.* Brighton: Harvester.

Dunning, Eric (1987) Comments on Elias's 'Scenes From the Life of a Knight'. *Theory, Culture and Society* 4 (2–3), 366–71.

Durkheim, Emile (1938) *The Rules of Sociological Method.* New York: Free Press.

Durkheim, Emile (1969) Individualism and the Intellectuals. Translated by S. and J. Lukes, in *Political Studies* XVII (1), 14–30.

Durkheim, Emile (1984) *The Division of Labour in Society.* London: Macmillan.

Edwards, Derek (1978) Social Relations and Early Language. In Andrew Lock (ed.), *Action, Gesture and Symbol: The Emergence of Language.* London: Academic Press.

Elias, Norbert (1969) Sociology and Psychiatry. In S.H. Foulkes and G. Stewart Prince, *Psychiatry in a Changing Society.* London: Tavistock.

Elias, Norbert (1970) Interview met Norbert Elias door J. Goudsblom. *Sociologische Gids* 17 (2), 133–40.

Elias, Norbert (1978a) *What is Sociology?* London: Hutchinson.

Elias, Norbert (1978b) *The History of Manners: The Civilizing Process*, Volume 1. Oxford: Basil Blackwell.

Elias, Norbert (1978c) On Transformations of Aggressiveness. *Theory and Society* 5, 229–42.

Elias, Norbert (1982) *State Formation and Civilization: The Civilizing Process*, Volume 2. Oxford: Basil Blackwell.

Elias, Norbert (1983) *The Court Society.* Oxford: Basil Blackwell.

Elias, Norbert (1984) Knowledge and Power: An Interview by Peter Ludes. In N. Stehr and V. Meja, *Society and Knowledge: Contemporary Perspectives on the*

Sociology of Knowledge. New Brunswick: Transaction Books.

Elias, Norbert (1987a) The Changing Balance of Power Between the Sexes — A Process-Sociological Study: The Example of the Ancient Roman State. *Theory, Culture and Society* 4 (2–3), 287–316.

Elias, Norbert (1987b) *Involvement and Detachment.* Oxford: Basil Blackwell.

Elias, Norbert (1987c) On Human Beings and Their Emotions: A Process-Sociological Essay. *Theory, Culture and Society* 4 (2–3), 339–61.

Elias, Norbert (1989a) The Symbol Theory: An Introduction, Part One. *Theory, Culture and Society* 6 (2), 169–217.

Elias, Norbert (1989b) The Symbol Theory: Part Two. *Theory, Culture and Society* 6 (3), 339–83.

Eysenck, Hans J. (1953) *The Structure of Human Personality.* London: Methuen.

Eysenck, Hans J. (1982) *Personality Genetics and Behaviour.* New York: Praeger.

Farr, Rob (1987) The Science of Mental Life: A Social Psychological Perspective. *Bulletin of the British Psychological Society* 40, 2–17.

Farr, Rob (1990) Waxing and Waning of Interest in Societal Psychology: A Historical Perspective. In H.T. Himmelweit and G. Gaskell (eds.), *Societal Psychology.* London and Newbury Park: Sage.

Ferrier, Linda (1978) Word, Context and Imitation. In Andrew Lock (ed.), *Action, Gesture and Symbol: The Emergence of Language.* London: Academic Press.

Feuer, Lewis S. (1970) Lawless Sensations and Categorical Defenses: The Unconscious Sources of Kant's Philosophy. In C. Hanly and M. Lazerowitz (eds.), *Psychoanalysis and Philosophy.* New York: International Universities Press.

Feuerbach, Ludwig (1972) *The Fiery Brook: Selected Writings.* New York: Anchor.

Foucault, Michel (1970) *The Order of Things.* London: Tavistock.

Foucault, Michel (1977) *Discipline and Punish.* London: Allen Lane.

Foucault, Michel (1979) *The History of Sexuality*, Volume One: *An Introduction.* London: Allen Lane.

Foucault, Michel (1980) *Power/Knowledge* (ed. Colin Gordon). Brighton: Harvester.

Foucault, Michel (1982) The Subject and Power. In H.L. Dreyfus and P. Rabinow, *Michel Foucault: Beyond Structuralism and Hermeneutics.* Brighton: Harvester.

Foucault, Michel (1986a) *The Use of Pleasure: The History of Sexuality*, Volume Two. London: Viking Penguin.

Foucault, Michel (1986b) What Is Enlightenment? In Paul Rabinow (ed.), *The Foucault Reader.* Harmondsworth: Peregrine.

Foucault, Michel (1988) *The Care of the Self: The History of Sexuality*, Volume Three. London: Viking Penguin.

Foulkes, S.H. and Anthony, E.J. (1957) *Group Psychotherapy: The Psycho-Analytic Approach.* Harmondsworth: Penguin.

Freud, Sigmund (1900) *The Interpretation of Dreams.* Harmondsworth: Penguin, 1976.

Freud, Sigmund (1930) *Civilization and its Discontents.* London: Hogarth.

Frisby, David (1984) *Georg Simmel.* Chichester and London: Ellis Horwood and Tavistock.

Garfinkel, Harold (1967) *Studies in Ethnomethodology.* Englewood Cliffs, N.J.: Prentice-Hall.

Gay, Peter (1984) *The Education of the Senses.* Oxford: Oxford University Press.

Gay, Peter (1986) *The Tender Passion.* Oxford: Oxford University Press.

Geras, Norman (1983) *Marx and Human Nature: Refutation of a Legend.* London: Verso.

Gergen, Kenneth J. (1982) *Towards Transformation in Social Knowledge.* New York: Springer-Verlag.

Gergen, Kenneth J. (1985) The Social Constructivist Movement in Modern Psychology. *American Psychologist* 40 (3), 266–75.

Gergen, Kenneth J. (1989) Warranting Voice and the Elaboration of the Self. In J. Shotter and K.J. Gergen (eds.), *Texts of Identity.* London and Newbury Park: Sage.

Giddens, Anthony (1971) *Capitalism and Modern Social Theory: An Analysis of the Writings of Marx, Durkheim and Max Weber.* Cambridge: Cambridge University Press.

Giddens, Anthony (1979) *Central Problems in Social Theory: Action, Structure and Contradiction in Social Analysis.* London: Macmillan.

Giddens, Anthony (1984) *The Constitution of Society.* Cambridge: Polity Press.

Goffman, Erving (1961) *Asylums.* New York: Doubleday.

Goffman, Erving (1969) *The Presentation of Self in Everyday Life.* London: Allen Lane.

Goffman, Erving (1983) The Interaction Order. *American Sociological Review* 48 (February), 1–17.

Greenfield, Patricia Marks (1978) Structural Parallels Between Language and Action Development. In Andrew Lock (ed.), *Action, Gesture and Symbol: The Emergence of Language.* London: Academic Press.

Habermas, Jürgen (1972) *Knowledge and Human Interests.* London: Heinemann

Harré, Rom (1979) *Social Being: A Theory for Social Psychology.* Oxford: Basil Blackwell.

Harré, Rom (1983) *Personal Being: A Theory for Individual Psychology.* Oxford: Basil Blackwell.

Harré, Rom (ed.) (1986) *The Social Construction of Emotions.* Oxford: Basil Blackwell.

Harré, R., Clarke, D. and De Carlo, N. (1985) *Motives and Mechanisms: An Introduction to the Psychology of Action.* London: Methuen.

Heidegger, Martin (1967) *Being and Time.* Oxford: Basil Blackwell.

Heller, Agnes (1976) *The Theory of Need in Marx.* London: Allison and Busby.

Helminiak, Daniel A. (1984) Consciousness as a Subject Matter. *Journal for the Theory of Social Behaviour* 12 (2), 211–30.

Henriques, J., Hollway, W., Urwin, C., Venn, C. and Walkerdine, V. (1984) *Changing the Subject: Psychology, Social Regulation and Subjectivity.* London and New York: Methuen.

Hirst, P. and Woolley, P. (1982) *Social Relations and Human Attributes.* London: Tavistock.

Honneth, A. and Joas, H. (1988) *Social Action and Human Nature.* Cambridge: Cambridge University Press.

James, William (1912) Does 'Consciousness' Exist? In W. James, *Essays in Radical Empiricism.* London: Longmans.

Joas, Hans (1985) *G.H. Mead: A Contemporary Re-examination of His Thought.* Cambridge: Polity Press.

Keat, Russell (1986) The Human Body in Social Theory: Reich, Foucault and the Repressive Hypothesis. *Radical Philosophy* 42, 24–32.

Kelly, George A. (1955) *The Psychology of Personal Constructs*. New York: Norton.

Kenny, Anthony (1968) *Descartes: A Study of his Philosophy*. New York: Random House.

Khan, M. Masud R. (1983) *Hidden Selves: Between Theory and Practice in Psychoanalysis*. London: Hogarth.

Körner, S. (1955) *Kant*. Harmondsworth: Penguin.

Kozulin, Alex (1990) *Vygotsky's Psychology: A Biography of Ideas*. Hemel Hempstead: Harvester Wheatsheaf.

Lacan, Jacques (1977a) *The Four Fundamental Concepts of Psycho-Analysis*. London: Hogarth.

Lacan, Jacques (1977b) The Mirror Stage as Formative of the Function of the I as Revealed in Psychoanalytic Experience. In Jacques Lacan, *Écrits: A Selection*. London: Tavistock.

Laing, R.D. (1965) *The Divided Self*. Harmondsworth: Penguin.

Laplanche, Jean (1989) *New Foundations for Psychoanalysis*. Oxford: Basil Blackwell.

Larrain, Jorge (1979) *The Concept of Ideology*. London: Hutchinson.

Lasch, Christopher (1979) *The Culture of Narcissism*. New York: Norton.

Lasch, Christopher (1985) Historical Sociology and the Myth of Maturity: Norbert Elias's 'Very Simple Formula'. *Theory and Society* 14 (5), 705–20.

Lee, Benjamin (1985) Intellectual Origins of Vygotsky's Semiotic Analysis. In J.V. Wertsch (ed.), *Culture, Communication, and Cognition: Vygotskian Perspectives*. Cambridge: Cambridge University Press.

Leontyev, A.A. (1981) Sign and Activity. In James V. Wertsch (ed.), *The Concept of Activity in Soviet Psychology*. Armonk: M.E. Sharpe.

Leontyev, A.N. (1972) The Problem of Activity in Psychology. *Soviet Psychology* 9, 4–33.

Leontyev, A.N. (1978) *Activity, Consciousness and Personality*. Englewood Cliffs, N.J.: Prentice-Hall.

Leontyev, A.N. (1981) *Problems of the Development of the Mind*. Moscow: Progress Publishers.

Lévi-Strauss, Claude (1975) *The Raw and the Cooked*. New York: Harper and Row.

Lichtman, Richard (1982) *The Production of Desire: The Integration of Psychoanalysis into Marxist Theory*. New York: Free Press.

Lock, Andrew (1978) The Emergence of Language. In Andrew Lock (ed.), *Action, Gesture and Symbol: The Emergence of Language*. London: Academic Press.

Lukes, Steven (1973) *Individualism*. Oxford: Basil Blackwell.

Luria, A.R. (1976) *Cognitive Development: Its Cultural and Social Foundations*. Cambridge, Mass.: Harvard University Press.

Luria, A.R. (1981) *Language and Cognition*. New York: John Wiley.

MacDonald Ross, G. (1984) *Leibniz*. Oxford: Oxford University Press.

Marcuse, Herbert (1970) *Eros and Civilization*. London: Allen Lane.

Marx, Karl (1875) Critique of the Gotha Programme. In K. Marx and F. Engels, *Selected Works*, Volume Two. London: Lawrence and Wishart, 1968.

Marx, Karl (1973) *Grundrisse*. Harmondsworth: Penguin.

Marx, Karl (1977) *Selected Writings* (ed. David McLellan). Oxford: Oxford University Press.

Marx, K. and Engels, F. (1970) *The German Ideology.* London: Lawrence and Wishart.

Mead, George Herbert (1909) Social Psychology as Counterpart to Physiological Psychology. In Andrew J. Reck (ed.), *Selected Writings: George Herbert Mead.* Chicago: Chicago University Press.

Mead, George Herbert (1910a) Social Consciousness and the Consciousness of Meaning. In Andrew J. Reck (ed.), *Selected Writings: George Herbert Mead.* Chicago: Chicago University Press.

Mead, George Herbert (1910b) What Social Objects Must Psychology Presuppose? In Andrew J. Reck (ed.), *Selected Writings: George Herbert Mead.* Chicago: Chicago University Press.

Mead, George Herbert (1913) The Social Self. In Andrew J. Reck (ed.), *Selected Writings: George Herbert Mead.* Chicago: Chicago University Press.

Mead, George Herbert (1917) The Psychology of Punitive Justice. In Andrew J. Reck (ed.), *Selected Writings: George Herbert Mead.* Chicago: Chicago University Press.

Mead, George Herbert (1924) The Genesis of the Self and Social Control. In Andrew J. Reck (ed.), *Selected Writings: George Herbert Mead.* Chicago: Chicago University Press.

Mead, George Herbert (1929) National-Mindedness and International-Mindedness. In Andrew J. Reck (ed.), *Selected Writings: George Herbert Mead.* Chicago: Chicago University Press.

Mead, George Herbert (1934) *Mind, Self and Society, From the Standpoint of a Social Behaviourist.* Chicago: Chicago University Press.

Mennell, Stephen (1989) *Norbert Elias: Civilization and the Human Self-Image.* Oxford: Basil Blackwell.

Merleau-Ponty, Maurice (1963) *The Structure of Behaviour.* London: Methuen.

Mills, C. Wright (1963) *Power, Politics and People: The Collected Essays of C. Wright Mills.* New York: Oxford University Press.

Mills, Peter J. (1986) *The Early History of Symbolic Interactionism: From William James to George Herbert Mead.* Leeds: Leeds University Ph.D Thesis.

Mischel, Walter (1971) *Introduction to Personality.* New York: Holt, Rinehart and Winston.

Mixon, Don (1980) The Place of Habit in the Control of Action. *Journal for the Theory of Social Behaviour* 10 (3), 169–86.

Morss, John R. (1985) Old Mead in New Bottles: The Impersonal and the Interpersonal in Infant Knowledge. *New Ideas in Psychology* 3 (2), 165–76.

Munch, Richard (1981) Talcott Parsons and the Theory of Action. 1. The Structure of the Kantian Core. *American Journal of Sociology* 86 (4), 709–39.

Munch, Richard (1987) *Theory of Action: Towards a New Synthesis Going Beyond Parsons.* London and New York: Routledge.

Natsoulas, Thomas (1985) George Herbert Mead's Conception of Consciousness. *Journal for the Theory of Social Behaviour* 15 (1), 60–75.

Nietzsche, Friedrich (1968) *Basic Writings of Nietzsche.* New York: Modern Library Giants.

Ollman, Bertell (1976) *Alienation: Marx's Conception of Man in Capitalist Society.* Cambridge: Cambridge University Press.

Parker, Ian (1989) *The Crisis in Modern Social Psychology – and How to End it.* London and New York: Routledge.

Parsons, Talcott (1962) Individual Autonomy and Social Pressure: An Answer to Dennis H. Wrong. *Psychoanalysis and Psychoanalytic Review*, 49 (2), 70–9.

Parsons, Talcott (1964) *Social Structure and Personality*. New York: Free Press.

Petrunik, M. and Shearing, C.D. (1988) The 'I', the 'Me', and the 'It': Moving Beyond the Meadian Conception of Self. *Canadian Journal of Sociology* 13 (4), 435–48.

Piaget, Jean (1926) *The Language and Thought of the Child*. London: Routledge and Kegan Paul.

Reck, Andrew J. (ed.) (1964) *Selected Writings: George Herbert Mead*. Chicago: Chicago University Press.

Roberts, Brian (1977) G.H. Mead: The Theory and Practice of His Social Philosophy. *Ideology and Consciousness* 2, 81–108.

Rorty, Richard (1982) *Consequences of Pragmatism (Essays: 1972–1980)*. Brighton: Harvester Press.

Rose, Nikolas (1989) Individualizing Psychology. In J. Shotter and K.J. Gergen (eds.), *Texts of Identity*. London: Sage.

Rotter, Julian (1982) *The Development and Application of Social Learning Theory*. New York: Praeger.

Sacks, Oliver (1985) *The Man Who Mistook His Wife For a Hat*. London: Picador.

Sampson, E.E. (1986) What Has Been Inadvertently Rediscovered? A Commentary. *Journal for the Theory of Social Behaviour* 16 (1), 33–40.

Sampson, E.E. (1989) The Deconstruction of the Self. In J. Shotter and K.J. Gergen (eds.), *Texts of Identity*. London: Sage.

Saussure, Ferdinand de (1974) *Course in General Linguistics*. London: Fontana.

Sayer, Derek (1987) *The Violence of Abstraction: The Analytic Foundations of Historical Materialism*. Oxford: Basil Blackwell.

Sayer, Derek (1991) *Capitalism and Modernity: An Excursus on Marx and Weber*. London and New York: Routledge.

Schwalbe, Michael L. (1988) Meadian Ethical Theory and the Moral Contradictions of Capitalism. *Philosophy and Social Criticism* 14 (1), 25–51.

Sève, Lucien (1978) *Man in Marxist Theory and the Psychology of Personality*. Brighton: Harvester Press.

Shames, Carl (1981) The Scientific Humanism of Lucien Sève. *Science and Society* XLV (1), 1–23.

Shames, Carl (1984) Dialectics and the Theory of Individuality. *Psychology and Social Theory* 4, 51–65.

Shotter, John (1976) Acquired Powers: The Transformation of Natural into Personal Powers. In Rom Harré (ed.), *Personality*. Oxford: Basil Blackwell.

Shotter, John (1978) The Cultural Context of Communication Studies: Theoretical and Methodological Issues. In Andrew Lock (ed.), *Action, Gesture and Symbol: The Emergence of Language*. London: Academic Press.

Shotter, John (1983) 'Duality of Structure' and 'Intentionality' in an Ecological Psychology. *Journal for the Theory of Social Behaviour* 13 (1), 19–43.

Shotter, John (1984) *Social Accountability and Selfhood*. Oxford: Basil Blackwell.

Shotter, John (1989) Social Accountability and the Social Construction of 'You'. In J. Shotter and K.J. Gergen (eds.), *Texts of Identity*. London: Sage.

Simmel, Georg (1971) *On Individuality and Social Forms* (ed. D.N. Levine). Chicago: Chicago University Press.

Simmel, Georg (1978) *The Philosophy of Money*. London and Boston: Routledge and Kegan Paul.

Skinner, B.F. (1953) *Science and Human Behaviour*. New York: Macmillan.

Skinner, B.F. (1971) *Beyond Freedom and Dignity*. New York: Knopf.

Smith, Robert J. (1985) Propositions to a Marxist Theory of Personality. *Human Development* 28, 10–24.

Thorlindsson, Thorolfur (1983) Social Organization and Cognition. *Human Development* 26, 289–307.

Turner, Bryan S. (1984) *The Body and Society: Explorations in Social Theory*. Oxford: Basil Blackwell.

Valsiner, Jaan (1988) *Developmental Psychology in the Soviet Union*. Brighton: Harvester Press.

Van der Veer, R. and van IJzendoorn, M.H. (1985) Vygotsky's Theory of the Higher Psychological Processes: Some Criticisms. *Human Development* 28, 1–9.

Vološinov, V.N. (1973) *Marxism and the Philosophy of Language*. Cambridge, Mass.: Harvard University Press.

Vološinov, V.N. (1976) *Freudianism: A Marxist Critique*. New York: Academic Press.

Vygotsky, L.S. (1962) *Thought and Language*. Cambridge, Mass.: M.I.T. Press.

Vygotsky, L.S. (1978) *Mind in Society: The Development of Higher Psychological Processes*. Cambridge, Mass.: Harvard University Press.

Vygotsky, L.S. (1981) The Genesis of Higher Mental Functions. In James V. Wertsch (ed.), *The Concept of Activity in Soviet Psychology*. Armonk: M.E. Sharpe.

Vygotsky, L.S. (1987) *The Collected Works of L.S. Vygotsky,* Volume One: *Problems of General Psychology*. New York and London: Plenum Press.

Weber, Max (1968) *Economy and Society: An Outline of Interpretive Sociology* Volume 1. New York: Bedminster Press.

Weber, Max (1985) *The Protestant Ethic and the Spirit of Capitalism*. London: Counterpoint.

Wertsch, James V. (1979) From Social Interaction to Higher Psychological Processes: A Clarification and Application of Vygotsky's Theory. *Human Development* 22, 1–22.

Wertsch, James V. (1985) *Vygotsky and the Social Formation of Mind*. Cambridge, Mass.: Harvard University Press.

Wertsch, James V. (1987) *Voices of the Mind*. Inaugural Lecture, Faculty of Social Sciences: University of Utrecht.

Whitehead, A.N. (1920) *Concepts of Nature*. Cambridge: Cambridge University Press.

Willis, Paul (1977) *Learning to Labour: How Working Class Kids Get Working Class Jobs*. Aldershot: Gower.

Wilshire, Bruce (1982a) The Dramaturgical Model of Behaviour: Its Strengths and Weaknesses. *Symbolic Interaction* 5 (2), 287–97.

Wilshire, Bruce (1982b) *Role Playing and Identity: The Limits of Theatre as Metaphor*. Bloomington: Indiana University Press.

Wittgenstein, Ludwig (1953) *Philosophical Investigations*. Oxford: Basil Blackwell.

Wouters, Cas (1977) In-formalization and the Civilizing Process. In P.R. Gleichmann, J. Goudsblom and H. Korte (eds.), *Human Figurations: Essays for Norbert Elias*. Amsterdam: Sociologisch Tijdschrift.

Wouters, Cas (1986) Formalization and Informalization: Changing Tension Balances in Civilizing Processes. *Theory, Culture and Society* 3 (2), 1–18.

Wrong, Dennis H. (1961) The Oversocialized Conception of Man in Modern Sociology. *American Sociological Review* 26 (2), 183–93.

Index